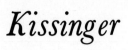

Kissinger

Kissinger

The European Mind in American Policy

BRUCE MAZLISH

Basic Books, Inc., Publishers

New York

The author gratefully acknowledges permission to reprint excerpts from the following:

"Kissinger: Action Biography," ABC News Documentary. © American Broadcasting Companies, Inc., 1974. Reprinted by permission.

"60 Minutes," October 13, 1970. © 1970 CBS Inc., all rights reserved.

"Henry," popular German song translated in *The New York Times*, July 13, 1975. © 1975 by The New York Times Company.

Library of Congress Cataloging in Publication Data

Mazlish, Bruce, 1923–
    Kissinger: the European mind in American policy.

    Includes bibliographical references and index.
    1. Kissinger, Henry Alfred.   2.   United States—Foreign relations—1969–1974.   3.   United States—Foreign relations—1974–   I. Title.
    E840.8.K58M38   973.924′092′4   [B]   76–18120
    ISBN: 0–465–03727–5

Copyright © 1976 by Basic Books, Inc.
Printed in the United States of America
Designed by Vincent Torre
76 77 78 79 80   10 9 8 7 6 5 4 3 2

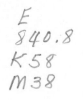

Contents

v

PART III

Kissinger in Power:
Policies and Procedures

Preface

ENRY KISSINGER is a most paradoxical "hero" of
our time. This improbable "superman", with clay feet, has
contributed to what I refer to as the "Europeanization" of
American foreign policy. One of the key elements in this
transformation has been a ponderously conceptualized and
updated version of the balance-of-power doctrines of the nineteenth century, especially those of the Congress of Vienna, that
Kissinger had studied so intently. Mediated through his
personal experiences in Nazi Germany and then his Americanization, Kissinger masterfully applied these doctrines to the
world of nuclear weapons.

The paradox is that Kissinger's world, and ours, has been
irretrievably revolutionized at the very moment he sought to
stabilize it in the old-fashioned terms. In the nuclear age, as he
himself recognized, no one and no one nation is invulnerable;
power, in fact, has been alchemized into powerlessness. At the
same time, an explosive increase in communications technology
and in economic relations has made the world more inter-

dependent. Thus, the old concepts associated with the term "balance of power" no longer suffice. The very success of Kissinger's policies has made plain that they are based on a flawed foundation; his world view is anachronistic.

Vietnam made this state of affairs self-evident. In the glare of that experience, we have become intensely conscious of the inadequacies of the old doctrines and of the need for a new synthesis. Henry Kissinger is the natural place to begin the necessary reexamination. His style of diplomacy, his views of foreign affairs, and his personality have stamped themselves on the problems of our time and the future. Because he has stood at the center of American foreign policy for the last eight years and more, the paradox of his rise and fall is ours, too.

There are evident difficulties in writing a book on a contemporary figure. One such difficulty is to justify the enterprise as "history." I take refuge in the comment of the Roman-Jewish historian Flavius Josephus, made almost two thousand years ago: "To place on record events never previously related and to make contemporary history accessible to later generations is an activity deserving of notice and commendation. Genuine research consists not in the mere rearrangement of material that is the property of others, but in the establishment of an original body of historical knowledge."* In short, to paraphrase a well-known assertion, history is too important to be left solely to future historians.

Another difficulty is that new material may appear in the interval between the writing of one's book and its actual publication. To cite a few examples, after my book had already been copy edited three interesting works appeared: Matti Golan's report of Kissinger's supposedly secret conversations,

---

* Flavius Josephus, *The Jewish War*, in *Greek Historical Thought*, ed. A. J. Toynbee (New York: New American Library, 1952), p. 62. Arthur Schlesinger, Jr. quotes this in "The Historian as Participant," *Daedalus* 100, no. 2 (Spring 1971):339–58. This article is an excellent defense of contemporary history as a worthy aspect of the historian's practice.

Edward R. F. Sheehan's article on Kissinger's Middle East negotiations, and Woodward and Bernstein's account of the final days of the Nixon administration.† In Golan's case, the "secret" material was anticipated by the Israeli government and much news coverage was given to their censoring of the book; in the flesh, the book is disappointingly jejune. In Sheehan's case, the author had already been kind enough to share with me the essentials of his fine article. As to Woodward and Bernstein, while they make more dramatic the expression and extent of Kissinger's contempt for Nixon's personality, they do not tell us anything we did not know as early as 1968. What they add are details. As Richard Reeves remarks in his review of *The Final Days*, "The small surprises are details we did not know... But there is little in the book that will change ... [our] basic perceptions."‡ Thus, we are told about the now famous prayer scene, about Kissinger's disdain for Nixon's mental capacities, about his annoyance with his crumbling leader's weakness. Such vignettes, however, leave us with a rather partial and one-sided view of the matter because the relationship is depicted out of context and out of time.

Interestingly, however, my relating Kissinger to Nixon is, if anything, reinforced by Woodward and Bernstein who slyly, if implicitly, impale Kissinger on his own leaked stories, and show him to be more like Nixon than he would have us believe. But while they highlight the similarities, I also depict the important differences. Rather than retailing particular "revelations," as they do so well and so readably, I have tried to describe and analyze the basic elements of Kissinger's personality, his fundamental patterns of behavior, the deeply rooted ways in which he views the world; if I have done my

† Matti Golan, *The Secret Conversations of Henry Kissinger*, trans. Ruth Geyra Stern and Sol Stern (New York: Quadrangle, 1976); Edward R. F. Sheehan, "Step by Step in the Middle East," *Foreign Policy*, no. 22 (Spring, 1976); Bob Woodward and Carl Bernstein, *The Final Days* (New York: Simon and Schuster, 1976).
‡ *New York Times Book Review*, 18 April, 1976, p. 1.

work well my interpretations should stand fast against any new "evidence." Such an assertion may be bold, but at least it puts the issue on the line.

Nor, in my view, do more recent events—Angola, Brazil, a falling-out with Congress, the pyrrhic victory over former Defense Secretary James Schlesinger leading to Kissinger's own loss of position as head of the National Security Council, the weakening of détente—cause me to wish to change my analysis. Unless that analysis had been wrong from the beginning—and, needless to say, I do not believe it has been—it should inform the new events, while the events should merely lend additional nuances and testing to the analysis.

What has changed is Kissinger's own power position. He has clearly become a major issue in the 1976 Presidential campaign. His enemies now come hot and heavy at him from both the right and the left. There has been agreement among all of Ford's opponents, from Reagan through Jackson, Carter, Humphrey, Udall, and Brown, that Kissinger is the wrong leader for American foreign policy. All sides attack his policies and suggest that he ought to be discharged (and by the time this book is published he may well have been forced to resign, though I doubt it). Paradoxically, the very liberals who would have been expected to support his policy of détente are so distrustful and annoyed at Kissinger that they oppose him even on this issue. After eight years of great public success, Kissinger has now allowed his enemies on both the right and left to coalesce—a fatal mistake in politics. The Savonarola effect, of which I speak in the book, appears about to manifest itself with a vengeance.

Nevertheless, all of these developments, and others, must be understood in the context of his achievements and debacles of almost a decade of activity and thought, and must not be allowed to obscure the total picture. As stated earlier: Kissinger's life and work already belong in a significant way to the history of our times.

That is sufficient reason for our persisting interest in him. Beyond this, however, is the sheer fascination of his personality. He is one of those figures, like a Churchill or a de Gaulle, who bestride their eras and dominate by the sheer weight of their character. Such figures take on mythical, as well as historical, attributes even in their own time.

In the course of writing this book, I sought an interview with Henry Kissinger, without success. The day before I had to return the copy-edited manuscript to the publisher, chance stepped in and gave me an opportunity to exchange some words with him. An account of that meeting, and its effect on me, might be of interest to the reader.

Kissinger had come to Boston on March 11, to receive the annual award of the World Affairs Council and to give a major address. On our being introduced, he said he knew very well that I was working on a book about him. He then said that he would have liked to have spent hours talking to me, that one hour would not have been enough. I replied that I understood his point. He added that, in any case, he was deeply suspicious of psychiatry. I said that I was aware of his feelings. Then, in a most appealing, rather small-boyish way, he asked, "Will I be unhappy with your book?" I answered that I hoped not—I had tried to be understanding as well as impartial—but that I couldn't be sure of its effect on him.

We then talked about a number of other matters: a personal relationship, a brief touching on the problem of détente and why liberals were not supporting him, a concern for a "Cambridge stereotype" about him (which I agreed existed, but which I assured him I did not share), a fear that, with Nixon gone, he had become the substitute target, and so forth. The entire interchange had been most friendly, with Kissinger entirely forthcoming.

I had, in fact, been exposed to Kissinger's charm. Kissinger's aides had been very frank with me. After my interviews with them they told me that they had advised Kissinger to see me. I was a serious scholar, they informed him, and, just as importantly, they believed he would be able to charm me. They were right; from the first moment of our meeting, I felt that Kissinger realized he had made an error and should have seen me. At least he made me *feel* that that was what he was feeling. In addition, he conveyed to me that small-boyish air of vulnerability that I mentioned, saying, "I'm defenseless, don't pick on me" (let me hastily add that this was coupled with a sense of his presence, for at the same time he exuded confidence and prosperity).

I tell this story for its intrinsic interest, and because it left me feeling that the book was better, more impartial, for my not having been exposed earlier to Kissinger's charms. I would have been beholden to him, brought into his confidences in a way that would have inhibited my final analysis and evaluation. Whatever the gains of a personal interview, the losses probably would have been greater, at least in this particular case. Such are the strange ways and perils, gains and losses, of doing contemporary history.

My debts in writing this book are many. First, to Henry Kissinger, who himself perceived in history the revelation of a personality, in this case his own, and thus provided me with the materials for my study. Next, to the numerous individuals, and in some cases institutions, who so generously shared with me their knowledge and views on Kissinger and American foreign policy. With only two exceptions, everyone I asked responded favorably and cooperatively to my request for an interview; moreover, they were astoundingly forthright and candid in their comments. Some were Kissinger's declared enemies, many more were his friends. It is a tribute to Kissinger that so many, in spite of seeing the warts in his character or disagreeing with some of his policies, hold him in such warm regard.

Needless to say I did not interview everyone who has known

Henry Kissinger. At a certain stage of my work I reached a point of greatly diminishing returns. Once I had the firm outlines of his personality and life fixed, and increasingly confirmed by interviews that followed, I merely did spot checks. These last, in addition to the well over 100 full and formal interviews, themselves number in the hundreds, but are not of the same importance as my earlier inquiries.

It would have been difficult, if not impossible, for me to have done the research necessary for this book without the support of an M.I.T. Ford Foundation Research Grant, and I wish to record my appreciation here. As always, I am indebted to the secretarial staff of the Department of Humanities at M.I.T. for struggling with my penmanship and producing clean and clear typescripts. To Linda Zieper, I owe the index. My wife, Anne, was invaluable in reading the draft chapters of this work.

Cambridge, Massachusetts
May, 1976

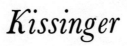

Kissinger

Introduction

THE KISSINGER EPOCH: PERSONALITY AS POLICY

HERE IS A STORY, possibly apocryphal, that a psycho-analyst in Cambridge, Massachusetts, has as a patient a person named Superman, who think's he's Henry Kissinger. That such a story exists about an American Secretary of State tells us much about this extraordinary man, whose life reads more like a piece of fiction than a serious biography.

Our purpose, however, is indeed serious.[1] Kissinger's life is not only novellike; it has been the fulcrum of American foreign policy for over eight years. As one observer commented on a *Newsweek* cover depicting Kissinger as a Gulliver swarmed over by lilliputian figures representing his various international and domestic problems, "The Kissinger personality has replaced the traditional Uncle Sam figure and literally dwarfs the biggest issues of the day."[2] Without question Kissinger's personal attributes, his views, and his procedures have all entered, subtly or blatantly, into the formation and execution of American foreign policy during a critical period marked especially by the problems of deterrence, détente, and America's involvement in the Vietnam War.

The personalization of American foreign policy by Kissinger

has become an issue in itself. Thus, for example, Thomas L. Hughes has attacked him for substituting personalism, the intrusion of his own personality, for institutional and policy-oriented handling of America's international relations. In Hughes' indictment, in place of issues we have had a man; personality has upstaged policy. Americans "have made . . . an exceptional overinvestment in one exceptional man—Henry Kissinger. . . . In the process, our national priorities have perforce become his preferences. Our national interests have become whatever he has time for at the moment."[3]

What sort of person is this "exceptional man," Henry Kissinger? What are his views? His policies? How, if at all, are these related? Obviously, policy is more than a given person, or, indeed, the sum of the personalities involved in its formation. It is, however, not separate from these personalities, not an entity which takes shape mechanically, utterly independent of the motives of key actors and groups. To understand historical events and policies, one must also understand the human beings involved with them. This, surely, is a truism. As Abba Eban remarks, Kissinger's "personal role refutes the view that history is the product of impersonal forces and objective conditions in which the personal human factor doesn't matter."[4]

The Kissinger Phenomenon

Even if one does not wish to go as far as Eban or Hughes, it is clear that Kissinger's personality has intruded on the normally colorless realm of foreign policy making in an unexampled fashion. One is faced, in fact, with the "Kissinger phenomenon," which has become as important, in terms of historical interpretation, as Kissinger's personality. The phenomenon of his rise, and perhaps fall, is as much a part of history as his actual diplomatic actions.

The Kissinger story begins with the ascent of an obscure German-Jewish refugee to American Secretary of State, regarded by many as the President for Foreign Affairs. In his heyday Kissinger has commonly, even if often with tongue in cheek, been referred to, as in our opening paragraph, as Superman. A popular German song, called "Henry," lyricizes,

> Henry! La la la la, la la.
> Kings, beggars, gypsies wait for
> Henry's kiss.
> A baby wails; "My little one, don't
> cry, you can tell your troubles
> when Uncle Heinz comes by."
> What are Tarzan and Superman
> against his tricks.
> Hercules, the Commissar, are out—
> A new star—Henry—has all the
> clout![5]

Time eulogized him as having probably "more impact than any other person in the world. Quite possibly, he has now become the world's indispensable man."[6] Gallup polls showed him as the man Americans most admired. Improbable as it seems from his physical appearance, he also became a sex symbol, the darling of film stars, and even the unlikely hero of a racy novel, *President Kissinger*. A Superman, indeed!

On the other side are those who see him in quite a different light, as a Dr. Strangelove or a Frankenstein (who was, incidentally, also a doctor, the creator of a monster who went out of control). Anthony Lewis, the *New York Times* columnist, calls him a "war criminal," whose negotiating techniques "amount to deception."[7] Daniel Ellsberg, a former deputy Assistant Secretary of Defense and co-worker with Kissinger, as well as leaker of the Pentagon Papers, privately thinks of Kissinger as a "murderer" for his bombing of Indochina.[8] Morton Halperin, a former Kissinger aide on the National Security Council, believes that his erstwhile boss committed "an indictable offense of perjury" on the wiretap matter.[9]

Kissinger, in fact, has been built up by admirers and detractors in the media, as well as by events, into both a culture hero and a villain. Most of the writing about him has tended to take the form of either hagiology or demonology. He is fast becoming a legendary figure of light and dark, with the legacy of Kissinger-ianism, just as that of Machiavellianism, potentially taking on the features of mythology as much as history.

An Overview

Personality and phenomenon; the two seem to go together. Just as there is Kissinger, the subject of hagiologic and demonic interpretation, so is there the Kissinger perceived by those who know him well as a mixed and complicated man, a "Dr. Kissinger and Mr. Henry," as one of them jokingly referred to him. There are two Kissingers, I was constantly being told: the paranoiac and the trusting man, the courtly and the boorish, the generous and the insensitive, the straightforward and the duplicitous. Given to "extreme and sudden changes of person-ality," exhibiting more than the usual mixed motives, an in-tellectual as well as an activist, Kissinger, in addition to being an important subject, is obviously a fascinating one.[10]

In seeking to understand him, I shall go back to his earliest roots in Europe. In one sense Kissinger can be regarded as among those European immigrants, refugees from Hitler's perse-cutions, such as a Von Neumann in science or a Marcuse in philosophy, who have strongly influenced American intellectual or political life. Putting Kissinger's claim at the highest pitch, one can say that he has "Europeanized" America in the foreign policy area.

If Kissinger has been able to "Europeanize" American policy, however, it has only been because he himself has gone through

6

the process of Americanization. Perhaps his major characteristic is his ability to change and grow. Outwardly, his is a fairly typical story: the European immigrant who takes on American culture and becomes a new man—and a success. (I always think of that wonderful autobiography, *The Americanization of Edward Bok*.)[11] What is atypical, as we shall see, is that Kissinger's Americanization took place primarily in terms of his military experience in World War II.

Kissinger, as a German Jew, responded naturally to the notion of assimilation. He was prepared by his own culture to take on, in large part, the trappings and spirit of another culture while retaining his inner integrity. We shall trace out, therefore, how he came to terms with the years of his early experience in pre-Nazi and Nazi Germany, and then entered into the mainstream of American life through the army, then Harvard, and then the wider world of the American foreign policy establishment. His use of patrons, of teachers, of "connections," and of councils must be studied. So, too, his own career as a teacher, and the transition from being a mere intellectual to being an activist as well, thereby mirroring the movement of American universities in the postwar years, will call for our rapt attention.

We shall wish to study his evolution of a "world view," or ideology, and his compulsive attention to such themes as holocaust, tragedy, limits, goodwill, and will. The fact that he has developed a "conservative world view" is of prime importance for us. His style of work, his procedures as head of the National Security Council and as Secretary of State, will engage our attention. We shall seek to understand the sources of his unique negotiating skills, and to see how he exercises them in various situations. The subject of power, and what it means for Kissinger, will be inquired into, and even the way in which women and sex figure in the drive toward power. These are some of our subjects in studying the personality of Henry Kissinger.

We must also study his policies and see how, if at all, they are related to his personality. Strictly speaking, they are not simply Kissinger's policies, for almost all of them were initiated or carried out as the assistant to a President—Nixon (and now Ford, but with Ford, the policies are almost entirely inherited ones). Therefore, we need first to examine Kissinger's relations to Richard Nixon. Only then can we go on to an examination of Kissinger's policies concerning the Strategic Arms Limitation Talks (SALT), the Soviet Union, China, the Middle East, and so on, limiting ourselves, however, to consideration of how they bear on the observations that we have made about his personality, and vice versa.

An Interpretation

My approach throughout is interpretive. This fact must be underlined from the very beginning. By now there are a number of acceptable and sometimes fine studies and articles on Kissinger's thought, policies, or actual negotiations. Often weakened by an uncritical adulatory or condemnatory bias, such works are nonetheless fundamental in helping to establish some of the "facts" about Kissinger in his many guises. They rarely, however, center on Kissinger's personality in the sense I undertake here.[12]

On the other hand, it must immediately be added that psychological insights into Kissinger's patterns of behavior have become almost commonplace. Such a state of affairs points to the widespread acceptance by the media and the public, especially after the Nixon experience, of the intrusion of personality onto the public stage. What I can add to these discussions is a greater effort at depth and accuracy and a sustained attempt at understanding the meaning of the insights.

I believe, for example, that I have had certain advantages in undertaking this study which have given me access to persons and areas of knowledge not available to most inquirers. I, myself, am an intellectual, involved in the same academic milieu as my subject. My interests have been in fields related to those of Kissinger's interest: if he wrote a doctoral dissertation on the "conservative" settlement of 1815–1822, I did my thesis on "Burke, Bonald, and De Maistre: A Study in Conservatism"; if Kissinger wrote his senior thesis, *The Meaning of History*, on the philosophy of history, I wrote a book called *The Riddle of History*, taking up the same subject;[13] if Kissinger has been absorbed with the revolutionary forces of history, I have taught and written on the subject of comparative revolution. We share many friends and acquaintances in Cambridge and in Washington, D.C. We are of the same generation.

It hardly needs to be said that we differ in many, many ways. Where we diverge most is that he became an activist as well as an academic intellectual. For scholars this has always been an unresolved dilemma. However, I hope I have not been totally unaware of the pressures of bureaucracy and political power struggles.

Suffice it to say that I have tried to approach Kissinger compassionately and empathetically, as well as to understand the background of American foreign policy formation in as detached, i.e., nonpolitical, a fashion as possible. Of course I do have feelings and views, both about Kissinger and American foreign policy, and the reader will detect these, even where I have not made them overt, as I do to a certain extent in the last chapter. Where they color the facts unduly, rather than help to provide the inspiration for my empathetic interpretations, I shall have failed.

The major source for this book, aside from existing public data, has been oral history, that is, well over 100 interviews. Primarily in London, New York, Washington, and the Boston area, I have spoken to those who knew Kissinger in Fürth, Germany, in New York, Harvard, and the world of power in

Washington, D.C. With one or two exceptions they have been extraordinarily candid with me. The condition for their trust, aside from whatever faith they had in my scholarly intentions, was one that I proffered from the very beginning of my work: total confidentiality. I promised not to quote them by name, and not even to list their names in a preface.[14]

The price to be paid for this condition—a major requirement for obtaining the kind of data needed—is that I must violate the scholar's standard means of substantiating his statements: footnotes citing the references, which any interested reader may then verify for himself. Although many of my interviews are taped (I abandoned the practice as I got further into the work, contenting myself with notes), I can offer no proof in this book as to the accuracy of my quotations. The reader will simply have to decide for himself whether the statements have the ring of truth about them. It is my hope that the reader will so decide in terms of the total interpretation that I offer.

What of the subject, Kissinger, himself? Did I interview him? The answer is, "No." Though most of his top aides were very cooperative, did give me interviews (obviously with his knowledge, a testimony to the man's relations with them), and in at least two cases interceded with him to grant me an interview, in the end, after four months of weighing the possibility, it was reported to me that "He was intrigued, but had decided that he had better not do it." I could well understand how a busy Secretary of State, once burned by a trusting interview with Oriana Fallaci and suspicious of my approach, might come to such a decision.

I made no effort to talk to his parents or to his former wife, mainly out of my own feelings of delicacy, though I was also sure that at least the former would not talk to me without their son's approval. Kissinger's brother, Walter, again understandably, declined graciously to talk to me; thus, a key part of Kissinger's emotional life, his sibling relationship, will have to await a later unfolding by some other hand.

In spite of these gaps, I believe that the picture of Kissinger that emerged from my interviews is a "true" and "deep" one. Of course, I would have been interested in speaking directly to Kissinger about certain matters. But to do so would have been to meet him only as he is now: not as the young boy in Fürth, the thin army soldier, the intense graduate student, the young scholar putting on weight while writing *Nuclear Weapons*, and so on. As George Kennan remarked in speaking of Stalin, "The impression one gains of a public figure from seeing him at first hand is of course a different thing, and far less important, than the impression one gains from long and careful study of his public career."[15] For my purposes, I would widen this statement to include his private as well as his public career. And I would point out further that, although Kissinger is living, our treatment of him is also in terms of a long-range "historical" perspective.

In sum, I would go so far as to say that I "know" Kissinger better now than does any single friend of his or person whom I interviewed, and perhaps better than Kissinger knows himself; I hope the reader will be in the same position at the end of this book. Time and again I found that intimate acquaintances of Kissinger's either did not know something that I did, or were convinced about something that I knew to be wrong; they knew only one of the many Kissingers. As in the Japanese movie *Rashomon*, where six observers all tell the story of a murder differently, my interviewees gave me their versions of "what happened." Gradually, out of the evidence they supplied, one could evoke a composite picture with some claim to verisimilitude.

Throughout this work I have sought to avoid the mere repetition of already existing data (though some of that was unavoidable), but tried rather to add nuances and facts derived from the interviews, and, above all, to do all this from an interpretive point of view. Validation or repudiation of my facts and interpretation may eventually come when other participants, and Kissinger himself, write memoirs on the matters under consideration here. Still, even then, in "interpreting" the theses and views advanced in such memoirs, the explication and facts advanced here will have to be remembered. For example, for Henry Kissinger merely to deny the existence of sibling rivalry or to allege that he does not identify with his opponent, as I claim he does, is merely to add one more piece of datum which must itself be interpreted. In sum, validation is not just a matter of getting the facts right, but of interpreting these facts in relation to an internally consistent theoretical explanation.

The Importance of Henry Kissinger

Kissinger's life and work raise in passionate fashion some of the key problems of history in general and of our era in particular. In seeking to understand him we are forced to wrestle with such questions as morality and power, and the meaning of history. These abstract questions became dramatically real, especially in the events surrounding our policy in Vietnam, where the debate over moral idealism and pragmatic realism entered into a strange dialectic played out with real peoples. A Cambodian invasion, bombs, and wiretaps were actions fraught with moral meaning to achieve certain ends, themselves debatable.

Our relations to the Soviet Union and China, to expansionist communism, and our policies of deterrence and détente—these issues come into play vis-à-vis Kissinger's own personality. He has been intensely involved in our negotiations in the Middle East. He has had a strong hand in our policies and actions in relation to Cuba, Chile, India, Pakistan, Turkey, and Greece, to name only a few prominent examples. Whatever the specific case or country, Kissinger has subsumed his position toward it under his larger concern for international stability and order. All of his policies, just as is his own personality, are linked in covert or dramatic fashion to this overriding concern.

Above even this concern, or, rather, haunting it, is the concern with the nuclear threat. For Kissinger, if international stability and order fail to hold, if the center gives, there is the real and constant possibility of holocaust. For the first time in history the breakdown of international stability may entail the end of the human race. In dealing with Kissinger, therefore, we are dealing not only with an interesting personality, a present-day culture hero, and certainly an important statesman, but with the omnipresent dilemma of our time. We are dealing, in the end, with ourselves, and the possibility of our extinction. Perhaps these are apocalyptic terms, but today they are commonplaces, invested with a new and frightening reality. It is Kissinger, often accused of being inhuman or amoral, who personifies this new condition of the human species. We neglect to study and understand him at our own peril.

PART I

The Americanization of

Henry Kissinger:

From Fürth to

Washington

Chapter 1

BEGINNINGS:
FAMILY AND GERMANY

A Conservative "Hero"

HENRY KISSINGER was born a German and became an American. How was his soul shaped by the first and reshaped by the second experience? We talk, or used to, rather glibly about "Americanization," or the making of an American. In fact, the process is reciprocal, and America itself is remade by its immigrants, as we now know so well. As for the Americanization process, an abstract notion for the country at large is an intense personal experience for the individual concerned, in this case a boy named Heinz who became Henry Kissinger, and a Secretary of State.

An even larger question, beyond the specific socialization process called Americanization (which only applies to some individuals), is how *any* personality is formed. We can define personality as the habitual pattern of response to external and internal stimuli. A person is a complex interrelation of such factors as genetic inheritance, ethnic and cultural roots, national origin, social position, generational experience, particular family upbringing, and specific life experiences. Out of this welter a person has to try to secure a sense of self, a cohesive and satisfying way of reacting to the world around and inside him.

Nowadays we speak of the outcome of this process (if it succeeds) as an "identity," and this usage points to the fact that the self is formed to a large extent by the "identifications" we make with others: parents, people in authority, culture models, even enemies. Building on the work of Freud, Erik H. Erikson has popularized the notion of an "identity crisis" as central to the "life history" of a great man (as well as lesser ones). Erikson's "identity crisis," through which the hero in history must pass, is seen as a new *rite de passage*. Luther and Gandhi have been Erikson's major examples.[1]

At first glance, Henry Kissinger seems a strange Eriksonian hero, an unlikely candidate for their company. Both Luther and Gandhi reaffirmed their religious calling and then turned that reaffirmation to political power; Kissinger seems to have turned away from deeply based religious ties—his Judaism appears only nominal now—and then moved toward the political arena. Luther and Gandhi both affirmed their natal nationalities, leading other Germans and Indians to a heightened sense of national identity; Kissinger gave up his German nationality, has a difficult time with his Jewish identity, and has taken on a particular kind of American identity. Luther and Gandhi were both revolutionaries; Kissinger is a conservative in a revolutionary era. Only in a time when the "idea of progress" is no longer considered the master force in history could such a figure become a potentially new kind of Eriksonian hero.

Difficult as it may first appear, then, we must look at Henry Kissinger as a conservative "hero" whose development can be perceived in Eriksonian terms. Fairness and empathy require such an approach. Thus, we must ask in compassionate vein: How did young man Henry become middle-aged Kissinger? He himself has said that his early years in Fürth, Germany, "left no lasting impressions . . . that part of my childhood is *not* a key to anything." As he continued, "I was not consciously unhappy. I was not so acutely aware of what was going on. For children those things are not that serious. It is fashionable now to explain everything psychoanalytically, but let me tell you, the political persecutions of my childhood are not what control my life."[2]

The key phrase here is *"that* [my italics] part of my childhood." I believe Kissinger is right: that the Nazi experience per se, with Hitler coming to power when Henry was about nine, played a relatively small part in his basic formation. Of course, as we shall see, one must not underestimate or dismiss that part. Henry Kissinger himself undercuts his earlier remark when he declares to Ted Koppel that "I think the deepest impact it [the rise of National Socialism] made on me was that twice, once in 1933 when the Nazis came to power, then in 1938 [sic] when I came to the United States, all the things that had seemed secure and stable collapsed and many of the people that one had considered the steady examples suddenly were thrown into enormous turmoil themselves and into fantastic insecurities. So in this sense it was a rather unsettling experience."[3]

We can perhaps see here the seeds of Henry's desire for stability, his basic attraction toward conservatism. The personal underpinnings of what later became an intellectual attraction are even clearer. One of the "steady examples" suddenly called into question was Henry's father, who lost his job and status. Even more to the point, however, was the fact that Henry himself lost *his* secure and stable position. Thus, as he responds to Koppel's query as to what it was like to be transported to the United States, "having been within my circle, President in my class and unbelievable as it may seem now, Captain of the soccer team, not to speak the language and not to be part of the group was quite a transition. . . ."[4]

What was the "circle" of which Henry was a part? Who

were the "steady examples" whose existence as models and sources of support he could no longer take for granted? To ask such questions is to take us directly to Henry's birthplace, Fürth, Germany, and to the family and community in which he was born. Even though our information is necessarily sketchy, enough is available to give us the broad outlines concerning his formative years. Many, many Jews, including those of Henry's age, similarly experienced the coming to power of the Nazis. Only Henry Kissinger experienced them in terms of *his* particular family and community, and brought to this experience *his* unique endowment and development, with consequences that eventually led *him* to be an American Secretary of State.

Community and Family Background

In an amazingly large proportion of my interviews, the person to whom I was talking identified Henry Kissinger as a German, and seemed unaware of anything but the vaguest Jewish background. This accords with Kissinger's own sense of identification and belief, and thus gives a truthful picture. Yet, in his formative years, his entire milieu was influenced by an intensely Orthodox Jewish presence which permeated the entire daily life of all those whom it touched.

So, too, knowledge of his family was sparse. Although Kissinger, once in power and prominence, proudly shared his triumphs with his parents, few of those who worked with him or knew him as a colleague had any awareness of his early personal background. He seemed to have come from nowhere, to have always been Henry Kissinger, almost fully formed. Yet the reality is quite different. He has changed and developed over time, in very definable ways. He has been shaped by his family and by his early experiences in both obvious and subtle ways, and it is our task to try to understand this early shaping as best we can. That the connections with his later life are labyrinthian must not deter us in our effort to understand the original formative influences, nor should the fact that our information is necessarily sparser than we would wish, and much of it by now familiar to those who have looked at Kissinger with other intentions in mind.

Henry Kissinger was born on May 27, 1923, in Fürth, Germany. His mother, Paula Stern Kissinger, came from Franconia, and at the time of her marriage was living with relatives who ran a butcher shop. His father, Louis Kissinger, was a teacher and the son of a teacher. Both parts of the family seem to trace back a number of generations in the general area of Franconia, and the Kissingers probably took their name from a spa, Bad Kissinger, in that locale. Henry was named Heinz Alfred at birth (he was probably also given a Hebrew name at the time, from which the Heinz Alfred was derived). A year later, on June 21, 1924, a brother, Walter Bernhard, rounded out the family circle.

Fürth, to which Jews apparently first came in 1528, became part of Bavaria in 1806 as a result of Napoleon's reorganization. In the 1930s it was a town of about 70,000. The population was mainly Lutheran, although Roman Catholics formed a substantial minority (about 20 percent); the Jews of Fürth numbered about 2,500 to 3,000. The Jewish community itself seems to have been, not unexpectedly, informally divided along status lines. The few professional people were mainly doctors and lawyers, with about 90 percent of the community in business, mainly the wholesale or manufacturing trades, or small shops. There was one large synagogue surrounded by a number of smaller ones. Rabbis and religious teachers, incidentally, like all religious functionaries in Germany, were paid by the state. The "liberal" Jews, according to informants, patronized the large synagogue, which was poorly attended except for the High Holidays. Orthodox Jews, generally those who had more recently come into Fürth from the surrounding villages, numbered about 400 to 500, and worshiped in the smaller synagogues. In these synagogues the old ways prevailed, and services were held twice daily, in the morning and at dusk, not Friday night and Saturday morning only. In this setting the Kissinger family seems to have been typically Orthodox, attending a small synagogue of relatively low status (though the lines are blurred in this matter), but occupying a position of respect and dignity in the community.

Politically, most of Fürth's Jews were inactive. Almost all its survivors have only a vague memory: In the Weimar Republic, Fürth Jews, if they voted, would have voted for the Democratic party of the center. (Although one informant thought Louis Kissinger might have voted Social Democratic, all the others, some vehemently, doubted this.) Above all, Fürth Jews thought of themselves as "good Germans." Assimilation, *as Jews,* was the ideal, taken for granted. As Germans, the Fürth Jews served in the army in World War I (though exposed to much social anti-Semitism) and were loyal and sometimes ardent nationalists at least until 1936. Their disinterest in domestic politics was not because their loyalties lay outside of Germany, for they were mostly strongly anti-Zionist. Their Liberal or Orthodox Judaism, combined with their German "identity," somehow precluded most Jewish members of the Fürth community from being sympathetic to the creation of what eventually became the state of Israel.[5]

This was the setting in which Louis Kissinger grew up and then raised his sons. Of Louis Kissinger's parents we know little. His father, David, was a teacher in the lower schools, and was still living when Henry and Walter were boys. He is remembered as being of patriarchal appearance, with a long white beard, and attending synagogue frequently, for he was "very orthodox." During his retirement he rented a room in Würzburg; thus we know he was not living directly with the Kissingers. According to one informant, Henry loved and admired his grandfather greatly, and in later life had his picture on the wall; we also know that Henry Kissinger named his own firstborn son David after his grandfather. Of Henry Kissinger's grandmother we learn nothing.

Some day, perhaps when Henry Kissinger writes his memoirs, we may know more about the influences on him of his grandparents. For the moment we must settle for what we have. Henry had two uncles on his father's side (there were also two or three aunts but we have no information on them beyond the fact of their existence). Karl eventually emigrated to Israel, and was in the shoe business. Arno, the youngest brother, is of more importance in young Henry's life. He became the representative of an optical firm, Lehmann of Fürth, in the Scandinavian countries, and was a salesman of repute. Apparently he was considered a "swinger," with great charm and a somewhat mercurial personality. So outgoing a person was hardly likely to be a distant uncle, though he was often away. We can assume that the visits of the exciting and appealing Uncle Arno, and stories of his business successes, made a great impression on Henry and Walter.

Louis was a very different sort. All accounts speak of him as serious, cultured, refined, a person of courtly manners. He was also shy, a young man who did not go out with girls. A "man of utmost sincerity, genuine piety and kindness; unassuming and friendly": these are the ways in which friends characterize him. He was also apparently, as a good German, sometimes pedantic and bureaucratic, sometimes authoritarian. So, too, he is frequently described as a "strict" teacher in class, though there is some difference of opinion as to exactly how strict he was.

Apparently he was also strict with his own children. One of Henry's childhood friends recounts that the father was "always checking Heinz's [Henry's] homework" (which, according to the friend, he apparently neglected in favor of spending time with the girls), and generally keeping a close watch on him.[6]

Another contemporary of Henry's, Jack Heiman, who boarded with the Kissingers as a child, tells how, though he was treated leniently, the Kissinger children were not: "They never hit me, and they weren't bashful with Henry and Walter. They really got it. We were all in the same bedroom at night, sometimes too noisy and rambunctious while Mr. Kissinger was grading papers. He'd come in and hit them—but not me even though I was equally guilty." Pressed to explain, Heiman said that "hit" meant spanked.[7]

How much did Henry resent his father's strictness? It seems the attitude of a typical German Jewish patriarchical authority, perhaps exacerbated by somewhat narrow living quarters (they had a five-room apartment), and hardly unusual for the time and the milieu. Although Louis Kissinger did not play soccer or other sports with his children, everything points to his being a loving and concerned parent. A sense of humor—he is described as "witty"—surely helped. Nevertheless, though Henry in later life obviously loved and respected his father— one of the things all his friends noticed was how proud Henry was of his father, bringing him right into the midst of his triumphs—I cannot help suspecting (and general clinical data supports such a suspicion, as well as one knowledgeable informant who says he was definitely "afraid of his father") that as a child Henry's resentment toward his father's authority was strong, and strongly repressed. Whatever negative feelings he had, natural in the circumstances, were blocked, and all criticism of the "authority" figure muted or silenced in his conscious life.[8]

Let us leave such speculation for the moment, and return to Louis Kissinger. Though he never went to university (apparently he went only as far as a *Lehrerseminar*, what we might call a normal school), he did go beyond *his* father by teaching at a higher level. Moreover, he taught primarily at non-Jewish schools, until the Nazis came. At first he taught at the Heck-mannschule, a private school which, though Christian in directorship, had a student body that was between 40 and 65 percent Jewish, drawn mainly from the local bourgeoisie. Here he taught a range of subjects, including math, singing, and religion until the Weimar Republic dissolved all private schools, thus causing him to lose his job. There is a certain irony in the democratic Weimar Republic ousting Louis Kissinger from his post, just as the Nazis were to do later. But the result was different the first time, for Louis Kissinger got another job at the Hoehere Toechterschule—a girl's junior high school or lycée—and then at a business school (accounting and economics), the Handelsschule. Dismissed from these public positions by the Nazis, who had come to power, he was forced to teach at the Kaufmännische Berufsschule, a Jewish vocational school in Nuremberg. At this point his secure, dignified career as a teacher lay in ruins around him. Having risen higher than his father, he had now fallen lower.

Before this sad event, Louis Kissinger had led a moderately successful life. He earned a comfortable living and supported his family well. The terrible inflation of 1923, the year in which Henry was born, does not seem to have had a severe impact on the Kissingers. While of the middling rank economically in the Jewish community, Louis' position as teacher brought him not only sufficient money but prestige, for high school teachers in Germany were highly regarded. He seems to have been a good teacher, somewhat strict, as we have noted, and regarded by at least one observer as "ambitious." Curly-haired, he was nicknamed "Goldilocks" by the children.

An Orthodox Jew, Louis Kissinger seems also to have been a good German. It is astounding, therefore, that no one remembers clearly whether or not he fought in World War I. "Oh, he must have," a number of my informants declared, "Why, everyone did, as for example my father." Other informants, however, feel that he probably didn't, and vaguely suspect some disability. Given Henry Kissinger's later involvement with World War II and the military, it is of some point to know his father's experiences and attitudes in this area; but we can find no clear answer, itself a kind of commentary.

The coming of the Nazis obviously changed the roles of

Jews as "good Germans." For many the shock was traumatic. All observers are agreed, however, that there were no incidents with the Nazis for Louis Kissinger. Though not frightened, he was politically inactive, and behaved in an absolutely "correct" manner. In fact, it seems that he could not believe what was happening around him. When dismissed without notice from his teaching post, apparently he thought it was all a mistake, that somehow his job would be returned to him. It was his wife, Paula, who realized that they had better get out, and made the arrangements for their leaving.

The Kissingers left Nazi Germany in 1938. They went first to England, where Paula had some relatives, and then a few months later on to America, where, again, Paula had relatives who were able to secure the necessary affidavits for immigration. Louis Kissinger was apparently very ill with gall bladder problems when he first came to America, and made a slow recovery. In any case, America was difficult for him. He was fifty, without a secure command of the English language, and unable to obtain a teaching post. Eventually he took a job as a bookkeeper, a lowly though honorable position for the former high school teacher. Effectively, his "career" was finished, his "secure and stable" life in tatters. His son Henry's existence, on the other hand, was about to take on new shape, and his career about to begin. Such was the result of the coming to power of the Nazis and the consequent "unsettling experience" of the Kissinger family.

Mother

In later life Henry Kissinger stated rather injudiciously that women to him were merely a pastime or a hobby.[9] Whether this is in fact true of his mature life and casts a true light in any way on his own marriages, or rather is merely an offhand dismissal of his "swinging" existence, we shall consider in Chapter 7. We know it cannot be true of the first woman a child knows: its mother. The mother is both the source of a child's first attachments, and then a model, either positively or negatively (and this last can be out of overattraction as well as rejection), of the future women in his life. It is in some such terms, even if we cannot extrapolate them precisely, that we must regard Henry Kissinger's mother.

Paula Stern Kissinger was born in 1900 and grew up in Leutershausen, a small village about thirty miles from Fürth. Her father was a cattle dealer, described as a cultured man, and prominent in the Jewish community. Her mother, described as a "beautiful woman," died very young. The father, however, remarried, and Paula was therefore raised by a stepmother.[10]

We are told that Paula came to Fürth to go to school. There is the possibility that, coming from a small village with few eligible boys, her marital prospects may also have been a consideration in the move. In any case, she came to live with her aunt, Berta Fleischmann, who was married to one of Fürth's three kosher butchers. Berta Fleischmann has been described as "energetic," the head of the clan, and the heavyweight in the family. A number of sources believe that she arranged the marriage of her niece to Louis Kissinger.

We know that Paula was one of Louis Kissinger's former students, and that when she was 22 and Louis 35, they got married. Perhaps the reputed cultural interests of her father may have left their mark on Paula. By every account, the marriage was, and is, a great success. Louis adored his wife, and she respected him in return. Within exactly nine months Henry was born, and a year later, Walter. Then the childbearing stopped, not an unusual event in an Orthodox Jewish family, but hardly compatible with traditional teachings. While there is some controversy as to whether Paula was quite as religious as her husband—some sources say "yes," the New York Post[11] says "no"—it is clear that she was a good Jewish wife.

Paula, unlike Louis, had enjoyed an active social life before her marriage. She is described as an outgoing girl with a sense of fun and humor (even to the point of playing little tricks); as lively and attractive (with curly dark hair), and even a little bit vain; and as extremely bright and clever, adaptable, sharp, and very diplomatic. Apparently, as a mother she did not fuss over her children, and one source suggests that she may have seen her children occasionally as a bit of a burden, sometimes farming them out with relatives.

In the house she let her husband outwardly rule but, in fact, sha was the driving force in all decisions. As one Fürther described this not uncommon situation, there is a Jewish saying that "the voice is the voice of Jacob, the head of the house, but the woman runs the family" (I suspect this saying suffers in translation). Probably because of Paula, the Kissingers kept up a good circle of friends, and lived a sociable existence.

It was Paula Kissinger who pulled and pushed the family out of Nazi Germany. Once in America, they finally settled in an apartment in the Fort Washington section of New York (called, jokingly, the Fourth Reich by the refugee Jews, who thus implied that it would outlast Hitler's Third Reich and its thousand year boast), where they still live. Paula adapted quickly and competently. She began by serving as a cook at private parties, then established her own catering business. One must remember, of course, that she was only 38, compared to Louis' 50, and therefore presumably at a better stage to cope with a new life. But, youth aside, she was clearly the more energetic one by character. Her quickness and cleverness also stood her in good stead in learning the English language (in retaining an accent, Henry was perhaps unconsciously still holding on to parts of his father, although, as we shall see, retention of an accent depends considerably upon the age at which the mother tongue is given up). Clearly, it was she who became "Americanized" first and most.

Childhood

"The child is father to the man," says Wordsworth. In Kissinger's case, his childhood seems to have been a normal one, at least until the coming of the Nazis to power. There is no doubt that this event was of the utmost importance to the Kissinger family. Did the advent of the Nazis, occurring when Kissinger was about ten, cast a traumatic shadow over his coming adolescence (for he remained in Fürth until he was almost fifteen)? The answer is neither clear nor simple.

In fact, either Henry Kissinger's childhood was externally uneventful, which is probably the case, or evidence about it is lacking, which is certainly the case, or perhaps both. Details about his early years are sparse. There are no data whatever on how he was raised in infancy. Our first glimpse of him is in school, that is, after his sixth year. All sources agree that he showed none of his later brilliance here, doing only average work. Later, in high school, the same observation held. Thus Shimon Eldad, who taught English and French in the Jewish junior high school in Fürth in the 1930s, recalled Henry Kissinger as a good but not outstanding student: "He was a spirited and scintillating youth, but I didn't notice anything special in him. His English didn't exactly excite me, and it seems that way still today."[12] One informant attributed his average performance to his being lazy, without ambition. A further reason seems to have been his interest in girls. One of Henry's close friends, Dr. Menachem Lion (his name was also Heinz until he changed it in Israel), now a chemist at a biological institute in Israel, tells us that "Henry Kissinger spent many hours in my home. They lived near us and Heinz would ride over on his bike. He liked being with us. It seems to me he had a problem with his father. If I'm not mistaken, he was afraid of him because he was a very pedantic man, a teacher in a German high school for girls. His father was always checking Heinz's homework and kept a close watch on him. Heinz told me more than once that he couldn't discuss anything with his father, especially not girls."[13] According to Lion's story, as a result of Kissinger's paying too much attention to the girls, he once brought home a less than satisfactory report card. "He was only twelve at the time and the girls were already chasing after him, but he didn't pay any attention to them. His first love was a charming blonde." Lion also remembers "that he and Kissinger used to take their girlfriends for walks in the local park on Friday evenings. When he returned home late from one of these walks, his parents put the blame on Heinz Kissinger's influence and forbade their son to see the Kissinger boy for a whole week. Later they sent their son off for six weeks to a summer camp in Czechoslovakia to get him away from Heinz Kissinger, who had earned a reputation as a skirt chaser."[14]

We ought to take parts of these accounts with a grain of salt. What does emerge is Henry Kissinger's average school work and a possible interest in girls. In addition, we know that he had a strong interest in sports. According to Lion, he and Henry cycled together and hiked in the local woods and mountains. Henry was also an ardent soccer player, apparently playing at center half (his brother Walter was a forward); he still exercises this interest in spectator fashion.[15] One childhood acquaintance remembers him as being tall (one must allow for childish perspective), and substantiates this memory with a photo showing Henry as the only one in a group of children with his head cut off in the picture, i.e., being taller than the rest. He certainly grew to be taller than his parents, both of whom were short. In the eyes of both teachers and school chums, Henry was perceived as being "well grown" as a boy.

He also seems to have been something of a leader, thus supporting his remark to Koppel. As one of his childhood friends commented, Henry was, in those days, "more a leader than a negotiator." He conducted the synagogue choir and dominated a game of "battleships," played on rainy days. The other children followed him naturally.

Religious practice took up much of young Henry's time. Lion informs us that the two boys went to synagogue every morning before school. On Saturdays Lion's father taught them both the Torah. The Kissinger family, of course, observed the dietary laws and all the holidays. Henry knew Hebrew, and studied Jewish history and rabbinical literature. To prepare for his Bar Mitzvah at 13, Henry learned to chant the Torah (we remember that his father also taught singing) — and was excellent at it; apparently he had a good musical ear. Indeed, his training and abilities were so good that he also prepared his brother for the Bar Mitzvah, an unusual event. Outwardly, Henry as a child was an observant, practicing Orthodox Jew. It may be that, inwardly, seeds of rebellion were already planted. As one of his classmates recounted, the Rabbi who taught Jewish studies slapped the children too much, alienating many of them from their religion as a result. Whether Henry Kissinger was so affected, however, is not clear.[16]

In short, until the coming of the Nazis, Henry Kissinger's life seems that of a typical Jewish boy in Fürth, leading an existence filled with schooling, religious observance, sports, perhaps girls, and lots of games and excursions.

How serious were the reputed street fights with Nazi youth that presumably erupted in the 1930s? In interviewing survivors of Fürth, an extraordinary difference in memory emerged. The older people, of the generation of Henry Kissinger's parents, remembered no street fights involving their children. "Oh, no," I was told repeatedly, "that could never happen. It would have been too dangerous." The children remembered otherwise. Moving always in groups, the Jewish boys had to face frequent encounters with Nazi youths in which stones were chucked, and school briefcases had to be held high for protection. Sometimes the boys were spat on. Serious as these encounters were, they also held an element of risky fun known to all boys who have engaged in gang rivalries.

Such experiences were not traumatic, and no informant remembers any more serious anti-Semitic ugliness involving the Kissingers. Still, it left in the children a deep memory. Kissinger is not unique in recalling that on first arriving in America (for others it was England or South Africa, or any other country that had admitted them), he would cross the road if he saw a group of boys approaching on his side of the street. The feeling of constantly being liable to unpredictable violence was obviously laid deep in Kissinger's psyche, a kind of groundwork on which his later attitudes (even to nuclear warfare) could be built.

These Nazi experiences came at the end of Henry Kissinger's childhood—as we have noted, he was about ten at the time Hitler came to power—when the basic elements of his character had already been laid down by his family and by his life in the Jewish community of Fürth. Experience with the world outside that community was limited, for the Orthodox Jews of Fürth were a world unto themselves. The coming of the Nazis, of course, breached that existence, and sent Henry Kissinger spinning out into a much wider world.

The Sibling

A word must be said about Henry's brother, Walter. He is the silent presence, the unspoken shadow, I believe, behind much of Henry Kissinger's pattern of relating to other men, and especially to competitors in the larger sphere of the world. Freud has told us how his relations to his nephew John conditioned his development. "Until the end of my third year we had been inseparable; we had loved each other and fought each other, and, as I have already hinted, this childish relation has determined all my later feelings in my intercourse with persons of my own age. My nephew John has since then had many incarnations, which have revivified first one and then another aspect of a character that is ineradicably fixed in my unconscious memory."[17]

Now Walter was Henry's brother, not his nephew, and a year younger, not older, as was Freud's John. Nevertheless, I suspect a similar kind of impact on Henry Kissinger, *mutatis mutandis*. All of this is speculation, though supported in one part at least by a trustworthy observer who commented that the two boys "fought a lot" (what else should we expect from two healthy boys?). Strong sibling rivalry was in the air.

Leaving such speculation, we have only a few facts about Walter Kissinger's childhood at our disposal. We know that he was conceived shortly after Henry's birth; thus his mother probably had to give up nursing Henry, assuming she had been doing so, after two or three months, or as soon as she was pregnant again. The coming of Walter Bernhard (there was another Bernhard in the family, a cousin) must have diverted some of her attention from Henry. Though the one-year-old Henry would have been unaware of the cause of this withdrawal, a few years more would have made him fully cognizant of his rival. Nevertheless, the initial impact of this sibling rivalry was preoedipal, and obscure in its bearings; again we are left with speculation on the basis of a few facts.

Walter, called "Kissus" (from Kissinger; Henry apparently was also so nicknamed), favored his mother in looks, whereas Henry took after his father, with the same curly golden hair and long forehead. As we know, Henry eventually also wore glasses, like his father, whereas Walter did not, like his mother. Most observers feel that Walter was the better-looking boy, who eventually grew to be taller than his brother (though this would not be the case during childhood). He, too, was interested in soccer (as we have noted) and is reputed also to have been president of the local clubs.

Dimly, we see two active, healthy brothers, rivaling one another in many areas. Though the father thought of Henry as the thinker and Walter as the doer, the evidence, according to some of Henry's contemporaries, suggests that Heinz and Walter were both initially much like their mother in character: born leaders, involved in everything. Henry the student and negotiator had not yet come into significant existence. It was the Nazis and Hitler who, in forcing the Kissingers to emigrate to America, changed the child Heinz to Henry, and into a shy and studious boy.

The Heritage

What was the heritage from his family and community, as well as from the Nazis, that Henry took with him to America? In his own home he had the model of a good Jewish marriage, in which his quiet, studious father outwardly ruled in traditional patriarchal fashion, while his energetic mother outwardly obeyed, as tradition required, but in reality ruled the roost. Both his grandfather, David, and his father, Louis, provided Henry with the model of being a teacher, but a model that at the end was eroded. In the background, his uncle Arno provided an example of successful action as a businessman. As for the mother, there is the strong possibility that, though providing an opposite sex model of activity, she may have left Henry with some feelings of having been neglected, especially for his sibling.

From his community Henry inherited a strong Orthodox Jewish background, whatever his personal adherence to its dogmas and observances. With this went vague awareness of the Orthodox Jew's disinterest in domestic politics and a kind of basic political conservatism, or at least moderation. Such Jews were also generally anti-Zionist and good Germans, holding assimilation as a high value (as long as it did not require the relinquishment of their religion), and prepared to accept the values of their "host" country, now viewed as their own.

As Henry Kissinger himself has told us, the imprint of the Nazi coming to power was etched into this basic inheritance in terms of the loss of security and stability experienced by the "steady examples" to whom he had hitherto looked for guidance and protection, and who were now themselves in a state of "fantastic insecurities." Foremost among these figures was his father. Henry's deepest reactions, unconscious of course, must have been mixed and chaotic: great insecurity and fear for himself; a resentment of his father's "authority," which nevertheless could not protect those under it from the Nazi threat;[18] and a desire to redeem his beloved father's failure (coupled with feelings of guilt that, in doing so, he might "show up" his father and surpass him).

From this complex of feelings and experiences, he later drew many lessons. As we shall see, he came to feel deeply the "tragic" sense of life, the way in which what was ascendant in history could be brought low; this was a sense he felt totally lacking in the American people, and which he as a "European" felt he could supply. He turned against revolutionary movements, which could dispossess people of their lifelong status and humiliate them; thus, he emotionally deepened the political conservatism he already found at hand in Orthodox Judaism. And last, he became convinced that "goodwill" was not enough. As all informants emphatically observe, Louis Kissinger was a "good" man, a man of noble character, and, as Henry Kissinger underlines, a person of intense goodwill. Yet it had not been enough to save him (or his people). The lesson young Henry drew was that one needed somehow to acquire power. To protect men of goodwill, too weak to protect themselves, one might therefore have to grasp even the enemy's weapons, and, if necessary, resort to violence and destruction. It is a lesson, unexpectedly and paradoxically taught to him by his schoolmaster father, which Henry Kissinger has never forgotten.[19]

35

Chapter 2

AMERICA, WAR,
AND THE MILITARY

The Past and Its Price

OBVIOUSLY, the Nazi experience must have left its mark on Henry Kissinger. Nevertheless, one has to be impressed with the way he mastered his childhood experience, with how little crippling damage it inflicted on him. Largely, he outgrew it, and his refusal to talk much about it must be seen in this light. As a result, even as a young man he was someone not ostensibly in conflict with himself—hence, in part, his stamina, his ability to concentrate (which is the source of his "brilliance," so often commented on now, and so lacking in accounts of his earlier years).

Of course, a price, or many prices, had to be paid. By repressing so many of his memories, he never fully came to grips with them. Thus they were not so much resolved as put aside. Whatever energies would have been engaged by the need to come to a fuller resolution of the feelings evoked by the rise of the Nazis and his father's fall from a secure and respected position were, instead, sublimated into work and dedication. Moreover, as we shall see later, the past returned to haunt him in a way about which Henry Kissinger was, and is, totally unconscious: his identification, in part, with the aggressor, a trait which underlies much of his successes and failures.

Outwardly, however, Henry Kissinger not only sublimated, but largely expunged his past. Whatever the price, he was able, by leaving his past behind him, to prepare the ground for his new creation—and creativity. The "Americanization" of Henry Kissinger is the beginning of that story.

School in America

Millions of Americans have gone through the Americanization process. There is nothing unique in this part of Henry Kissinger's story. In Henry's case, however, arrival in America coincided with his puberty. All children go through puberty, but it is the special cultural and social aspects imposed on it in the twentieth century that make for the stage of psychosexual development we regard as "adolescence." For the young refugee, the acculturation shock, on top of the biological changes, added to the usual adolescent difficulties. Generally, the boy seems to have handled this phase of his life by a kind of withdrawal into shyness, a sense of insecurity, and a dedication to hard work. We can see how imitative these traits were of the father.

Henry also tried quickly, however, to assimilate. Within a few weeks of his arrival he was already learning about baseball and attending games at Yankee Stadium. He was enrolled at George Washington High School, where he first began to demonstrate his academic brilliance, doing especially well at math. After a year, family financial necessity made him shift to night school for his last two years. During the day he worked in a shaving brush factory, squeezing acid out of the bristles, and eventually being promoted to delivery boy.

These were some of Henry's first steps out of his home milieu. In fact, they were tentative and partial. Even in America, the Fürthers, and those like them, were able to create a fairly tight-knit community unto themselves (a similar group, incidentally, exists in London). Bonds of family and friendship snapped in Germany were reunited in America. Fort Washington may not have been the "Golden Ghetto," as it was called, of the lower West Side area around 90th Street, but it had many of the same qualities, without the money. Thus, in Washington Heights most of the young people, Henry included, joined the Beth Hillel Youth Group (where Henry may have first met his future wife, Ann). We are informed that Henry, shy and retiring, didn't enjoy the dancing class.

As for his experiences at George Washington High School, there appear to be almost no hard personal data obtainable, and one has to extrapolate from general observations made by other graduates. The school was large—around 5,000—and its student body, like that of the area it served, was extremely diverse. So was the teaching staff, with some being "old American schoolmarms" and others "youngish Ph.D.'s."

Every foreign student—and there were Hungarians, Austrians, and so on, besides the Germans—had to go through Miss Bachman's English for Foreigners and, if they failed, had to continue with class II. In fact, few had to take II. As one contemporary of Kissinger's reported, "Miss Bachman was a disciplinarian, and she worked us hard. She emphasized extemporaneous little talks, carefully correcting grammar and pronunciation." Here, obviously, the groundwork for Henry Kissinger's manipulation of the English language was laid.

Another teacher at the school was a Miss Chapin, who taught English and American literature. As one former student put it, "She loved us foreigners because many of us shared her appreciation of 'culture.'" Miss Bachman, on the other hand, was suspected by some students of not exactly liking the refugees whom she taught so rigorously and well.

38

The Jewish refugee students who piled into the school in the 1930s were typically, or so it is alleged, "bookish, bespectacled —and unhappy!" Their unhappiness arose from a number of sources. One reason was that they disdained the frivolities of their American contemporaries, who seemed to have no understanding of true *Geist*, and were disdained in turn for their overseriousness. Another reason was that almost all the refugee boys suffered greatly from their lack of attraction for the opposite sex. The refugee girls ignored them; *their* aspirations turned toward Americans. And the American girls, for obvious reasons, would have nothing to do with "foreigners" (Henry's "exotic" qualities would only appeal later, when in power). The fact that the refugee boys were also generally broke as well as shy compounded their adolescent problems.

The competition was strong, and the school is noted for its brilliant and successful refugee graduates. Within a year or so surrounding Kissinger's class, one can identify the president of a prestigious eastern college, earlier an accomplished scientist, a renowned theoretical linguist, also at a major eastern university, and a number of distinguished professors of history or political science at colleges and universities around the country. As one of them put it, "We were all outstanding students—I mean, what else was there to do?" As he goes on, "We all had miserable jobs, working in factories, etc., and the only road to salvation was via CCNY, where there were 30,000 equally bright types." He concludes, "The draft came as a liberation from that sort of drudgery."

Clearly, then, Henry Kissinger's experiences were not unique. What is unique is what he made of them, and the way in which, once formed, he entered so forcefully into his adopted country's history. But all this lay ahead. At the beginning of the 1940s he was still at George Washington High School. Upon finishing he decided to attend City College, at night, with the other "30,000 . . . bright types," and become an accountant. Obviously, the financial insecurity of his family, plus the fact that he was good at math, influenced his choice. We can also see in it echoes of his father's bookkeeping role, lifted to a slightly higher level. We can also note that no teacher at George Washington had inspired Henry to anything higher. There is no evidence of a strong interest in history or political science, or a similar subject. At George Washington, his school record noted that he had a "foreign language handicap" (in spite of Miss Bachman's efforts), and this problem affected his early work in mainly verbal subjects. At school in Fürth he had studied some English, but not much.

This leads us to the matter of Henry Kissinger's accent. Whereas his brother Walter, just one year younger, came to speak without an accent (or else a slight touch of an English accent), Henry could not, or would not, rid himself of one. As Henry Kissinger remarked years later, "I was terribly self-conscious about it [the accent]," although he then hastened to add, "but not because anybody made fun of it."[1] One possibility is that past a certain age, say 14 or 15, it is difficult to shed an accent; Henry at 15 may have been just past the critical point. Another is that shyness inhibits the mimicking ability necessary to acquire accent-free fluency in a foreign language. Yet another possibility—the one I favor—is that, inwardly, he did not really wish to part completely with his tie to Germany and his father and thus retained the linguistic affiliation (Bavarian, incidentally, not Prussian in accent and intonation). In any case, although self-consciousness about it disappeared, as Kissinger began to win academic success in the late 1950s, the accent remained, to bear witness to his German-American identity, and later to intrigue Americans as they listened to their strange and fascinating Secretary of State.

But, again, this is to anticipate our story. At the moment, Henry Kissinger was doing his best to cope with his new environment, while deriving what security he could from remnants of his past culture. His ambitions were distinctly limited. He neither knew the "culture cues" of any other sort of life, nor even dimly, as far as we can tell, aspired to such a life. In short, the "Americanization" of Henry Kissinger seemed about to take an ordinary path, somewhat removed from the great currents of history.

The Army and the War: The Enemy Within and Without

The army and World War II changed all this. It literally gave Henry his American identity—he was naturalized in 1943 —a new sense of self, a glimpse of larger horizons, and, indeed, the financial means by which to march toward them. By now the details of Henry's experiences are familiar; nevertheless, they bear some reexamination.

Henry Kissinger was called to service in February 1943 and sent to Camp Croft, Spartanburg, South Carolina, for basic training. The shock of being in the South for the first time, rather than being depressive for Kissinger, was "exhilarating."[2] He was discovering a wider America. The regimentation of army life seems to have been tolerable. In any case, he was taken out of this environment, and returned to school again. His army IQ and aptitude tests had qualified him for the Army Specialized Training Program (ASTP), an educational program that sent selected soldiers to colleges at government expense for presumed future purposes useful to the military (the program, as one biographer points out, was also useful in keeping open colleges whose campuses had been emptied by the war).

After a brush-up summer at Clemson College, Henry was sent to Lafayette College, in Easton, Pennsylvania, in a special engineering program. Here he spent all his time on his studies, and we note that they were mainly in science or technical subjects. His record as a student was outstanding. The army had given Henry Kissinger his first recognition as someone special, and he responded well. We can also see that he did well in terms of the fusion of his intellectual abilities and the military needs, a theme to be encountered throughout the rest of his life.

The military's needs in this case, however, suddenly changed. The exigencies of war called for front-line soldiers in greater numbers, and even the intellectual elite of the ASTP were required. Henry Kissinger was reassigned in April 1944 to the 84th Infantry Division at Camp Claiborne, Louisiana, as a foot soldier. Like almost all the rest of the 100,000 or so ASTP reassignees, Henry Kissinger was, as his father put it, "very unhappy."[3] Nevertheless, his unhappiness did not prevent him from lasting through the summer's grueling and accelerated retraining and shipping out with his division to the European war theater in late September. In November his company was in battle near Aachen, Germany. But Kissinger had just been reassigned again, as a driver-interpreter for the commanding general of Division Intelligence. Once more his intelligence and his German linguistic past (as well as his friendship with another German, Fritz Kraemer, to which we shall come later) had singled him out, and perhaps saved his life.

In any case, Henry Kissinger's military career was now connected for the rest of the war to Army Intelligence and Counter-intelligence, a link that persisted into his later civilian life. He never actually fired his rifle, it appears, but he did show good nerves and courage in combat situations. According to a family friend, for example, around June 1945 Henry was made a sergeant and proposed for the Bronze Star for taking 240 German soldiers as prisoners; he had entered a building, it seems, without knowing there were that many Nazis there. (The *New York Post*'s account is that he was awarded the Bronze Star "for slipping through the German lines in civvies in April to question retreating enemy troops about the chances of a suicidal counterattack," but anyone who has read in

Tolstoy's *War and Peace* knows how confused these accounts become).[4]

When in January 1945 the 84th Division occupied Krefeld, Henry Kissinger was made military administrator (again on the recommendation of Kraemer). He also officially became a CIC agent. Promotions, first to private first class and then sergeant, followed a few months later. The 21-year-old Kissinger restored the municipal government of Krefeld to working order in a matter of a few days, we are told. Such good work led to an assignment to run the district of Bergstrasse, with his headquarters at Bensheim, only 100 miles from Fürth. Here, again, he performed well (accounts of Kissinger's power and success, one feels, are exaggerated in the telling, but no matter). When demobilization came in 1946, Kissinger remained in Germany as a well-paid civilian instructor at the European Command Intelligence School at Oberammergau, teaching German history. His salary was about $10,000, a large sum for the former shaving brush worker—the army paid well, he might readily conclude—and he was in a position of authority, earned by his intellect, over men his superiors in rank and in age. Heady stuff!

Oberammergau was obviously important for Henry Kissinger. Here he could combine the inheritance from his father and grandfather—teaching—with his new inspiration—the military—in a highly satisfactory mixture. It is important to remember that Kissinger's real "Americanization" took place in terms of the army, an experience remote for most immigrants of the past. But that army experience was colored over by work in intelligence and administration. Moreover, though he never rose above sergeant (his brother Walter, serving in the Far East theater, rose to be a captain, a situation unquestionably bound to torment his older brother), Oberammergau allowed him to identify with the commissioned ranks, rather than the GI Joes, since he exercised authority over officers, at first as a noncom and then as a civilian.

Yet, with all the money and power that Oberammergau conferred on him, Henry Kissinger decided in the spring of 1947 to return to America, and to college. He was taking the long view, well realizing how little qualified he was as yet to wield the authority he had held for a time. He applied to a number of prestigious universities—Kraemer had told him that a gentleman did not go to City College—and when only Harvard College responded that it was willing to enroll him for September (the others required him to wait a year),[5] he "accepted" Harvard. His commitment to Harvard, however, was really no stronger than that.

At Oberammergau Henry Kissinger had a number of comrades who would play roles in his future life. One was George Springer, a Czech refugee (also Jewish) who, back in America, with his wife, became Henry's closest friend. There was also Helmut Sonnenfeldt, now Kissinger's counselor in the State Department, and Henry Rosovsky, later a colleague of Henry's on the Harvard faculty, and now Dean of the School of Arts and Sciences. All three of these men, like Henry Kissinger, were at Oberammergau and then came to Harvard to study on their return to America.[6] Thus, Oberammergau also provided Henry Kissinger with a circle of friends and fellow scholars, though the degrees of intimacy varied greatly among the relationships. It is the first instance, perhaps, of that extraordinary network of acquaintances that he was later to establish, and which plays such an important role in his rise to power.

These episodes, as we have outlined them, were the *events* of Henry Kissinger's army experience. What did they *mean* to him, and what must they *mean* to us? As all accounts agree, Sgt. Henry Kissinger, aged 22, suddenly came into a position of power, as administrator of Krefeld and then Bergstrasse, over those who had killed his people and driven him and his family out of the country. Instead of being vengeful, Kissinger acted in a detached and forgiving manner toward his enemies. His behavior at this point forms the first thread of a pattern that persists in all of his diplomatic action. He was able to enter into the other person's view, in a sense to identify himself with his opponent, and thus to seek accommodation rather than pursue animosities. As Kissinger explained recently, "Not vengeance. I felt, to the dismay of my family, that if racial discrimination was bad vis-à-vis the Jews, it was bad vis-à-vis the Germans. I mean, you couldn't blame a whole people."[7]

Later, in his senior thesis at Harvard, Kissinger was to give intellectual form to his rationalization of his treatment of erstwhile enemies. He declares that for the sage, "Reason teaches him that to respite hatred with kindness, and violence with gentleness increases his power over himself, over the effects of the body and over the environment."[8] Like an earlier Jew with an identity problem (and I push the imagery no further), Kissinger had learned that forgiving one's enemies can become a prime source of power: over oneself, and over the enemy.

Kissinger, in fact, went so far in his fraternization with the enemy as to take German mistresses. According to one who knew him intimately at the time, Kissinger professed no interest in American girls. Instead, though there was an army rule against fraternizing with German women, Kissinger broke the rules (made easier for him as a CIC agent) and showed a lively interest in his erstwhile enemies of the opposite sex. At one point, in fact, he engaged in a fist fight with another man at the Oberammergau school over the favors of a German lady friend. According to the account, the other person, a non-Jew, incidentally, provoked the fight—and came out second best!

Kissinger commandeered as his car a 1938 Mercedes-Benz sedan. While this can be explained as an expedient of those times, such an explanation does not apply to Kissinger's later choice of Mercedes while at Harvard and Washington, D.C. *Of course*, many other American military personnel took German mistresses and drove Mercedes cars; for non-Jews to be pro-German was an all-too-frequent commonplace at the time (one recalls General Patton's question of why we were fighting the Germans, our natural and admired friends, and not the Russians). What was unusual was for the son of Orthodox Jews, who had lost 12 or 13 members of his family in Nazi concentration camps, to take German mistresses, and to drive and buy Mercedes (after the war many American Jews fervently boycotted the purchase of German automobiles), and to forgive his enemy to the extent and in the way that he did (objectively viewed, incidentally, it can be argued that this was a praiseworthy attitude).

It is this pattern of behavior, technically described as "identification with the aggressor," that became Kissinger's way, finally, of dealing with the Nazi experience (and we must now add this explanation to the earlier ones of sublimation and forgetting).[9] By empathy and identification Kissinger was able to forgive as well as to forget the past. In so behaving, he was thereby picking up again, though in an odd form, the theme of assimilation that had been pursued by so many German Jews before him.

In addition to the personal evidence cited, there is abundant clinical evidence to support the possibility *in theory* of Kissinger's identification with his enemy. Thus, analysts have reported cases of Jews who identified with Nazi storm troopers. Kissinger, as a German Jew—he has always struck people on first acquaintance as German rather than Jewish, and most Americans, according to a recent poll, still so view him—of assimilationist background, rising in the army by virtue of his German language ability, retaining his German accent even in English, might very well take his former enemy unto himself, in a very special way. Such an analysis is emphatically *not* to suggest that Kissinger became a Nazi, or even came close to it, though this is what the Dr. Strangelove accusations are suggesting, and Bruno Bettelheim has shown this actually happening in the cases of some Jewish concentration camp victims.[10] Kissinger's case is *very* different. It is much more complicated and, in my view, more positive in its contribution to certain aspects of Henry Kissinger's growth and development (as we shall see when we come to analyze his diplomacy).

The fundamental evidence for Kissinger's partial identification with his opponent is, ultimately, the words and actions of his later life, as we shall come to hear and see them. (For example, Kissinger lectured one aide about how Americans needed more discipline, after having chortled about how easy it was for him to round up SS men during the war because Germans were so "disciplined.") That identification, if my thesis is accepted, also involved an acceptance, in this case, of the enemy's stress on power and the uses of violence. Of course, the power and violence were identified with, and transferred to, the American army and placed in the service of men of goodwill. Henry Kissinger could now redeem his father. To do this, however, Henry Kissinger first needed to be freed from his father and the latter's "failure." He needed an intermediary, a new inspiration, offering him strength and a path to security. Shaking off and loosening past affiliations and memories (while retaining and transforming them in the way we have suggested), Kissinger was now ready to move out from under his father's and his community's authority. He was ready, as are so many bright adolescents, for a new model of what it is to be a man. Into this breach stepped Dr. Fritz Gustav Anton Kraemer, personalizing what until now we have been treating abstractly.

Kraemer

Hypnotic qualities are often in the eye of the beholder, as well as in the eye of the mesmeric individual, and the unconverted do not recognize any special qualities in the person; thus, one student in a class given by Kraemer hardly even remembers him. But for many others, Kraemer has been a spellbinder and a man of extraordinary qualities.

He is actually a fairly short man, but because of his erect posture and jaunty vitality he gives the impression of being a sizable person. He has a large head and a large, sensual mouth. He is hard of hearing, and has been for a long time, and is short sighted (he wears a monocle); nevertheless, he has striking eyes, which he expands with great flashing effect, thus creating a hypnotic effect. Though he constantly talks today about how old he is (about 67), he creates the impression of a man of strength in the prime of his life. A short sword, encased in a riding whip-type scabbard, heightens the effect of power and strength. If this is Kraemer in his mid-60s, one can imagine the impact of a 35-year-old version on the impressionable Henry Kissinger of 20.

A man of simple tastes, living in a generally spartan fashion, Fritz Kraemer, on his own account, came from an aristocratic family in Germany, growing up in a 35-room house in Nassau am Rhein. His father, he says, was a Prussian officer; another account has his father as a businessman.[11] (The name Kraemer, incidentally, means "grocery" or "general store" in German, and is often a Jewish name. There was a Krämer in the Fürth community, known to the Kissingers, and this in a subtle way may have served in making Kraemer an acceptable transitional figure to young Henry.)

His early life reads in part like a sophisticated picaresque novel. At the age of ten he witnessed the efforts at communist revolution in Germany, and these events of 1918 contributed significantly to his antibolshevism. After private school in Germany, he went to Geneva to study French, and then to the London School of Economics for English; here he studied with Harold Laski and Philip Noel-Brown. Later, he went to Rome to study Italian. All in all, he claims to know 14 languages (and in Rome worked as an interpreter for the League of Nations International Bureau). Along the way in his varied schooling, Kraemer acquired a doctorate in law from Frankfurt and one in political science from the University of Rome.

When the Nazis came to power in Germany, Kraemer could not stomach them. They offended his aristocratic feelings as well as views, and affronted his conservative politics. When they began to arrest some of his friends, he knew it was unsafe for himself, with his outspoken nature, to remain. His story of his "escape" is a "Hairbreadth Harry" one. In any case, leaving behind with his mother his Swedish wife and infant son, neither of whom he was to see again until the armistice seven years later, Kraemer eventually made his way to America. In 1939 he was at Columbia University, rowing a Falk boat on the Hudson River from New York to Poughkeepsie to keep in shape.

With the coming of Pearl Harbor, Kraemer enlisted in the U.S. Army. He was willing to fight fellow Germans as the only way to rid Germany of the horror bestriding it. His comrades in the 84th Division suspected him of being pro-German because of his monocle and his family in Germany, but he convinced his commanding general to let him go overseas with his fellow soldiers, knowing full well why *he* was fighting the Nazis. Kraemer, a born orator—like a "machine gun," he describes himself—a man of broad education, was superb at explaining to his companions why *they* should be vigorously combating the Nazis.

This is the man with whom Henry Kissinger had his fateful encounter while at Camp Claiborne. According to Kissinger's account in the now well-told story, Kraemer, a PFC (only later did he become a lieutenant, as a result of a battlefield commission), drove up to army barracks in a Jeep driven by a lieutenant (an obvious exaggeration), a monocle dangling from his chest, and snapped out in a Prussian accent, "Who is in charge here?" When the commanding officer appeared, Kraemer ordered him to set up a lecture for the men. Kissinger was impressed by this self-assured man, 15 years his senior, who could order officers around and explain to the troops why they were fighting—or rather, *should* be fighting—and he responded by writing a pretentious note: "This is how it should be done. Can I help you somehow?" It is clear that what Kissinger really meant was "Can you help me? Help me to become like you"—a man of will, daring, and self-confidence bordering on arrogance. Kraemer, with his extraordinary sensitivity to other's gifts, responded immediately to Kissinger's subterranean message and took the awkward youth under his wing.

To be chosen in this fashion, by such a man, made an enormous impression on Henry Kissinger. Kraemer claims to have a strange ability to "guess" about people and events, a semi-occult power which frightens even himself. Thus, he has spotted a number of extraordinary young men, including Colonel Al Haig, whom he recommended to Kissinger. He also says he predicted the outbreak of World War II as well as of the Yom Kippur War.[12] Whatever the truth in these matters—and, in fact, there is no reason to doubt Kraemer's claims—he believes in his own intuitive powers and makes others believe in them by the force of his personality.

Kraemer's account of the meeting is that within 20 minutes he became convinced that "this little [actually Kissinger is the same height as Kraemer] nineteen-year-old Jewish refugee, whose people knew nothing really of the great currents of history that were overcoming them," possessed a most important historical mind. "Henry had the urgent desire," Kraemer recalls, "not to understand the superficial thing but the underlying causes. He wanted to grasp things."[13] In Kraemer's view, Henry Kissinger "is musically attuned to history. This is not something you can learn, no matter how intelligent you are. It is a gift from God."[14] Whatever the truth of these assertions at the time, the fact that this powerful, hypnotic figure chose Kissinger in this way turned the judgment into a self-fulfilling prophecy. It also turned Henry Kissinger into a follower.

What Kraemer did was to provide Kissinger with a new

model (as well as a patron), emancipating him from his bourgeois Jewish parents and community. He was able to do this because much of what he offered Kissinger was old wine in new bottles, that is, Kraemer actually reaffirmed aspects of Kissinger's past while partly emancipating him from it. Kraemer, as we shall see, was the perfect transitional figure for the adolescent Henry: a "second father" because he incorporated significant elements of the first, while transcending them.

Kraemer preached a message, derived from his orthodox Lutheran (he is, today, a staunch member of the Missouri Lutheran Synod) commitment, of being responsible only to God, not man. Within the conservative commitment to his inherited religious dogmas and values, therefore, Kraemer was extolling the necessity of autonomy from authority.

Kissinger was not put off by Kraemer's Lutheranism because he himself was slipping the bonds of his Jewish training. Away from his family for the first time, open to religious questionings in bull sessions among the men of his company, Kissinger was on the way to becoming a marginal Jew, respectful of his parents' views but no longer a practicing adherent of the faith. As a result, as we have already noted, those who first met Kissinger in college or later thought of him as "German," and in many cases only learned of his being Jewish months or years later. It was not that he falsified his Jewish past, only that he no longer faced the world as primarily a Jew. He had achieved autonomy from his father's religion, if not from his father's God.

Kraemer also made Kissinger reaffirm or discover part of his German background. It was Kraemer who made Henry Kissinger speak German to him in the army and got him his position as a *German* interpreter. It was Kraemer who made Kissinger study *German* history. The values that Kraemer preached were those of *German* conservatism. In going on to become an American, Kissinger would retain more of the German element in him than would otherwise have been the case. Kraemer was *not* an American, and it is of great importance that Kissinger's first and most important model was neither Jewish *nor* American.

By identifying with Kraemer, Kissinger was able unconsciously to overcome and bypass his father (in technical language, we might say to win through in his oedipal struggle). Henry's father was a teacher; Kraemer scorned academics, a scorn that later surfaced in Henry Kissinger's attitudes to Harvard and his colleagues there.[15] Henry's solution was to combine his parental heritage of teaching and scholarship with a disdain for it. His father was a shy, "weak" man, though typically German in his strict patriarchal, slightly authoritarian manner; Kraemer preached a message of strength and power and behaved in an "arrogant" fashion. Everyone has noted how Henry Kissinger combined in his own character shyness and insecurity with arrogance. By retaining parts of his father inside him, but fusing them with Kraemer's person, Kissinger at last was able to reconcile emotionally the needs of goodwill and power, of weakness and strength.

As a vigorous, dashing figure with enormous presence and a hypnotic quality, Kraemer preached a doctrine of lonely courage, of following one's convictions without the need for approval by others, of disdaining success, especially bourgeois monetary rewards. He acted out a conservatism based on absolute values, on aristocratic standards—"be a gentleman," he exhorted Henry —and on the notion that strength and manly power was what held the world together in the face of violence and savagery. Kraemer was also as much anticommunist as he was anti-Nazi, linking the two "barbarisms" for Kissinger (a link strengthened by the anticommunism of the CIC, for which Kissinger worked). Exuding vitality, an interest in women, and an adamantine self-confidence, he was just the model to fire Kissinger's imagination.

Thus it was under Kraemer's influence that Kissinger decided, upon his return to America, to give up his "bourgeois" notion of being a CPA, to go to a good college—"a gentleman doesn't go to City College," we have seen Kraemer tell him—and to become a "new man," an American with a transcended German-Jewish identity. Kraemer as a German in America was the perfect transitional figure for young Henry to follow.

In sum, Fritz Kraemer symbolizes and personifies the role played by the army in Henry Kissinger's development. He reaffirmed the conservatism that Henry had brought with him from his Orthodox Jewish past, but gave it new dress. Kraemer's conservatism, incidentally, was more a *Weltanschauung*, a world view, than a scholarly, philosophical position; even more than a *Weltanschauung*, it was an embodiment in action of conservatism. In the end, this conservatism provided the justification for the use of strength and power that Henry Kissinger so desperately needed in an effort to construct his new world, and his "new" self. "A man," Kraemer said, "does not know the world until he has been out alone on the docks of Marseilles, hungry and with only one suit, being stalked by another man who wants that suit. *Then being reasonable or good doesn't matter* [my italics]. Then a man has to stand up for himself or die."[16] In these words was the solution to Henry Kissinger's personal and political problems.

The context in which all this came to pass was World War II, and the power involved was military power. It is our thesis, therefore, that the army experience, which for so many Americans meant death or a hiatus in their prospective careers, meant a new life for Henry Kissinger. Henceforth, that life was intertwined, in one way or another, with the military. It was the money accumulated in the army, plus the G.I. Bill, that permitted Kissinger to go to Harvard. It was the Clausewitzian combination of war and peace ("war is only a continuation of policy by other means") that engaged his professional attention thereafter. Eventually, it was on the issue of nuclear policy, the ultimate war weapon, that Kissinger made his reputation and then, on this basis, his first entrance into the foreign policy-making world. His links to the military establishment have until recently been strong; they have thought of him as a "hawk," and therefore acceptable to them. (The recent struggle with former Secretary of Defense Schlesinger illustrates the limits of both his hawkishness and the military's acceptance of his policies.) The paradox is that in the pursuit of peace and the preservation of men of goodwill, Kissinger willingly embraced the world of weapons and the threat of violent power. As much as Napoleon, to whom, in what he jocularly referred to as his "megalomanic" moments, he frequently compared himself, Kissinger was made by the army and the military (personified by Kraemer). Instead of a marshal's baton in his knapsack, however, Kissinger carried a future appointment as Secretary of State.

Chapter 3

HARVARD
AND ACADEMIA

Postwar Harvard

Henry Kissinger

HENRY KISSINGER came to Harvard as a member of what the yearbook described as the "last of the predominantly veteran classes."[1] He was 24 at the time, not a typical peacetime freshman. He remained at Harvard as undergraduate student, graduate student, and faculty member for over 20 years, longer than his entire life in Germany. It is an understatement, then, to say that Harvard played a major role in the making of Henry Kissinger.

What was Harvard like in 1947? One can turn to the yearbook of 1950, Henry Kissinger's graduating year, for a partial account. On one hand, we are told that there was much new political activity. Chapters of both the Young Republican Club and Americans for Democratic Action were astir. Polled about its political preferences, the class of 1950 voted about 30 percent independent, 10 percent moderate Republicans, 10 percent liberal Republicans, and 10 percent Truman Democrats.[2] On the other hand, the yearbook notes that "the veterans, older and more mature, tended to replace college spirit, never a very high-priced commodity at Harvard, with an intense enthusiasm in specific individual enterprises." What these last are is never spelled out. It may well have been individual scholarly achievement, aimed at career catch-up, and this guess is supported by the next statement in the yearbook, that "they knew what they wanted as had no other generation in the recent past, and they approached college life with intensity and decisiveness."[3]

At the risk of giving a tendentious account, one can say that the gentleman's "C" and the rah-rah spirit were not prevalent, and high-minded and serious work was in. President Conant, former High Commissioner to Germany and a renowned former scientist, set the tone. It would be naive, however, to believe that the club system no longer prevailed, and that an air of snobbery—prep school boys still accounted for about 50 percent of the Harvard student body—did not envelop the "intense" veterans. Alas, most observers would also agree that genteel anti-Semitism was still strong, though Harvard as an institution was increasingly opening its gates to students of Jewish background.

The tension between the students' political interests and their commitments to "individual enterprises" appears mirrored in the comments of Charles R. Cherington, Associate Professor of Government, who wrote the section on social sciences. His tone is very critical. Pointing to the faculty's failure to meet the challenge of society's problems, he accuses his fellow political scientists of being "notably confused as to their mission." The government department has "attractive platform performers," who pack the students in; it purports to deal with the problems of power: "But when we come to examine genuine *intellectual* contributions to the University and to society, the record is, with a few exceptions, sadly deficient." In Cherington's view, the historians were in a slightly better position than the political scientists, since they had a traditional method. But in the end, he concludes that all social scientists lack a "sense of mission." Gropingly, Cherington was calling for a fusion of individual intellectual effort and "power" problems.[4]

The government department, incidentally, was the one in which Henry Kissinger would major. Most of its members would have considered Cherington a peripheral figure, but it is clear that he spoke out of a frustration caused by real, if muted, tensions within the department and the university.

What else should one note about Harvard and the class of 1950 at this time? The tuition had hit a record $600! By the time of graduation, 1 percent of the class had married. At least two of its members were later engaged with Henry Kissinger in foreign policy activities: George Cabot Lodge and Herbert John Spiro (a fellow refugee, though from Hamburg, who is now working in the State Department). Many others were to become famous in the arts, professions, government, and business world, and a large number were from socially prominent families, with fame and social position frequently overlapping.

Kissinger as an Undergraduate

Where did Henry Kissinger fit in all this? The record is sparse, for Kissinger seems to have gone through Harvard, at least as far as his fellow students were concerned, as an "invisible man." Aside from a roommate or two, he stayed to himself and his books. *Par excellence*, he exemplified his class's dedication to "specific individual enterprises." He was more mature, and mature looking, than most of his fellow undergraduates, and he expressed his maturity by an almost monastic devotion to his studies. As one who knew him reported, he was continuously reading, cracking the books until 1:00–2:00 A.M. every morning.

The picture is not completely unrelieved. He did go to

football games, continued his avid interest in New York Yankees' baseball games, and somewhere along the way became concerned with the Moral Rearmament Movement. Aside from such minor excursions, however, he kept close to the path of scholarship. His career plans at first seemed unsettled. Thus, he studied math, and toyed with the idea of going on in that direction. He was interested in logic and philosophy (an appendix of his undergraduate thesis concerns itself with logical positivism), and was much affected by one of his professors in this field, Henry Scheffer. Kissinger also spoke frequently of the ideas of Professor Percy Bridgman. According to his roommate, Arthur Gillman, he even thought, unlikely as it appears now in the light of his attitude to the field (see pp. 196–197), of becoming a psychiatrist, and took science courses with an eye to a premedical major. Eventually, however, he settled firmly into his destined studies in government (with little attention, it should be noted, to economics).

We shall refer later, in great detail, to some of the ideas in his undergraduate thesis, "The Meaning of History; Reflections on Spengler, Toynbee and Kant." Here we wish only to note his concern with the three thinkers mentioned, as well as such other thinkers as Spinoza, Hegel, Clausewitz, Marx, and Dostoevski. While Henry Kissinger never became a scholar in relation to these figures, it is obvious that he had at least a nodding acquaintance with the great political philosophers and their work. (Much of this, of course, was under the stimulus of his major professor, William Yandell Elliott, whom we shall consider shortly.) It is also clear that a large proportion of these thinkers were German—Kant, Hegel, Clausewitz, Marx, and Spengler—thus continuing the influence of Kissinger's earlier background, although now in highly reified form.

To all of this work, in fact, Kissinger brought the weight of his previous beliefs and experiences. He certainly impressed his younger roommate, Arthur Gillman, with his strong opinions and convictions, and his tremendous ability to concentrate on his work. According to Gillman, Henry frequently talked with him (though not with an eye to making an impression) about his experiences in military government and his continuing close relations with top people in the army, presumably as a part of his reserve officer status. His main concern was with the Russians, who he thought were out to dominate the world. According to Gillman, Henry predicted that the Russians would become powerful in the Middle East. His fear was not for the newly created state of Israel but for America. In fact, Henry Kissinger was not enthusiastic, as were so many of the other Jewish students, about the formation of Israel in 1948. Even then, he felt that a United States policy that favored Israel would turn the Arabs against America, and thus toward Russia, thereby permitting the Soviet Union to enter the Middle East. (Incidentally, Kissinger seems to have demonstrated his future charm and diplomatic skills with Gillman's pro-Zionist family when he was invited home to dinner. Without offending them, he managed to express his opinions.) All in all, Kissinger was very *American* in his cold war attitudes. Though he expressed no interest in domestic politics, his foreign policy concerns did lead him to the expressed view that Henry Wallace (the Progressive Party candidate in the 1948 election) was "soft" on communism.

If he talked at some length about his military experiences and foreign policy views, Kissinger refrained from saying much about his earlier experiences or background. He never mentioned being at City College, and he had little to say about his family (though not trying to hide anything and perfectly happy to have his brother Walter visit him). Gillman recalls that Henry did remark that his father was a teacher, or professor, and that he was a very Orthodox Jew. Henry himself, as we know, was no longer a practicing Jew at the time, and gave the impression that the reason for this was that religion had been the cause of the Jews' suffering, and therefore should be discarded. One catches a glimpse of the young Henry's disturbance over that which was weak and unable to protect him; indeed, over what seemed to jeopardize his existence.

There was some discussion about girls, but not much. Neither boy did much dating. Henry's girl, Anne Fleischer,[5] came to visit from time to time, and apparently he did talk over the question of his marrying her. When he arrived at his decision to do so, it ended his residence at Harvard, first at Claverly Hall and then at Adams House. He and Anne took a furnished apartment in Newton Center, about 20 minutes from Cambridge, thereby removing Henry even further from the mainstream of Harvard undergraduate life. His marriage, as we know, placed him with only 1 percent of his fellow students.

His dedication to work and studies also placed him with an equally small, or even smaller, group of students. He had all A's and was one of only 16 seniors to make Phi Beta Kappa. (Two of the others were also government majors, and one of the others was James Rodney Schlesinger, in economics, who later became Secretary of Defense.) It seemed only natural that so brilliant a student—he was, of course, also a summa cum laude—should go on immediately to graduate work. And this he did (with Anne working as a bookkeeper—reminiscent of his father—full-time in a furniture store). By going on to graduate school, he continued and strengthened the influence over him of his senior tutor, Professor William Yandell Eliott, the man who, with Fritz Kraemer, gave Kissinger the model of what it was to be conservative—and strong.

Elliott

In a real sense, Kissinger chose Elliott as his mentor, just as he had chosen Kraemer, and then, in turn, became chosen by him. Harvard, in its inimitable fashion, first assigned Henry Kissinger as an undergraduate to Professor Carl Friedrich of the government department. What more natural than to have a German-American student work with a distinguished German-American professor? What Harvard did not know was that this particular German-American student had already had a transitional figure of this kind in his life and was now on the way to becoming "more American than the Americans." He and Friedrich, therefore, never spoke in German.

There were other reasons why Kissinger asked for a change of tutor after six months. Friedrich was primarily a dedicated scholar, and Kissinger wished to be a "practical politician." Friedrich, a non-Jew, was nevertheless pro-Zionist, and the teacher and student argued over this issue. Moreover, Friedrich did not think his tutee's work in political theory particularly distinguished, although perfectly competent, and his teacher's lack of belief in his brilliance must have nettled Kissinger. In any case, teacher and pupil amicably agreed that a transfer was a good idea. It was Friedrich, apparently, who recommended Elliott to Kissinger, who promptly "chose" his new teacher. Friedrich recommended his former tutee to Elliott as one who was not potentially a great scholar, but who was bright and capable. Both Friedrich and Elliott, it might be noted, though they attracted different kinds of students—that generation of Harvard students frequently divided into disciples of one or the other—were adherents of the great humanistic and historical tradition, as opposed to the new behavioral and quantifying types in political science.

Professor William Yandell Elliott was just the man for Kissinger. Like Kraemer, Elliott was an "aristocrat," though Southern rather than Prussian, a "powerful" figure, possessed, in Kissinger's words, of a "seigneurial" presence. Dark and handsome, he was impressive in size and physique—he had been an all-American tackle at Vanderbilt University—an overpowering figure for teaching power, the perfect model of the scholar-activist, the teacher who combined thought with practical concerns.

A Rhodes scholar at Oxford, Elliott knew firsthand what the

genteel life of the mind was like, and he carried the tutorial attitudes of English university life into his Harvard teaching activities. Thus, though he shifted to a hillbilly accent when back in Tennessee, at Harvard he spoke with a Balliol accent. But he also fancied himself a bestrider of the corridors of real power: the military and government. During World War II he was a mover in the Office of War Mobilization, retaining his army commission into peacetime. In the 1940s he served as a staff director on the Herter committee. He never let anyone forget that he had once met Stalin. When Kissinger came to know him, he was a consultant to the House Committee on Foreign Affairs in Washington, and spent two or three days a week there. Possessed of tremendous physical energy, he maintained an unusually demanding schedule which included making himself available to students back on the campus.

Elliott was also an enormously ambitious person (some qualify this by saying he was not a driven or mean-spirited man). According to one friend, Elliott even thought of himself as a future President of the United States. Instead, it seems, he had to settle for a dominant role in the government department at Harvard. A number of his colleagues felt he was obsessed with his own importance. At departmental softball games, it was Elliott who had to bash the ball farther than anyone else. He tried, apparently, to be a kind of Renaissance man, friend not only to the mighty in Washington but also to the poet John Crowe Ransom of Vanderbilt University. Elliott himself was constantly writing novels. His nickname of "Wild Bill" Elliott apparently suited him partly because of his bull-like energies, and partly because of his boundless ambitions ("Wild Bill" also has a cowboy connotation—one thinks of Wild Bill Hickok—and Kissinger's later fantasy of being a lone cowboy riding into town, as in his Fallaci interview, may derive in part from this inspiration).

Unfortunately, Elliott's family life was tinged with tragedy and unhappiness. His first wife had a mental breakdown, and his oldest son had similar problems. There is additional talk of domestic troubles, and in the end Elliott and his wife were divorced. His second wife apparently was a solid and faithful supporter. All in all, however, one sees in Elliott a tormented, almost demonic, figure of incredible promise and unfulfilled ambitions. Alas, in his later years he was perceived by many as a shadow of his former self, a dull poseur, a man who had not realized his great gifts: a "burnt-out case," sarcastically referred to as the "Senator from Tennessee."

But at the time Henry Kissinger first met him, Elliott was still a seemingly dynamic and dominant figure. In truth, he may have needed Henry Kissinger as much as the latter needed him. In the view of some who knew him well, Elliott was deep down "a very frightened man," paying the price inwardly of being a hillbilly at Harvard. In any case, with his oldest son disturbed, Elliott apparently saw in Kissinger the son he always wanted, an "adopted" son (and one might well argue that Henry has fulfilled in his own person his tutor's great ambitions). Inwardly insecure and unsatisfied, Elliott was highly vulnerable to the flattering attentions that his young tutee could provide in a courtly manner. Together the two men took long walks, discussing the important things of this world.

In many ways, of course, it was an odd relation. Elliott was an ardent Christian Scientist, a faith he had inherited from his mother. He was also given to anti-Semitic remarks. Those who knew him well argue strenuously over the meaning of this trait in Elliott. For many, it was part of Elliott's general antagonism to "foreign" elements in American society: he didn't like Italians any more than Jews, for example, and made all kinds of ethnic slurs (à la the White House tapes, apparently). For others, it was simply part of "Wild Bill" Elliott's directness: in today's world he would say something like, "Why don't the damned Jews stop supporting Jackson?" As these people forcefully argue, Elliott's anti-Semitic remarks do not indicate he was anti-Jewish, for too many of his close friends were Jews. Nevertheless, it is clear that there was an Archie Bunker-like insensitivity to Elliott, strange in one otherwise so sophisticated. Or perhaps it was just the commonplace social anti-Semitism of Elliott's Southern background, and not particularly rare at Harvard either at the time. In any case, it apparently did not diminish the relationship between Elliott and his Jewish-German-American student and disciple.

For Kissinger, the flattery involved in having such a person as Elliott interested in him was great. It confirmed his own sense of growing self-esteem. All in all, emotionally as well as intellectually, the effect of Elliott on Kissinger as model and patron was far-reaching and deep.

Intellectually, one of the most important things Elliott gave Henry Kissinger was a true political philosophy, a theoretical underpinning for and confirmation of his conservative leanings. Elliott at Oxford had become steeped in the Hegelian idealist tradition, mediated through such English thinkers as T. H. Green, Bernard Bosanquet, and A. D. Lindsay, the Master of Balliol College. Elliott, of course, emphasized the conservative side of Hegel, and turned him to his own uses (expert opinion, incidentally, does not credit Elliott with being a particularly sound Hegel scholar). The effect of Elliott's Hegel on Kissinger was profound, and some observers profess to see the mark of the dialectic in Kissinger's later thinking; one observer, in fact, sees Hegel's notion of *aufgeheben*—literally not solving problems as such, but outgrowing them, i.e., solving them on another level—as a clue to Henry Kissinger's general approach.

Elliott was also intensely, even rabidly, anticommunist. Eventually his oral diatribes found their way into print, coloring over his erstwhile scholarship. If Hegel had, in historical reality, led to Marx, Elliott gave no sign of understanding this, adhering religiously to the idealistic perspective of the great German philosopher and denigrating the materialist interpretation of his disciple. In fact, Elliott was not so much concerned

with Marx and his errors as he was with the Bolshevik en-
shrinement of atheistic communism in Russian, a great and
threatening world power.

The enhancement of Kissinger's already existing anticommunist feelings by Elliott's teachings is obvious. Elliott also
had intense moral feelings about life and politics. One commentator has described him as a "Manichean" in this regard.
In any case, politics was not a value-free "science" for Elliott
but a proving ground of high moral purposes. In the light of
Kissinger's apparent amorality of later years (a question that
needs to be discussed at much greater length; see pp. 273–278),
we must note that in his senior thesis under Elliott, on "The
Meaning of History," Kissinger wrestled with problems of
ethics and power. As viewed by his critics, Kissinger was
"giving" his teacher what the latter wanted.

Beyond the specifics of anticommunism and moral postures,
Elliott gave Kissinger an introduction to the wider world of
culture and feeling in general. In an oft-quoted remark, Kissinger
has stated, "We met every week for years. Bill Elliott made
me discover Dostoevski and Hegel, Kant, Spinoza, and Homer.
On many Sundays we took long walks in Concord. He spoke
of the power of love, and said that the only truly unforgiveable
sin is to use people as if they were objects [incidentally, this is
a charge often leveled against Kissinger by his critics; was
Elliott warning his pupil against a danger he sensed in him?].
He discussed greatness and excellence. *And while I did not
always follow his words* [my italics], I knew that I was in the
presence of a remarkable man."[6] In his own person, Elliott
embodied the views that he expounded. By "style" of life and
bearing, the teacher gave additional meaning to his words.

Elliott's influence on Kissinger was due in part to the fact
that the two had very similar types of minds. Both were concerned with the essential dynamics of history, and liked to
think in grand, sweeping terms. Both were intensely aware of
the problem of freedom of choice, and the dilemmas encased

therein. They shared a tragic sense of history. And both were ambitious to do something about their ideas, by involving them in the actual power struggle of daily life.

There is little reason, given the "fit" of Elliott and Kissinger, to wonder why each chose the other. Both were admirably suited to offer the other something he needed. Kissinger, especially, could flatter and imitate; in the process, he could turn imitation to personal development and growth. Elliott, however, had one additional thing he could offer to Kissinger: the powerful support of a patron. Having looked at Elliott as a model, we must now turn to this other side of the relationship, thereby resuming the story of Henry Kissinger's life in academia.

Graduate Student

Henry Kissinger's life as a graduate student was somewhat unusual, in that, as a summa, he did not need to prepare for the so-called general examinations, which hung like a minor nightmare over the rest of the students in the government department. Instead, he could concentrate on his thesis.

His thesis subject was itself somewhat unusual, for instead of choosing a contemporary topic, or one tinged with the behavioral approach becoming so fashionable at the time, he chose a *historical* subject—the Congress of Vienna settlements, broadly construed as running from 1812 to 1822—which only crept up on current international relations concerns by means of an analogy. We shall not attempt to paraphrase that book —this has already been done conscientiously by other scholars —but rather, later in our own work, to extract from it certain leading themes.[7] Here we need only note how consistent Kissinger's choice was with the Elliott mold of mind.

Even more unusual for a graduate student was his being chosen by Elliott in 1951 to become director of the Harvard

International Seminar, and in 1952 being backed as editor of a journal, *Confluence*. The "load" on Kissinger, a beginning graduate student, was extraordinary; so was the responsibility—and the opportunity.

The inspiration for the International Seminar seems to have been Elliott's. It was part of his cold war against communism, though accomplished very subtly. The idea was to invite the future leaders of other countries for a paid two-month seminar during the summer, and thus to expose them to the American way of life and American views. Financial support was secured from the Rockefeller Foundation and, as later disclosed, in small amount from the CIA. (Henry Kissinger apparently was unaware of this at the time.) To be director of the seminar, Elliott named his protégé, Henry, who then gave life to the project, doing all of the drudgery essential to such an institution. Stephen Graubard, one of Henry's friends in graduate school, apparently also helped plan the early seminars.

The purpose of the seminar (as stated, for example, in the 1965 Report) was as follows: "The Harvard International Seminar attempts to promote international understanding and cooperation by giving its members an opportunity: 1. To increase their stature as individuals and their general competence in their various fields. 2. To study and discuss the relations of the various countries of the world and to develop and deepen the sense of community among them. 3. To acquaint themselves with the attitudes and values underlying American life and thought. 4. To bring foreign concerns and thinking to the attention of Americans." It was designed "for persons between the ages of twenty-six and forty-five who are on the verge of reaching positions of leadership in their own countries."[8]

The Academic Program consisted of two formal groups of about 20 each, one in humanities and one in political and economic concerns, each under the leadership of a faculty member. In 1965, to take an example, the chairman of the Politics and Economics Section of the seminar was Professor Samuel H.

Beer of Harvard University, who dealt with domestic affairs, while Professor Henry A. Kissinger of Harvard University considered international relations. (The chairman of the Humanities Section was Professor Jack Ludwig, novelist, critic, and chairman of the department of English at the State University of New York, Stony Brook, thus giving some indication of the "Renaissance" breadth of the seminar.) In addition, there were many eminent and diverse guest speakers. "Visits to American Institutions and Enterprises" and "Open Forums" rounded out the formal program, while a social program, including an open-air concert at Crane's Beach, Ipswich, Massachusetts; Charlie Chaplin and Marx Brothers movies; and a Boston Red Sox baseball game, gave spice to the summer's study.

Henry Kissinger directed these International Seminars during 18 successive summers, with two exceptions: in 1966 he was on sabbatical leave and in 1968 he was on partial leave while advising Governor Nelson Rockefeller on foreign policy during Rockefeller's campaign for the Republican presidential nomination.

It takes little imagination to see how Henry Kissinger was able to use the seminar to build up a network of acquaintances in key positions in other countries; all recent commentators have pointed this out, listing the important names such as Giscard d'Estaing (now President of France), spotted as a comer back in 1954. What has attracted less, or no, attention is how, *as a beginning graduate student,* Henry Kissinger was able to hand out invitations and kudos to those closer to home. Academics, even prestigious ones, are often not adverse to invitations, honoraria, and summer jobs. Moreover, long before the John F. Kennedy Institute of Politics at Harvard deliberately tried to mix academics with political figures, the International Seminar had pioneered in making a connecting link between the corridors of political power and of mind (in 1965 the seminar also met with the Policy Planning Council of the State Department, with McGeorge Bundy, the Special Assistant to the President, and with the Honorable John T. McNaughton, Assistant Secretary of Defense for International Security Affairs in the Pentagon). In turning over the International Seminar to Kissinger, Elliott was giving him an unusual power base, midway between the life of the scholar and the life of the "practical politicians"—one more powerful because not perceived as such by the casual observer (and perhaps not even at first consciously so perceived by Henry Kissinger himself).

In its beginning in 1951, the seminar was conducted as a pilot project, with 20 participants drawn from West European students already in the United States. In 1953 Asians were invited for the first time; in 1957 Africa was represented; in 1959 the seminar was extended to include Latin Americans. East Europeans and Russians, though invited toward the end, never actually made it. But Arabs and Israelis, Pakistanis and Indians, Chinese (The Republic) and Japanese, Greeks and Turks all had their chance to argue with one another in a friendly atmosphere. It was a foretaste of, and a training ground for, Kissinger's now-famous mediating efforts. It also gave Kissinger the habit of establishing links between right- and left-wing groups, as well as seeking constituencies in both these rival camps, a pattern which persists up to the present.

Although the seminar and its details eventually became a burden to him—no wonder, with all his other commitments!— Kissinger obviously derived enough benefits to remain as its director for almost his entire academic career at Harvard. (It folded in 1969, when he left to become head of the National Security Council for Nixon.) By then it had served him well as one of his springboards to *real* power in the foreign policy-making world of Washington, D.C.

Another such vehicle, though of slightly lesser importance and duration, was *Confluence, An International Forum*, a quarterly journal which Kissinger founded in 1952 with the aid of a $26,000 grant from the Rockefeller Brothers Foundation. As its name suggests, its claim was to bring together

European and American thinkers. Who better to bridge the gulf than Kissinger, a German American whose split identity needed healing as much as did the relations of the erstwhile allies? Moreover, we can see Kissinger's personal concerns mirrored in the topics of some of the magazine's issues: "What Are the Bases of Civilization?", "Tradition in Culture and in Politics," mainly concerned with the problem of conservatism, and "The Problems of Religion." A perusal of the letters to the editors gives us hints as to Kissinger's particular directions. In vol. 3, no. 3, an English correspondent says, "The anti-Communist slant of *Confluence* gives me feelings of discomfort." In vol. 3, no. 4, there is a letter complaining about the inclusion of an article by a German reactionary, Ernst von Solomon, who had been involved in the murders of "leftist" political opponents (e.g., Walter Rathenau, a German Jew) during the Weimar Republic; what is interesting is Kissinger's reply defending the publication of Solomon's article. This is again a demonstration of empathy for and partial identification with the enemy, Kissinger's particular conservative form of the traditional liberal plea for tolerance.

For his editorial board, Kissinger had assembled a varied group: McGeorge Bundy; Harold Lasswell, the political scientist (and pioneer in personality and politics studies!); John Crowe Ransom, the poet and friend of Elliott; Arthur Schlesinger, Jr.; Arthur E. Sutherland, of the Harvard Law School; Huntington Cairns; Harry D. Gideonse; and Brian A. McGrath, S.J. Subscriptions were listed as $3.00, with single copies $1.00, but, in fact, the magazine was widely distributed gratis. As with the International Seminar, *Confluence* could serve as an ideal means of acquiring friends and influence. Kissinger neglected few opportunities to solicit a judgment from the great on the magazine's quality and thus on his own efforts. Also, as one friend put it, the young editor could write to prominent men and women requesting a contribution; he could then hold out to his Harvard contemporaries the flattering chance of being in the same journal as the luminaries. It is extraordinary how many of the people to whom I talked about Henry Kissinger traced their acquaintance with him back to an invitation to contribute an article to *Confluence*.

If the magazine didn't succeed in joining European and American intellectual life, it certainly accomplished the purpose of uniting Henry Kissinger with a number of important figures. More importantly for our purposes, Kissinger's use of the journal, as of the seminar, even if unintentional, revealed a manipulative skill that would stand him in good stead —nay, be essential—in his later climb to power.

Whatever its service to Kissinger, as a journal *Confluence* was not really successful as an intellectual enterprise. By its fourth volume, in October 1955, it had become thinner, and acquired an assistant editor, Kissinger's friend, Steve Graubard, who obviously became important that year because Kissinger himself went off to the Council on Foreign Relations. (Graubard later put his experience on *Confluence* to good use when he became editor of *Daedalus*, the prestigious journal of the American Academy of Arts and Sciences.) By the summer of 1958, the magazine had reached its unheralded end. Although it announced the articles to appear in the next issue, the issue itself was never published. (Oddly enough, those connected with the journal cannot remember what happened; one wonders whether subscribers got their money back or authors an apology for their articles being returned?) *Confluence* had run dry.

Europe: The Hand of the Past

The failure of *Confluence* intellectually to bridge the gap between America and Europe points to a later failure—and success—which has puzzled almost all observers of Henry

Kissinger's foreign policy. It is simply that his "successes" have come in non-European areas of the world, about which initially he knew almost nothing, and his "failures" primarily in regard to his relations with European countires. Let us pause to examine this situation, pending a later analysis of Kissinger's negotiating skills and successes.

With Europe, Kissinger is involved with himself, and his own past. His feelings, therefore, are unusually mixed and complex, as might be expected. First, however, one must acknowledge the "objective" fact that Europe, as an area of developed countries, poses exceptionally difficult problems. They are primarily problems of an economic and technical nature which do not lend themselves readily to personalistic negotiations and solutions, Kissinger's forte.

There is another factor that rests on the border between the objective and subjective. Most European countries, by and large, operate in a democratic or semidemocratic fashion, i.e., as parliamentary democracies. They are not generally headed by autocratic leaders who can speak without extensive limits on their power, and without the necessity of consulting a broad constituency. Thus, quick, dramatic agreements are extremely difficult, if not impossible, to reach.

The problem for Kissinger is compounded because of his basic distaste for left-wing or socialist regimes at a time when much of Western Europe has gone socialist, although in a democratic manner. It is no secret that Kissinger greatly admired de Gaulle, while not being particularly keen about the likes of Brandt. Although, as with *Confluence*, he cultivated both left and right groups, his sympathies for the latter were bound to color his attitudes to European matters.

Again on the border of the objective and subjective is the fact that Europe is neither an adversary, such as the Soviet Union or China, nor a group of obviously weaker parties, nor a collection of client states, such as Israel and the Arab nations, where Kissinger and America enter as a mediating power. Thus, Europe poses for Kissinger the nearest thing to a sibling or peer group situation, and we have already suggested his possible difficulties in such an environment.

His difficulties with Europe are compounded by two other, more personal elements. One is that Kissinger has become very American, and identifies strongly with American power (in the process partly rejecting his European identity), to the extent that Europe is seen as no longer powerful, as a possible candidate for being pushed into dependent status. Thus, all of Kissinger's dislike for the weak is mobilized. His temptation to play the autocrat in this situation is great.

The other personal element disturbing Kissinger's attitudes to Europe is his assumption that, as a past European, he automatically knows how Europeans think and feel. (One may call this, technically, a transference problem, itself a danger in any effort at psychological understanding.) Thus, Kissinger has real difficulty in allowing for and respecting European values and aspirations as being different from those of Americans, and therefore of himself. In short, he has trouble maintaining his "distance," his vaunted diplomatic ability to be "objective" in understanding another person's needs. Perhaps we can understand this better if we bear in mind Sadat's observation that Kissinger's success in the Middle East was due to the fact that he was the first American Secretary of State who came without preconceived ideas, who set out to learn the mechanical details of the problems, as well as the psychology of the peoples involved—i.e., both the specific nature of the problems and how they were perceived subjectively—and then acted accordingly.[9]

America's relations with Europe are complex and multi-layered. So are Kissinger's feelings toward his former homeland (the fatherland, for him, whereas for most immigrants it would be the "mother country"). Emotions that are logically contradictory are, nevertheless, psychologically consistent in Kissinger; often however, they lead to contradictory and "irrational" behavior on his part toward Europe.

Much of what we are talking about was prefigured in *Con-*

fluence. Though it claimed to be an "international forum," it was basically a European–American dialogue. As such, it mirrored the contradictory and unresolved aspects of Kissinger's own split personality. While I believe Kissinger has the capacity to learn and grow—the story of his life—and thus to modify in the future his attitudes and policy toward Europe, the past that he wished to forget can never let him go completely. To use a Spenglerian image, Destiny, or "Fate," takes a hand in his diplomacy, whether invited or not.

Bowie: A Failed Relationship

If Elliott and the International Seminar can be thought of as the patron successful, Robert Bowie and the Center for International Affairs can be considered the patron failed. For our purposes, in trying to understand the patterns of Kissinger's behavior, the failed relation is equally as important as the successful one. Both point to the way Kissinger would handle similar situations in the future.

The context for Kissinger's encounter with Bowie must be seen as one in which Harvard, as one of a number of universities, was involving itself increasingly in the world of governmental and military policy. A new "style" of university life was emerging, in which the ideal was no longer aloof and genteel scholarship set in ivy-covered cloisters but direct involvement with the actual day-to-day decision-making process of the centers of power. The new faculty hero was the one who spent half his time in transit to Washington, D.C. and who, back on the campus, set up centers and secured the funding for them through his "connections." (The Kennedy years were to be the epitome of this life style for Cantabrigians.) World War II had brought the universities, and their research facilities, directly into the national effort; no less was expected of

74

them in the cold war that ensued. Put in more flattering terms, the universities were still being drafted for public service (in some ways this was the new version of the old land-grant philosophy).

It is this great sea change in the nature of many universities, including Harvard, which must be seen as the background for Kissinger's emergence to power. Kissinger, of course, was not unique; Walt Rostow, McGeorge Bundy, and a host of others preceded him, while closer to home, Elliott had set a personal model. Bowie was another possible model, but one to which Kissinger would not bow down, for reasons we need to examine.

Robert Bowie had been on the faculty of the Harvard Law School, but then during the war was called to government service, assisting John Foster Dulles in running the State Department and serving as director of policy planning. On his return to Harvard he did not wish to resume his faculty appointment at the Law School. Instead, he helped bring forth an idea already in the air, a Center for International Affairs. Securing money from the Ford Foundation, he began planning for the Center in 1957, and made it operational in 1958. He accepted Henry Kissinger as Associate Director, at the suggestion of McGeorge Bundy. Bowie had known Kissinger at the Council on Foreign Relations (a story we shall have to tell in our next chapter), and had also been impressed by the book that emerged from Kissinger's work there.[10] For Kissinger, the associate directorship was a complement to his appointment as Lecturer in Government (when he left Harvard temporarily in 1955 to go to the Council, he had been a lowly Instructor). What Bowie did not know at the time was that Kissinger had aspired to the directorship itself and felt slighted at not having gotten it.

To say, as Stephen Graubard does, that Kissinger's "relations with the Director, Robert Bowie, were never close," is a major understatement.[11] They were, in fact, exceedingly acrimonious. There are two basically different accounts of what happened. According to one informed version, Bowie had carefully explained to Kissinger beforehand his conception of the Center and its operations, had made it clear who would be in charge, and had asked if Kissinger would be "interested in collaborating." Bowie was therefore unpleasantly surprised to discover Kissinger aggressively asserting himself as an equal partner, and at the same time contributing little during that first year to the work of fund raising, planning, and so on. Apparently Henry was too busy spending time on the Rockefeller Commission. Nevertheless, at first Bowie was apparently willing to give Kissinger the benefit of the doubt, to arrange for him to head the Defense Studies Program, and to support him in his claim to tenure. Not until about 1960 did Bowie's disenchantment with Kissinger become firm, as he realized the full nature of his Associate Director's work and character. A result was Kissinger's resignation from his post in that year, though formally he remained a member of the Center.

According to another informed version (or composite thereof), Kissinger started out with a natural tendency to be deferential to a former Assistant Secretary, but was rapidly alienated by Bowie's snubbing of him. Thus, almost from the start, the two men moved toward a dislike of each other. Quite quickly, Kissinger came to view Bowie's abilities with some contempt, to despise his lawyerlike approach to foreign affairs, and to scorn his belief that all problems could be settled by a "conference" or "panel discussion." The personal animus coincided with, or spread to, policy differences. Kissinger opposed Bowie's Multilateral Force (MLF) scheme (which envisaged a NATO naval force of surface ships carrying nuclear weapons and manned by crews of mixed nationalities) and poured scorn on it. Broadening his attack, Kissinger launched into a critique of the entire Eisenhower-Dulles conception of foreign policy, which Bowie largely supported.

Where is the truth in this matter? Obviously, it lies in elements of both accounts. The relationship was clearly a failed one on both sides. Kissinger, as in his relations with Kraemer and Elliott, needed ego support, a concerned attention. Bowie wanted an assistant or underling of sorts; neither socially nor intellectually would he have considered Kissinger as a possible disciple, and certainly not as an equal. Bowie could not "give" or else did not have what Kissinger wanted.

In attitudes of mind, the two men were also far apart. Bowie had the reputation of being relatively liberal (at least compared to Dulles).[12] Whereas Kissinger, like Elliott, prided himself on his broad philosophical and historical approach to foreign affairs, Bowie's was more that of the courtroom lawyer, the legalistically oriented government servant. He personalized for Kissinger this point of view, and we can be sure that a lasting remnant of the quarrel with Bowie was Kissinger's attack on the legal-bureaucratic attitude to international relations (cf. pp. 152, 203). So, too, in style a yawning gap divided the two men. Kissinger admired Renaissance types, men of seigneurial presence. Bowie gives more the impression of being the foxy Yankee, the quintessential WASP. The wonder, all in all, is not that the two men did not get along well, but that they got along at all.

Perhaps Kissinger was past the stage of needing a patronizing figure, or had already secured a new one in Nelson Rockefeller, as we shall soon see. Or perhaps Robert Bowie, as we have suggested, was simply not the man for the role. In any case, the Director and his Associate Director competed openly and aggressively. Kissinger would make decisions unilaterally, and then be reversed by Bowie. Both men sought money individually and competitively in Washington for what became the Center for European Studies at Harvard. On a couple of occasions Kissinger threatened his resignation (a forerunner, perhaps, of his behavior at Salzburg?), but, apparently counseled otherwise by McGeorge Bundy, withdrew it. Eventually, however, as we have noted, he did resign as Associate Director (though remaining Director of the Defense Studies Program) in 1960.

Obviously the Center relation with Bowie is important and

revealing. For one thing, it evinces no sign of Kissinger's famed ability at diplomacy and negotiations. Clearly, his passions and personality were too seriously involved to leave room for his vaunted empathy and psychological understanding. The conflict with Bowie had become "personalized" beyond the point of "practical politics."

Failure at Harvard, and Return

The Center for International Affairs was only one part of Kissinger's life at Harvard. Backed by Elliott, he had also been trying to climb the academic ladder in terms of formal faculty rank. Elliott was constantly singing his protégé's praises and intriguing for him. On one occasion, for example, as a member of an ad hoc committee, Elliott opposed the appointment of a particular individual to a chair, not because he opposed the individual, but because he wished the chair held for Kissinger, eulogizing him as "coming along rapidly."

Not everyone agreed with Elliott's exalted views; indeed, most of Kissinger's possible colleagues were put off by what they perceived as his arrogance, boorishness, and ambition, though clearly recognizing that he was a possible "young comer." In any case, in the early 1950s Kissinger had served as a teaching fellow in the famous undergraduate course, Social Sciences 2, headed by Professor Samuel Beer. Here, broad philosophical and historical questions were discussed in lectures and then in small sections presided over by the teaching fellows. For most of them, it was one of their most important and memorable experiences at Harvard, and a warm feeling of camaraderie still exists among the distinguished alumni of this "faculty." For Kissinger, apparently, the experience meant nothing— perhaps he was too busy not only with his own thesis but with the International Seminar and *Confluence*, or else felt he knew it all from Elliott—and even a favorable commentator admits that Kissinger "learned remarkably little from doing it."[13] Tutorials, in which Kissinger had learned so much from Elliott, were also not his forte.

In 1954 Kissinger was awarded his Ph.D., having completed his voluminous thesis on Metternich and the Congress of Vienna, later published as A World Restored.[14] His hopes for promotion from Instructor to Assistant Professor, however, were dashed, much to his shock and disappointment. Elliott had not been able to prevail in the academic power struggle. To anyone familiar with such matters, it is clear that Kissinger's character had subverted his qualifications, for his record and abilities were obviously such as to warrant the relatively routine promotion. The whole episode undoubtedly rankled deep in Kissinger's soul.

In turn, the offer of a tenured professorship at Chicago must have been temporary balm. Kissinger apparently accepted, then reneged. There is much academic gossip about this matter, with Kissinger's critics accusing him of "using" Chicago and then unfairly leaving it in the lurch at the last moment. Academic life is filled with such events and stories; while this particular story is not "pretty," it cannot be said that Kissinger was doing anything more reprehensible than playing the academic game.

In any case, instead of going to Chicago, he took a position as *rapporteur* for a study group at the Council for Foreign Affairs in New York in 1955. Out of that came a book[15] and a lasting connection with the Eastern Establishment-Rockefeller foreign affairs world, which ultimately led to the Secretary's office in the State Department. We shall tell and analyze that story in a later chapter. Meanwhile, on the strength of his Council work and the book, Kissinger was rehired at Harvard, but in the anomalous position of Lecturer rather than as a tenured Professor.

On the undergraduate level his teaching consisted primarily

of "Principles of International Organization." On the graduate level he taught a seminar in national security policy and another on Western Europe (with Professor Stanley Hoffmann). At the same time, as we know, he was Associate Director of the Center, and to this was joined the directorship of the newly established Defense Studies Program at Harvard. In the background still stood his directorship of the International Seminar, as well as his editorship of *Confluence,* now nominal.

No wonder he was a busy man! What stands out is the way Kissinger was zeroing in on military-government problems, i.e., defense policy, thus continuing his identification with the army established during the war. The other outstanding feature is his base in Western European studies. Noteworthy, too, are the omissions. The heavy tones of philosophy, and philosophy of history, are now missing. Apparently he spoke little or not at all on Nazi Germany as part of his lectures. The subject of the United Nations and underdeveloped countries was largely ignored. China, perhaps naturally, did not loom on Kissinger's mental horizon.

As is to be expected, opinions vary on Kissinger's abilities as a teacher. Most accounts agree that, himself overloaded, he often shortchanged his students. Though he spiced things up by often bringing in outside luminaries, he himself was frequently less than well prepared. Fortunately, he was a rapid reader, or matters would have been much worse. One observer recalls Kissinger in Government 289A as uninterested, reading his newspaper and correcting galleys for a book while an assistant tried to give the class. "Sleepy isn't quite the word," the observer commented. "He was sort of sitting and waiting like General Kutúzov in Tolstoy's *War and Peace.*" Kissinger gave one a "heavy" feeling, partly because of his physical heaviness and partly because he often repeated himself, worrying a problem like a dog with a bone. It all added up to "presence." If not at the beginning of his teaching career, within a few years he had learned to interweave with his "heaviness" his new use of self-mocking, sardonic humor.

A supporter of Kissinger gives a more positive evaluation. In this account, Kissinger was "a first-rate teacher, very gifted in large lectures and small seminars, a superb questioner who enjoyed the interchange with students. He had an excellent sense of irony, wit and humorous understatement . . . if he was interested in what you were doing he paid a great deal of attention to you."[16] For most of his students, however, Kissinger was unavailable. For special ones (like himself earlier?), he made a "great deal of attention" available.

What emerges from almost all accounts of Kissinger's teaching is that his real engagement was with "practical politics," with day-to-day, contemporary affairs. These were at the center of his interests, and in his most successful moments as a teacher he could communicate to the students a rare excitement about them. He enjoyed (at least up to the point of really being challenged) the give and take of discussion, accepting with equanimity even radicals as students and assistants if they were gifted.

Uppermost in any analysis of Kissinger's classes and teaching is the conclusion that he was not committed to the academic world, to the teaching profession. He was intent on moving well beyond his father's passive pedagogical role. He seemed most content when engaged, not with the world of mind, but with, for example, arms control and Defense Studies seminars. Here, sitting magisterially at a large table, surrounded by students, section men, and secretaries, falling asleep, drawing pictures, giving only occasional presentations of his own, calling generally upon outside guests—Jerome Wiesner, Tom Schelling, and even Gerald Ford—discussing Atlantic relations or general strategic problems, Kissinger seemed in his element.

It was excellent preparation for his transference to the larger tables of government, to the National Security Council, and ultimately the State Department. But till that breakthrough occurred Kissinger continued his climb up the academic ladder. In 1959 he was finally appointed Associate Professor, and in 1960 achieved full professorship.

At this point, he had more or less reached the top of the academic tree. Like Elliott before him, moreover, he was mixing the life of Cambridge and Washington, D.C. (with New York thrown in as well), the life of teaching with extensive consulting. It was an arduous, taxing existence. As one of his friends put it in understated fashion, "Kissinger guarded his time less well than he ought to have done."[17] On the level of day-to-day obligation to his academic life, this was, of course, true. On the higher level of Destiny, however, Kissinger at Harvard had "guarded" his time superbly.

Chapter 4

IN MEDIAS RES:
A MIDLIFE PORTRAIT

KISSINGER was at Harvard, in one sense or another (with important interruptions) from about his twenty-fifth to his forty-fifth year. If we were to paint a portrait of him in the middle of his life, say at 40, on the brink of his real entrance into public affairs, what sort of character would emerge? The result, I believe, ought to be like a Rembrandt, with its play of dark and light, or, in more modern dressing, a Picasso, with at least two faces emerging from the numerous planes; it should not be a highly polished, single-toned "official" picture.

Such a portrait must summarize his role at Harvard, his pattern of behavior, especially as revealed at the Center for International Affairs, and his enduring traits, viewed developmentally rather than statically. It must also be a portrait that highlights some things and leaves out others. And last, while showing empathy for and interest in its subject, it must nevertheless be a psychically true picture that gives us Henry Kissinger, warts and all.

Alma Mater

Basically, Kissinger was anti-Harvard. One might have thought that a man so concerned with making his way in the Eastern Establishment might have identified quickly with this cultural bastion of that establishment. Many others, superficially like him, have become more Harvardian than those born to the crimson. Such was not the case with Kissinger (perhaps to his credit?).

Two reasons may be advanced to explain this fact. The first is simply that Harvard rejected and snubbed him too much and too often. Although accepted by the admissions department as an undergraduate, it was clear to someone of his sensitivity that he was not part of the "real" Harvard: the Harvard of clubs, sports, and weekend parties. He was always on the periphery, a tolerated guest in the drafty halls outside the warm banquet room. As a Jew, he felt alien and hampered. "A Jew wouldn't get anywhere at Harvard," he is reported to have said on a number of occasions. Why should he have much loyalty to such an alma mater? It was merely an institution for him to use, and he used it well, especially through Elliott. Yet even Elliott was not able to protect him against the direct snub of being turned down, and away, from the expected assistant professorship. Kissinger had to return in 1957 via a sort of back door.

Even as a faculty member Kissinger was a kind of outsider, with a growing reputation for brilliance but also for boorishness. While the latter trait might serve him in good stead later in negotiations with the Soviets, it did not exactly endear him to many Harvard wives. Thus, while most of their neighbors in fashionable Belmont, where Henry and his wife, Ann, moved as he climbed up the academic ladder, liked her, they found him objectionable. There is little question that, socially and sometimes academically, Henry Kissinger was snubbed. Though he snubbed back in turn, such relationships were hardly likely to awaken warm feelings in him toward Harvard and Cambridge.

He displayed an obvious scorn for most of his colleagues. Except for one or two, such as Tom Schelling, he did not like them. Not keen on peer group competition at any time, he was doubly antagonistic in the academic arena at Harvard. It is true that he had a small circle of friends of roughly similar background to his own. Just as at Oberammergau he had met Springer and Rosovsky, acquaintanceships which continued at Harvard Graduate School, so he now had a circle made up of his colleagues Stephen Graubard and Klaus Epstein. They were, however, not rivals. Though Epstein especially was a recognized intellectual "heavywright," he was too serious and dedicated a scholar to encroach on Henry's activist territory; instead, Epstein's historical and personal commitment to the study of German conservatism made for common intellectual ground between them.[1] But aside from this circle (later augmented by Guido Goldman, a graduate student of Henry's), Henry Kissinger seems to have had little in the way of friendly feelings toward, or friends on, the Harvard faculty.

This attitude was made easier for him by the second reason for his basic anti-Harvard stance: his scorn for ivory tower academics in general. Kraemer had taught him that, and, in an odd way, so had Elliott. Their teaching fell on prepared psychic ground, as we have suggested, involving Henry's feelings toward his father, a "failed" teacher.

Negative feelings toward Harvard may have played a role in Henry Kissinger's noninvolvement with university academic power and politics. Somewhat surprisingly, perhaps, he showed none of the negotiating skills or flair for political infighting that he would demonstrate so superbly later in the White House. Though he dutifully attended government department meetings, he was almost always silent. He seemed to have an infinite capacity for listening to silly, boring conversation. Apparently, however, he never attended general faculty meetings. Those who knew him well agree that Henry Kissinger simply didn't feel that the academic power struggle, in this sense, was worth the candle. The example of Elliott, who did involve himself heavily in academic politics, apparently convinced Kissinger of their pallidness, their triviality as a substitute for the real thing. Viewing his colleagues as dull, petty, self-serving individuals, representing no greater constituency than themselves, Kissinger disdained to wheel and deal for trivial stakes in such a vacuous environment. Academic politics, therefore, can hardly be looked upon as a training ground for Henry Kissinger's later accomplishments.

His ambitions obviously lay elsewhere. And in the view of almost all his colleagues, he *was* ambitious. His ambitions at the time did not seem to extend as far as becoming Secretary of State (though he may have role-played a bit, as when he asked a student on an oral exam, "What if you were Secretary of State and . . . ?"). At first they were more mundane and limited. Apparently, he badly wanted to be invited to become a member of the prestigious Junior Fellows at Harvard, to no avail. He obviously wanted promotion and tenure, hardly unusual, of course. What was unusual was that Henry Kissinger clearly wanted these things in order to make his way into the world of foreign policy formation, not just study. His ambitions went beyond Harvard, and to ends other than the merely academic. As a measure of that deeper ambition, we can note the peculiar fact that Henry Kissinger, who as Secretary of State flies everywhere, all the time, has a deep fear of flying. So vaulting were his larger ambitions that he was even willing to wrestle with and overcome this terrible unsettling emotion.

At Work

At the Center for International Affairs Henry Kissinger displayed most prominently his style of work, in the sense of having a staff which he directed. Here, unlike in academic politics, he showed early and enduringly his characteristic way of interacting with associates. What was it like to work for Henry Kissinger? First, as all his former secretaries and associates attest, one worked for "Dr. Kissinger," or "Professor Kissinger," or "HAK," or even "Mr. K.," but not for or with "Henry." In name as well as behavior, he kept his distance. It is therefore especially interesting to note that, alone among recent Secretaries of State, Henry Kissinger is frequently referred to as "Henry" in the media (can one imagine journalists referring to Acheson as "Dean," or Dulles as "John"?). Unable to relax his dignity in personal relations, Kissinger as culture hero is uniquely able to unstiffen the image of the Secretary of State, which surely is part of the reason for his unequaled popularity with the American people at large.[2]

Dr. Kissinger impressed all those who worked with him at the Center as terribly hard working. Demanding much of himself, he seemed to have the moral right to demand much of others, which he did. Though he allowed his assistants to work their own hours, he required them to put in extra time simply to cope with the pressures of writing, and rewriting, papers that he assigned them. Many ended up hating him for his relentless taskmastery, often exercised in humiliating fashion; others became intensely loyal, gratified by his eventual praise.

Ungenerous and petty at times, he could also be surprisingly thoughtful, coming back from trips with gifts and memorabilia. Badly needing editorial assistance with his own books, he could often evoke in those who helped him, especially women, a sense of involvement and personal commitment, making them feel they had a share in this brilliant man's achievements.

87

If these be the positive sides of Kissinger as "Director"—and we have taken for granted the high level of his intellectual activity—there were, and are, also many negative features. One is told repeatedly about his arrogance: "the second most arrogant man I have ever met" is a frequent comment (with no hint as to the first, a typical academic safeguard). The required formal address, instead of a friendly "Hello Henry," is perceived as a small part of this arrogance. He was intensely suspicious, in circumstances where such an attitude was uncalled for. Secretaries, falsely accused of "betraying" him in some way, were left in frustrated and confused anger (later, however, a letter of apology might follow). Sometimes Kissinger's "paranoia" may have been justified—he *did* have enemies, some self-created—but the outbreaks and the intensity were overreactions.

Quick to criticize others, Henry Kissinger was, and is, himself intensely sensitive to criticism. One could compile a whole book made up of stories on this score. He is notorious for calling up journalists who have written about him and bawling them out for their criticisms. He responded to one critical review of his *Nuclear Weapons* book with a letter of almost 150 pages (shades of his overlong undergraduate and graduate theses!).[3] As viewed by most of his colleagues, Kissinger's sensitivity to criticism is a reflection of his basic insecurity, his lack of confidence in his status, role, and worth. As one colleague observed, he was "short, fat, and ugly"—why shouldn't he be insecure? According to this view, Kissinger's nervousness and insecurity, expressed physically by biting his nails, manifested itself psychically in terms largely of suspiciousness and extreme sensitivity to criticism.

A Depressed Personality?

An important part of our midlife portrait must deal with the "tone" of Kissinger's attitudes toward the world, what could perhaps more pretentiously be called the tint of his "world view." One study of Kissinger holds that he is a "depressive personality."[4] As part of this syndrome, we are told that the dysmutual (a term used synonymously with depressive personality) is "perpetually depressed." Is this true of Kissinger?

According to those who know him intimately, Kissinger is better described as what I shall call a "conditional optimist." He is, indeed, often moody and melancholic—and one can add, morose, capricious, and negative. There is also a deep strain of pessimism in Henry Kissinger (he would probably say realism). Nevertheless, while these states are relatively chronic, one must add that they are not, as perceived by penetrating observers, expressed in terms of deep depression. As one person commented, "He may be philosophically dark, but not so psychologically." Other, more positive qualities—his detachment, enormous tenacity, sense of humor, and, indeed, his deep-rooted faith in creativity—all temper his temperament, and bring him out on balance as what I have called a "conditional optimist." As one colleague remarked, he is certainly not a "Götterdämmerung" man. If nothing else, his limitless self-confidence in his intellectual powers, his sheer "arrogance," keep Kissinger from falling into deep and lasting depression, and fantasizing his way out of it by seriously imagining the destruction of the world.

Instead, Kissinger, as he insisted in his very revealing undergraduate thesis, believes that history is a matter of freedom, not causality.[5] Mystically expressed in its Spenglerian costume, it is nevertheless clear that Kissinger believes that individuals, and societies as well, can transcend the conditions making for their possible downfall and emerge with creative solutions.

While there is a deeply "tragic" sense to Kissinger's view of the world, it is a kind of Promethean tragedy in which man, at great pain, snatches the firebrand of creativity from the gods who seek to doom him. Kissinger presumably plays out this view of life in his personal history as well as in history at large (indeed, the two histories are sometimes fused).

Lying and Lying Abroad

By now we have already sketched many of the traits Kissinger brings to his role as actor in this historical drama: his distrust of goodwill, intense desire for stability, ability to identify with opponents, wish to assimilate, keen intellectual abilities, hard work, "heaviness," tendencies to megalomania and paranoia, arrogance, and so forth.[6] Let us conclude our midlife character sketch by dealing with three more traits, all extremely difficult and delicate subjects. First, we must examine closely the accusation that Kissinger is given to frequent lying, deviousness, and plagiarism. Next, the question of Kissinger's originality of thought, aside from the plagiarism issue, must be confronted. And last, at this point, it seems well to consider more deeply Kissinger's style of work, his "loner" quality, as it manifested itself in these years.

A diplomat has been defined as "one sent abroad to lie for his country." As originally used, "to lie" (as in "lie down") meant to rest or reside abroad, in order to assist and represent one's country in another country. Only later did the pun emerge, and to lie mean to falsify for diplomatic purposes. Is Kissinger's "lying" in the diplomatic or in a more personal, less forgivable, mode?

Bearing in mind the adage, "He that is without sin among you, let him cast the first stone," the evidence is nevertheless very strong that Kissinger, while at the Center and elsewhere, has resorted to subterfuge and evasion, both on trivial and large matters. One might doubt this if the evidence came only from enemies, but, alas, it also comes from friends. Many of the latter, in fact, are puzzled over why Kissinger has lied to them when the lie was so useless or self-defeating. As they also point out, at other times Kissinger is scrupulously truthful. How are we to understand this wart on Kissinger's character?

One explanation is that Kissinger lied the way a schoolboy lies: to avoid an unpleasant reality. Without sufficient self-esteem or strength of character at that precise moment to suffer the consequences of telling the truth, one evades or fabricates. Then, as Kissinger learned to substitute sardonic wit as a means of acknowledging unpleasant reality, lying became unnecessary. And it is clear that, though little in evidence at the beginning of his Center years, wit and humor became a major Kissinger character trait from the 1960s on.

Another explanation, by no means contradictory to the first, is that Kissinger does not realize at the given moment (or, indeed, afterward) that he is being untruthful. He actually believes his lie, and he believes it "sincerely." Kissinger noted this trait without condemnation in Bismarck. Describing Bismarck's use of rather astonishing "tactics" in his courtship of his future wife, Kissinger comments:

Ever since these letters became public, German historians have debated the degree of Bismarck's sincerity. But if Bismarck was insincere, it did not necessarily have to be in the letter to his future father-in-law. In any event, sincerity has meaning only in reference to a standard of truth of conduct. The root fact of Bismarck's personality, however, was his incapacity to comprehend any such standard outside his will. For this reason, he could never accept the good faith of any opponent; it accounts, too, for his mastery in adapting to the requirements of the moment. It was not that Bismarck lied —this is much too self-conscious an act—but that he was finely attuned to the subtlest currents of any environment and produced measures precisely adjusted to the need to prevail. The key to Bismarck's success was that he was always sincere.

This extraordinary passage by Kissinger (incidentally, one that shows unusual psychological insight) is made more extraordinary by Kissinger's later admission in his interview with Oriana Fallaci that "I am always convinced of the necessity of whatever I'm doing. And people feel that, believe in it. And I attach great importance to being believed: When one persuades or conquers someone, one mustn't deceive them."[7]

Obviously, there is a spectrum between the small fibs or lies one tells for the protection of one's own ego or interests and the "lying abroad" one does for presumed national interests. Lying, or at least shading the truth, seems generally to be essential to the life of politics (a politician changes his message generally, as we know, depending on the constituency he happens to be addressing). In diplomacy, it becomes an art of sorts. The statesman juggles those lies—or bluffs, as he may consider them—that he must tell other countries abroad (for example, "of course we shall support you if you are invaded") and those he must tell his countrymen at home ("of course we shall not send American boys to fight overseas"). For Kissinger, like Bismarck, the act is, and must be, unself-conscious and sincere.

The justification for such behavior is the belief that higher purposes and policies are involved and must prevail. There is an awesome morality, or lack of ordinary morality, in such realpolitik. It can, for example, justify wiretapping domestically and secret bombing in Cambodia in the name of this higher purpose. Kissinger's reading of Hegel would have told him that the World-Historical Hero must trample on existing morality to fulfill the purposes of the Idea or Spirit. Almost monomaniacal self-confidence by a Bismarck—or a Kissinger—that one has insight into the higher moral purposes of spirit is required for the hero to proceed "sincerely." In an ordinary person's case, self-consciousness, as in psychoanalysis or psychohistory, might shake one's confidence that the end justified the means. In Kissinger's case, insofar as he identified with Bismarck and the

Hegelian strand of German philosophy, with its emphasis on the historical hero, he was affirming the identification with the aggressor that we postulated earlier. In addition, of course, he was justifying his personal patterns of behavior.[8]

Kissinger's lying, therefore, stands far removed from the sort of fundamental character trait exhibited, for example, by former President Richard Nixon. For Nixon, massive and compulsive denial was a basic way of dealing with certain aspects of reality and of his own feelings.[9] Kissinger is well in touch with reality, and prevarication or deviousness is only occasional, and occasionally contrived. Where it does exist, it coexists with a strong desire to tell the truth, or at least a higher truth.

While it is clear that in his negotiating behavior Kissinger tells the other party, if possible, what the latter would like to hear, Kissinger himself does not blatantly lie. It would be utterly self-defeating. Higher purposes would hardly be effectively served. Deviousness, therefore, seems a better word to describe what generally goes on in diplomatic negotiations, rather than lying.

On the same spectrum, however, lies (if the further pun is allowed) duplicity. Again, there are a number of accounts charging Kissinger with this characteristic. One rather famous instance concerns his allegedly encouraging a subordinate colleague to proceed with the writing and publishing of a book on international relations and then writing a letter to the publisher involved, saying that he, Kissinger, had talked with them and the colleague about such a book, the material was his, and that he would sue if they went ahead with his colleague's book; as a final touch, Kissinger then sent a copy of his letter to his colleague, thus ending their "friendship." (Such bizarre behavior, of course, may have an explanation known only to Kissinger, or may stem from his self-admitted paranoid suspicions as to other's motives.)

Another unhappy incident involved plans at the Center to bring out a collection of essays, tentatively called "In Search of Germany" (presumably to duplicate Stanley Hoffmann's *In Search of France*). Although a number of people were brought to the Center for this purpose, and essays written, Kissinger apparently blocked final publication. Supporters of Kissinger claim that he didn't think the essays were very good. Opponents believe that he had a "thing" about the book. In any case, he did not write his own introduction, and scuttled the publishing plans, leaving a number of very embittered contributors (some now high up in German affairs).[10] At least one of these believes Kissinger's actions emanated from his ambivalent feelings toward his former homeland: "He has Mautthausen eyes," he commented, referring to the concentration camp and its guards, thereby classifying Kissinger with a rather special group of "blue-eyed Germans."

Whatever the truth in these various cases, many of those involved thought of him as characteristically duplicitous.[11] Many others believe that Kissinger not only stops the appearance of other people's work, but that he frequently "borrows," that he plagiarizes. There are a number of accounts of his signing his name to position papers worked up by others. Without excusing them, such incidents must be understood as a frequent procedure by bureaucrats and professors who piggyback on the work of their aides; undoubtedly, Kissinger's own position papers were often so treated by those above him. Other accounts, however, have Kissinger going much further, and publishing as his own in prestigious journals, such as *Foreign Affairs*, paragraphs and large sections of other people's work. One victim of such plagiarism, however, is convinced that Kissinger hadn't the slightest idea that he had gone beyond the bounds of good taste and friendship; he simply lacked sensitivity to the nuances of authorship. Kissinger, who was frequently suspicious of others' infringement on *his* work, as in the episode of his forbidding a publisher to put out the work of one of his subordinate colleagues, may have been projecting in such cases his own acknowledged tendency to "borrow" material.

Originality

Another partial explanation of Kissinger's tendency to plagiarize brings us to our second issue: the question of Kissinger's originality. Not one of those to whom I talked thought of Kissinger as an original thinker (an echo of his early teachers, not noticing any brilliance?). Instead he was perceived, correctly, I believe, as having a special kind of creativity, of absorbing whatever fits into his own intellectual framework. Kissinger can be called a "creative synthesizer." He may at times incorporate memorized turns of phrase and even passages into his "own" work, without being aware he is borrowing verbatim, or take written passages unaltered and "digest" them in his own article.

It is not, therefore, originality as generally understood, but this special kind of absorptive, synthetic work that is Kissinger's claim to originality. He was always ambiguous about being a teacher and a scholar, and his scholarship has always been a secondary matter for him. He prizes ideas not for themselves, but as tools with which to accomplish something. If he read Marx, or Max Weber, or Freud, it was not with any intrinsic interest in their ideas as such, but for their service, if any, to a "practical politician."

Instead of intellectual originality, what Kissinger creates is an effect of "weightiness." It is not so much what he says as how he says it that is impressive. There is something about his voice —that deep bass—that can't be ignored. The accent and the slow delivery contribute to the air of ponderousness. Coming from that large, disproportionate head, his voice possesses a tremendous authority which simply exerts itself. Kissinger has the capacity to make others feels both that what he is saying is weighty and *that the person spoken to is also weighty*. Indeed, on this score, Kissinger appears to have the ability in a one-to-one situation to give his listener the feeling that both share a common view, and that he and his listener are both more intelligent and clever than the "others." (In part, of course, this is an element in his alleged deviousness.) It does not matter, therefore, that Kissinger is not original. He is a creative and weighty synthesizer who is expert at overawing his audience.

Dependency

The other trait that emerges from a consideration of Kissinger's years at Harvard and at the Center for International Affairs is his "lone wolf" quality. He is clearly unable to serve well as part of a team such as the Center, to subordinate himself to a large organization. He *is* a solitary actor—or nothing. This is clearly his self-image, as made evident later in his fantasy, as told to Oriana Fallaci, of being the "cowboy leading the caravan alone . . . the cowboy entering a village or city alone on his horse."[12] His university behavior generally confirms his confession that "I've always acted alone." Such behavior, of course, sits well with his notorious dislike of rivals, of peer competitors. It also accords with his dislike of bureaucracies, his fear of being enmeshed in organizations. It fits equally well with his scorn for those in a dependent situation, i.e., those not able to stand alone.

Kissinger's fears of being dependent are vividly exemplified in his attitude to Harvard, as manifested at the time he and Ann were contemplating buying a house. Ann wanted to buy the house, but Henry was loath to borrow the money from Harvard, which provided unusually low interest loans. One colleague reported him as saying he didn't want Harvard "to get their hooks into him." (Nevertheless, Ann won out, and they took the mortgage.) So, too, according to this colleague, Henry wanted "no strings on him in the International Seminar" and took only a pittance as pay from it. Thus, his dislike of dependency in others mirrored his feelings about himself.

Kissinger's dislike of dependent persons was first obvious at Harvard, where, as a teacher and director, he clearly exhibited the utmost contempt for those dependent on him, e.g., students, section men, and Center assistants. Unwilling to associate much with peer group competitors, he surrounded himself with subordinates whom he could downgrade and often humiliate (subsequently even to the point of eavesdropping on them?). If they were perceived as weak and dependent, he despised them. He could not abide their leaning on him, needing him, making emotional demands on him, or indeed, anyone "touching" him. Much of this is symbolized by Kissinger's repugnance when, later, a politician put his arm around him, and Kissinger confessed to a friend, "I can't stand people to touch me" (how much Kissinger would change in this respect, as others, can be symbolized by the embraces he exchanged with Sadat!).[13]

Kissinger admired strong, independent men, and looked up to them. But he, whose career was so dependent on patrons, could not tolerate emotionally those who were dependent on him (this may also have been part of the story of his marital breakup). This is not a particularly pretty picture, and forms one of the more unappealing warts. Ingratiating himself with those above him, he frequently denigrated those beneath him. As one analyst commented, he demonstrated a classic submissive-dominance syndrome. Yet to leave it at that would be simplistic and unfair. In spite of his desperate emotional requirements, born out of his life's experience of somehow having to integrate weakness and power—here, clearly, he has not done it well or gracefully—Kissinger was able to retain a surprising integrity vis-à-vis his "superiors" and patrons. At the core, I believe, he kept his own sense of what it is to be a man—the message Kraemer had preached to him—living his life creatively and independently. Flattering and courtly, boorish and sadistic, Kissinger has wrestled with his own boils in the face of God as he has conceived Him. Necessarily, it is a solitary struggle.

As such, it is also a major source of Kissinger's "loner" quality, and his famous one-man shows. The "loner" qualities, of course, correspond splendidly with his personalized version of old-fashioned diplomatic negotiations, which he had studied so assiduously in the historical record of the Congress of Vienna. Such qualities work less well in complex, more bureaucratized matters, such as economic planning. But they do allow for, nay promote, the extraordinary emergence of Henry Kissinger as a culture hero in the midst of the grey, anonymous State Department bureaucracy.

A Changing Picture

This, then, in brief, is the character Kissinger had formed for himself while at Harvard. Built on his earlier years of experience, it was the character he would take with him into government service (for the moment we are treating the latter, which in fact was partly underway at the same time as his academic life, as if it came later). It was a character with great strengths, especially of intellect, memory, hard work, stamina, devotion, and commitment. It was also a character of great weaknesses, marred by excessive suspiciousness, deviousness, arrogance, and exaggerated disdain for "weakness" and respect for power (and we have not yet explored how Kissinger's personal disdain for dependent individuals might extend to dependent nations).

Along with such flaws in our hero at midlife, one must include as a major trait of Kissinger's character his ability to grow and develop. Therefore, to our Picasso-like efforts we must add the technique of the futurist painter, Marinetti, and his ability to show movement on a fixed canvas. Basically insecure and suspicious, Kissinger came gradually in his 40s (as his personal achievements, his work, began to secure widespread recognition) to exhibit a growing sense of security. He became less compulsively arrogant with a measure of success. Further, the light touch of wit and humor began more and more to replace the heavy hand of stuffy ponderousness. Kissinger was in transit from being a boorish, self-conscious academic to becoming, in the next decade, a swinger.

Especially evident in the areas mentioned, such shifts symbolize for us Kissinger's basic ability to change within certain givens, to develop inside a process of reaffirming permanent elements of his personality. Thus his own character is "conservative," in the sense of echoing his conservative ideological commitment to change—what he calls creativity—within set, stable conditions.

Chapter 5

THE WORLD OF
WASHINGTON AND
POWER

Onward

IN OUR ACCOUNT of Kissinger's life at Harvard and academia, we touched briefly on his increasing involvement with Washington, D.C., and the real world of foreign policy and political power. The links for Kissinger had never been totally broken since his army days, but they were attenuated. Thus, in the 1950s he served as a consultant both to the army's Operations Research Office in Washington and to the Psychological Strategy Board of the Joint Chiefs of Staff. In 1951 he was sent by the army to South Korea to study the effect upon the Korean people of military occupation.[1] Whatever he may have known about military occupation, he clearly knew nothing about Korea, but this would be only the first of many situations in which Kissinger's abilities as a quick learner, and a synthesizer of other people's work, would be called into play.

Such consulting was the very small change of the new academic game of serving as professional mercenaries, combining intellectual expertise and power politics. As a member of this corps, Kissinger was extremely low in the pecking order. This was quite natural; he was both young and very insecure at Harvard. In fact, as we know, in the mid 1950s he was refused promotion to Assistant Professor, and thus forced to look outside of Harvard Yard for his future prospects. Harvard's rejection, and the way Henry Kissinger rebounded from it and found another path, marks a turning point in his life and suggests a persistent pattern of adaptiveness. Rejected by Harvard, Kissinger, as we have noted, in turn rejected the University of Chicago (after apparently having first accepted the job) and, instead, took a position as Study Director at the Council on Foreign Relations. It was undoubtedly the most important single *political* decision of his life.

The Council on Foreign Relations

In Henry Kissinger's view, the Council on Foreign Relations was "unique" in its "combination of practical experience and scholarly standards supplied by its study groups."[2] Seen thus, it was clearly the ideal setting for Kissinger's synthesizing of desire and ability. The Council was also the most prestigious private foreign policy group in the country. As such, it brought together an extraordinary collection of men of wealth, governmental power (civilian and military), and intellect, and its membership reads like a confirmation of C. Wright Mills' "power elite."[3]

In 1954 the Council set up a discussion group on the subject of "Nuclear Weapons and Foreign Policy." The idea for the group appears to have originated with Gordon Dean, former chairman of the Atomic Energy Commission, aided by Carroll Wilson, formerly general manager of the same body. Both had retired to private business, but retained their concern over the "revolutionary changes in the weapons of warfare stemming from the production of atomic and hydrogen bombs and the advance in the means of delivering them."[4] Now they wished to clarify the implications of the new weapons for American foreign policy. They also made the important decision to work "outside the government and without the use of classified information,"[5] though, of course, many of the group members did have such information. Dean became the Chairman, and Wilson the Secretary.

Through the year 1954–1955, the discussion group, its members picked by Dean and Wilson with the advice of Council staffers George Franklin and William Diebold, met and considered a large array of questions. As the "Annual Report" tells us, meetings were held on the following topics:

Destructive Effects of Nuclear Weapons
> Discussion leader: Dr. Shields Warren, New England Deaconess Hospital

Defense Against Nuclear Weapons
> Discussion leaders: Robert Amory, Jr., Central Intelligence Agency; Mervin Kelly, Bell Telephone Laboratories

Nuclear Stalemate; The Problem of Alliances
> Discussion leader: Paul Nitze, Foreign Service Educational Foundation

Adaptation of Armed Forces to Nuclear Weapons; The Possibility of Keeping Local Wars Local
> Discussion leaders: General James McCormack, Jr., U.S. Army; Frank C. Nash, Nash, Ahern and Abell

Nuclear Warfare and the Situation in the Far East
> Discussion leader: Thomas K. Finletter, Coudert Brothers

Nuclear Warfare and the Situation in Europe and the Middle East
> Discussion leaders: General James M. Gavin, U.S. Army; Arnold Wolfers, Yale University.[6]

Encouraged by the success of these meetings, and the interest taken by its members in the work, the Council decided to continue its investigation "with the aim of producing a book that will be of help to the American public in understanding this immensely important subject."[7] To this end the Council, after debating whether to employ one of its own senior members as author, went looking for a bright young person to write the book.

Enter Henry Kissinger! Memories are divergent and unclear as to exactly how he was hired, but the composite version is as follows. Turned down at Harvard, Kissinger had been interviewed earlier at the Council for the job of managing editor on its journal, *Foreign Affairs*. Presumably, his experience as editor of *Confluence* would apply here, and a letter of recommendation from Arthur Schlesinger, Jr., helped. Interviewed by the magazine's Editor, Hamilton Fish Armstrong, and in spite of making a favorable personal impression, Kissinger was not given the job. Wisely, Armstrong had realized that writing style was not Kissinger's forte; Kissinger himself, it is alleged, realized he was not right for the position. Instead, Philip Quigg, a Princeton man who had worked there on the *Alumni Bulletin* (Armstrong had also gone to Princeton), was named as managing editor. All turned out well for Kissinger in the end, however, as we shall see; moreover, his relations with Quigg were later of the best (giving support to the view that Kissinger had not really been a serious rival for the editorial post). In fact, Quigg was the only one at the Council for whom Kissinger would stand as editor of his own writings.

Apparently, Armstrong passed Kissinger's name on to George Franklin, who was in charge of finding that bright young man to write the nuclear book. Franklin, an engaging, warmhearted person, was impressed by the fact that this particular bright young man came with recommendations not only from Schlesinger, Jr., but from McGeorge Bundy and William Elliott. (Today, Schlesinger, Jr., would not give such a letter; in fact, one can attribute to him a deep detestation of his former protégé.) Anyone who could be approved of by such diverse minds, Franklin concluded, must have something going for him. Franklin, we can now see, had been exposed to one of Henry Kissinger's major strengths: his ability, as in his negotiations, to engage the support of differing parties who perceived in him a sympathizer, if not an ally.

Franklin was also impressed by Kissinger's self-confidence. The Council had decided from the beginning that access to classified data was not required; now it decided that expertise in, or even real knowledge of, the subject was not essential. In fact, it perceived a virtue in having someone who was not steeped in inside views. Kissinger certainly seemed to fit the bill, for there is little evidence of his involvement with the nuclear problem before this time; indeed, as we know, up until 1954 he had been working on his doctoral dissertation on the Congress of Vienna. However, Kissinger's self-confident condition—"If I'm going to come, you've got to let me do it exactly my way"[8]—was not threatening, but reassuring (for the Council, it seems, was not really clear what *it* wanted). Interviewed further by Wilson and others (folklore at the Council has it that Walter Mallory was also involved), he impressed everyone favorably, and was offered the job. Clearly, however, the key figure in Kissinger's being hired was George Franklin, later to become, with his wife, a close friend of Kissinger's.

The impression of confidence that Kissinger created is crucial to our understanding of him. A very junior person, insecure in many ways, his situation at Harvard precarious, to say the least, he nevertheless impressed Franklin and others as decisive and strong. These same perceived character traits colored his whole time at the Council. As Study Director, awarded a Carnegie Research Fellowship for 15 months, he was entitled to "draw heavily" on the continuing discussions of the group, "which included men distinguished in the military arts and in the theory and practice of science as well as others with broad background in international affairs,"[9] but not bound to do so in any specific way. Kissinger did seem to benefit from discussions with some of his seniors, especially General James Gavin. But what stands out from all accounts of his work at the Council is how *he* dominated the distinguished men who surrounded him.

One informant, who had spent a number of years in government service and much time on the subject of the study group, recalls how staggered he was by the "arrogance" of this newcomer, "throwing his weight around." Kissinger had never really served in the government, yet he pontificated on the subject of governmental policies. He seemed to have no fear of contradicting his "superiors," men with great practical knowledge, background, and power. Whereas the staff man, serving on the middle levels of the Washington bureaucracy, had looked up to his superiors in awe, Kissinger had no difficulty in standing up to, for example, the Joint Chiefs of Staff (as he did in the chapter of *Nuclear Weapons*[10] in which he takes them to task). Kissinger's self-confidence became a partial source of his dominance over others. At the end of the study group, if not before, Kissinger had established himself as an oracle, a teacher, whose brilliance and leadership were accepted by the others. As we would interpret it, Kissinger, drawing on family tradition and his brief years in the Army Intelligence School and at Harvard, was reactivating these experiences, especially the military one, in a new and more favorable environment.

Kissinger's sense of assurance, according to one observer at the time, came from the qualities of his mind. Able to place things correctly and to arrange them rigorously, his sense of process gave him a feeling of order and control. At the Council, too, he felt a "European" superiority to the Americans, no matter how high their rank. While Americans believed everything to be a success story, Kissinger knew that history was made up of tragedies, with the United States no exception. To American naïveté, he could oppose the quiet confidence of one who knew the true nature of history and events.

As one staff member put it, Kissinger, with his ponderous manner, conveyed the feeling that he "walks with kings." Thinking of himself as a very important person, he demanded to be treated that way. (And we would add that this trait is related to his megalomania, of which he jokes so much; the megalomanic claims become self-fulfilling, forcing us to treat such a person, if he does not go over the edge, in terms of his self-image.)

Kissinger's task at the Council was made easier for him by

the fact that the study group really had no integrating quality of its own. Its members were busy men who in a sense were merely "keeping their hand in" on foreign policy debates. Like many intellectual "outsiders" before him—an Edmund Burke, a James Mill—Kissinger discovered how malleable, how easily led and impressed some members of the "upper class" could be. What for some of them was often a dilettantish interest (it goes without saying that many other members of the Council were vitally involved and informed in these matters) was for Kissinger a career matter, figuratively of life or death. As one participant remarked, "With his mind made up on most things," not very flexible, rather Germanic, with penetrating analytical capabilities, terribly articulate and persuasive, he "really lectures you" and, in turn, "doesn't give an inch."

Kissinger was more than a lecturer and teacher. He was a "presence." It was a trait that he first began to manifest at the Council and which he has since developed to an increasingly greater degree. As one observer has put it, "It's a physical thing; you feel it even if your back is turned." It emanates from a restless energy: "If Kissinger did something, it was an event." One knew, even on first meeting him, that he was someone clearly on the way up.

Another observer grudgingly concedes Kissinger's "presence," which he sees as coming from his intellect, but minimizes its extent as compared to that of other really great men (Harriman, for example). Nevertheless, he admits that Kissinger seems to "swell" in public; thus, with ambassadors and other important people he lowers his voice and speaks more slowly—as becomes a "man of affairs." (In staff meetings and with people whom he is not trying to impress, the ponderousness is set aside.)

We spoke earlier of Kissinger's "weightiness" as a psychological effect.[11] There is also a physical aspect to the "weighty" trait: Kissinger tends to eat too much. Though he doesn't smoke or drink—he takes a glass of wine out of politeness—he eats excessively out of nervousness or tension and at a party is hardly able to wait for the meal to be served. Yet his physique is obviously strong—most observers have remarked on his stamina—and he is bursting with energy. Thus the physical weight does not evoke the impression of flabbiness, but instead adds to the sense of psychological "weightiness," which in turn forms part of the general air he exudes of "presence."

Confidence, weightiness, presence: these are the character traits that Kissinger increasingly developed in the 15 months or so he spent at the Council on Foreign Relations. Having come to the Council on the brink of a kind of academic failure, he had proved himself—and his character—at the cutting edge where "practical experience and scholarly standards" meet. Such a success had to contribute powerfully to Henry Kissinger's sense of self-esteem, and to strengthen the very confidence that played so strong a role in its achievement.

Nuclear Weapons and Foreign Policy

Working at the Council meant a move to New York. First the Kissingers took a garden apartment in Hartsdale, later moving to a small apartment on East Seventy-third Street in order to eliminate the need to commute, thereby affording Henry more time for his arduous work load. Back in New York, where he had started, the great metropolis might just as well not have existed for all the impact it made on his senses or mind. Aside from visits to Cambridge, and spending the summers there— for he was still running the International Seminar and *Confluence*—he spent almost all his time at his Council office or at home.

Although the Council's own main quarters, an impressive town house, were on Park Avenue and East Sixty-eighth Street, Kissinger was given an office in another building, on Sixty-fifth Street, while the Council renovated and expanded its offices.

Kissinger had his own secretary and all the facilities of the Council at his disposal; he made good use of them. Though not quite as "invisible" as during his undergraduate days at Harvard, he spent most of his time in semiisolation, working on his own project. Obviously involved in the study group meetings, such as they were, occasionally having lunch or conversation with a staff member, Kissinger at the Council wasted little time socializing, aside, it seems, from a growing friendship with George Franklin and his wife.

The result of his single-minded dedication was *Nuclear Weapons and Foreign Policy*, an unexpected best-seller. Written under tremendous pressure—in the last months Kissinger, as we shall see, was also serving as Director of the Rockefeller Special Studies Project—Kissinger was able to revise and publish the book in less than two years. The Council would not have been unduly surprised to have discovered that no book could be written from its loosely organized discussion group notes; a summary report, to be filed away like many others, would probably have done, and any public response at all would have been gratifying. For the members of the discussion group to have exchanged ideas and achieved some clarifications would be justification enough for the exercise. To have a serious Council book, on a subject of strategic importance, become a 1957 Book-of-the-Month Club selection, be made required reading for all students of foreign policy, and be photographed in the hands of Vice-President Nixon, was as unexpected as it was gratifying. As one Council member summed it up, Kissinger was the Council's "single greatest success story."

We shall look later at some of the significant themes in the book itself. Here our concern is with the book's role in Kissinger's life. At one bound it clearly established him as a major figure in the foreign policy field. Although heavily criticized by authorities in the field as derivative or badly grounded in facts or poorly argued in theory, the book firmly installed him in the estimation of the establishment, i.e., the kind of people represented in the Council, and began that romance with the general public which eventually resulted in Kissinger's becoming a culture hero in the mid 1970s. At least as importantly, *Nuclear Weapons* marked the successful integration of Kissinger's scholarly abilities and political interests, the union of mind and action, which he had merely adumbrated in his work on the Congress of Vienna. If Harvard can be said to have served as a kind of ivory tower, the Council on Foreign Relations became Kissinger's battle tower from which he fired his own first nuclear salvo, fusing thought and power.

Friendships

The publication of *Nuclear Weapons* also brought Kissinger an unexpected and important friendship, that of Max Ascoli, publisher of *The Reporter*. The way this came about demonstrates anew and vividly a number of Kissinger's persistent traits: a deep resentment of criticism, a tendency to overwrite and transgress the ordinary limits of length, and an ability to turn initial opponents into eventual friends.

A member of *The Reporter* staff assigned *Nuclear Weapons* to be reviewed by Paul H. Nitze. Nitze, as a former director of the Policy Planning Staff of the Department of State and author of an article on atomic warfare for *Foreign Affairs*, was a natural choice. His reaction to the book was one of absolute horror. Himself a Council member and participant in the original study group, he did not believe that Kissinger had faithfully reflected the ins and outs of the discussions. While willing to acknowledge Kissinger's brilliance, Nitze was convinced that Kissinger knew little about the field in which he was writing. His review, naturally, reflected these feelings. When *The Reporter* sent a prepublication copy of the review to Kissinger, he apparently threatened the Council with a libel suit if the review were not revised (as a result, Nitze made a few minor changes). Kissinger also wrote and sent to Nitze a rebuttal of well over 100 pages, again going beyond the normal limits of length.

The upshot of all this is extremely interesting and revealing of Kissinger's way of behaving. On reflection, apparently, and after further discussion with Nitze, Kissinger admitted that perhaps he hadn't really thought the whole thing through sufficiently (later he would publicly change his mind on the advisability of limited nuclear war), and that, in any case, his rebuttal was unnecessarily long. The incident ended with Nitze and Kissinger claiming mutual respect for each other. (One observer, however, asserts that Kissinger never really forgave Nitze and tried thereafter to avoid meetings at which Nitze was present.) If this version of the story can be believed, Kissinger had once again "won" over an enemy.

There is an even more important consequence to this story, a reaffirmation of the point just made. Max Ascoli, a distinguished political exile from Italy since the 1930s, a writer and scholar in his own right, and the publisher of *The Reporter*, was returning from a trip abroad when the Nitze review was sent to him on board ship. Ascoli apparently thought the review too harsh and indicated where revisions could be made. Unfortunately, communications between the ship and the magazine in New York somehow broke down, and the review was printed in its original form. Incensed, Kissinger wrote Ascoli a long letter, expressing his shock and anger and accusing *The Reporter* of making an unfair attack. Ascoli suggested they have a drink together to talk things over. Though Ascoli was himself critical of the book, even if for reasons different from those of Nitze, the two men ended the talk as friends, on a first-name basis.

Further conversations followed, eventually including much talk about the Korean War and the Truman-MacArthur conflict. Kissinger asked Ascoli if he would like to publish a manuscript of his[12] in which Kissinger wrestled with an issue, policy making and the intellectual, that held intense meaning both for him and, as he must have perceived, for Ascoli. In any event, he accepted Ascoli's editorial assistance, flattering him that he was the only one whose advice he would take. Other articles followed, and *The Reporter* (along with *Foreign Affairs*) became a major vehicle for the expression of Kissinger's views on current issues.

Soon the editorial connection became a social one as well. Ascoli and his wife (the former Marion Rosenwald) lived in a luxurious town house on Gramercy Park, and Henry and Ann were invited for dinner. Henry also became a frequent visitor to Ascoli's office and to his second home in Croton-on-Hudson, New York. (In turn, Ascoli visited the Kissingers in Belmont.) Ascoli, an émigré from Italian fascism and thus a "liberal," was also strongly anticommunist. Two other staunch anti-communists, Kraemer and Nelson Rockefeller, with whom Kissinger was increasingly engaged, were also good friends of Ascoli's. Thus political and social bonds were joined together in a circle of convivial friendship.

Again we see that with Ascoli, as with Nitze, Kissinger had converted an opponent into a sympathetic acquaintance, and in this case even a warm friend. The friendship with Ascoli also served to further Kissinger's policy-making ambitions, providing a useful vehicle for the expressions of his views. Besides, an aura of luxury hung over this happy situation, and it is clear that Kissinger enjoyed being in the presence of good living, wealth, and power. The move from Washington Heights to Gramercy Park was one that Kissinger took gratefully, and even graciously, in his stride. It was all part of the "Americanization" of Henry Kissinger, reflecting his ability to grow and broaden himself while leaving much of his past behind him.

Connections

No one at the Council recalls being struck by any signs of Kissinger's future negotiating skills. What shone through was his intellect and his dominating certainty. Nor was there the slightest sense that here was a potential Secretary of State. Only in hindsight can we perceive that Kissinger was developing aspects of his negotiating powers, as in the Nitze and Ascoli episodes, learning, as one observer put it, a subtlety of vocabulary so that people came away from private encounters with him with different impressions. He was also sharpening his intellectual ability to understand a number of points of view, and thus the lines of possible development in any given negotiating situation.

Above all, Kissinger was developing his connections. It is the same pattern he demonstrated in the International Seminar and *Confluence*. Kissinger would use an initial connection— a William Elliott—to secure a position from which he could then dispense "favors"—a summer lectureship, an article, an invitation to an event—and in turn serve his original connection by offering his ever-expanding knowledge of who could and would do what for the particular enterprise involved. It is a pattern Kissinger developed to perfection in serving Nelson Rockefeller, and then put to public use as Nixon's Special Assistant for National Security Affairs. To put it another way, Kissinger became the center of an extensive communications network, giving him enormous leverage of a very special sort, virtually undetected by those around him.

At the Council and shortly thereafter, Kissinger was able to expand his circle of connections in the widest and most important fashion. Many scholars receive foundation grants; few, like Kissinger, can acknowledge the personal "inspiration and intellectual support" of John Gardner, the President of the Carnegie Corporation, and James Perkins, the Vice President, in the preface of his book (in this case, *The Necessity for Choice*).[13] Indeed, to read the prefaces of Kissinger's books is to read a sort of "Who's Who in the American Foreign Policy Establishment." If any single trait can be said to have carried Kissinger to the Secretariat of State, it is, I believe, his careful and astute cultivation and adroit use of connections. Other academics have Kissinger's intellectual abilities, and more; none have played the connection game with his cleverness. It is clear now that Kissinger saw in the study directorship at the Council an extraordinary entrance into the foreign policy power world, and that he took brilliant advantage of it.

The single most important connection, of course, was that with Nelson Rockefeller. It colors all of Henry Kissinger's future life and career and persists unabated today. It demonstrates to perfection almost all of the skills in this area we have been attributing to Kissinger.

The power of the Rockefeller family in international affairs is vast, but since it is often exercised in subtle and almost intangible ways, it frequently escapes widespread attention. Because many members of the family are personally decent and unassuming people, neither they nor we tend to be fully aware of the extent of their power and influence. When vice-presidential nominee Nelson Rockefeller disclaimed the allegation of great power made by a member of the Senate committee inquiring into his fitness, he was merely responding in terms of this self-image.

Certain other evidence, however, suggests the real power and influence of the Rockefellers. After World War II the United Nations was *the* prime symbol of the commitment to international affairs of all the nations of the world. The question of where this global body should have its home was crucial. To emphasize America's commitment to the United Nations President Truman offered the beautiful Presidio site on the shore of the Pacific at the Golden Gate: it seemed fitting to establish the United Nations in the city of its birth.

But, as Dean Acheson puts it, "The misplaced generosity of the Rockefeller family, however, placed it in a crowded center of conflicting races and nationalities."[14] New York was a center of Rockefeller philanthropy; unconsciously, and with the best intentions, they placed the United Nations in the same category.

Did John F. Kennedy need an acceptable Secretary of State in 1960? One was available at the Rockefeller Foundation, in the person of its President, Dean Rusk, earlier an Assistant Secretary of State for Far Eastern Affairs in 1950. Rusk had been promoted to President of the Foundation on the recommendation of John Foster Dulles, who, in 1952, as Chairman of the Board of the Rockefeller Foundation, was about to leave to become Eisenhower's Secretary of State.[15] Did the United States in the early 1970s need to reexamine its policy toward Europe and Japan, and strengthen its extragovernmental links with leaders in this area? David Rockefeller generously financed a Trilateral Commission to do what official Washington could not or would not do. One could go on with innumerable other such examples, till the list began to look like a kind of conspiracy theory. Such a conclusion would be simplistic and misleading. The point is merely that the Rockefellers were interested in foreign affairs. Whether they wished it or not, through their personal power and wealth, through their foundations, and through their network of connections they exercised enormous indirect, and frequently direct, influence on who got appointed to what, and what got done.

In turn, the Rockefellers were always on the lookout for bright young men to serve them. Taking their responsibilities seriously, they recruited what they considered the best brains available, irrespective of background, to help them. Henry Kissinger was one among many such choices; he made, as we know, the most of his opportunities. Serving Nelson Rockefeller well and loyally, he also served himself, making exceptional use of the connections afforded him by this, immeasurably his most important, connection. Henry Kissinger's instinct for power and status was infallible and unerring.

The Rockefeller Connection

The two men first met at an arms control conference at the Quantico Marine Base near Washington in 1955. It was a fitting place and subject, for, as we have seen, Kissinger's entire career has been advanced in a largely military setting. We are told that General Theodore Parker, a key White House aide of President Eisenhower who was later on Rockefeller's staff, recruited the panel members, and selected Kissinger on the recommendation of either Elliott or Kraemer, or both.[16] The inspiration for the conference had come from Nelson Rockefeller, then Eisenhower's Special Assistant for International Affairs and on the lookout for new ideas to present to his boss. As Rockefeller now recalls his impression of Kissinger: "I was tremendously impressed. He had the capacity to mobilize all the facts and arguments and to give both sides. And he was a conceptual thinker—he thought in broad terms."[17]

Later events may have been coloring Rockefeller's memory. In any case, there were few immediate results from this meeting. Naturally, Nelson was a member of the Council on Foreign Relations, but apparently he only attended a few meetings during Kissinger's two-year stint. David, Nelson's younger brother, was more active, serving as President of the Council for a number of years. Only when Nelson decided in 1956 to set up a special studies project, established under the Rockefeller Brothers Fund, to make projections as to the nation's major domestic and international problems over the next few years, did his thoughts seem to turn again to the bright young "conceptual thinker" of Quantico. According to one excellent source, however, it was probably Oscar M. Ruebhausen, Rockefeller's trusted advisor, who reestablished the contact and recommended Kissinger for the job of Director of the project.

It is incredible that Kissinger, still only partially through the writing of *Nuclear Warfare*, could take on the new position.

His work schedule grew necessarily heavier, as Kissinger toiled 12 to 16 hours daily on his two commitments. In accepting the original Council post, Kissinger had written to Franklin that one of the reasons was "not only because it seems directed in the main line of my own thought, but also because the Council seems to furnish a *human environment* [my italics] I find attractive."[18] As a friend recalled, Kissinger now ignored his wife, telling her not to talk to him, as he toiled away. " 'Henry,' " the friend remembers saying to him, " 'this is *inhuman*' [my italics]. . . . He was not even aware of that."[19] One must understand, therefore, that "human environment" meant something special to Henry Kissinger, and that the special studies project was simply a desired extension of the Council and not an unwanted and resented burden. Indeed, it was a fulfillment of Henry Kissinger's style of operating, his search for and use of connections.

As at the Council (and before that at the Army Intelligence School), Kissinger found himself overseeing the work of men who were his superior in rank and experience. Established, prestigious figures such as Chester Bowles, Arthur Burns, Lucius Clay, John Gardner, James Killian, Henry Luce, Charles Percy, Dean Rusk, David Sarnoff, and Edward Teller served on the various panels.[20] Kissinger added to this list, by means of his connections, many in academic and government service of lesser stature, but more expert on some particular phase of the panel's work. In my interviewing I was impressed by the number of times people would say to me, "Henry rang me up in 1957, and asked me to do a position paper on _____ for the panel." At one and the same time, therefore, Kissinger rewarded his friends and served his new patron. As Nancy Hanks, Executive Secretary of the group, summed it up, "He was the man with the contacts, and in the course of 1956–58 we developed a community of the best minds in the country."[21] Everyone was aware, of course, that Rockefeller was not only extraordinarily rich, but that he was potentially headed for the highest office in the land.

The final report came out in 1958, just as Rockefeller entered upon the first of his successful campaigns for Governor of New York. The 486-page book[22] was a good launching platform, though its plotted trajectory was obviously aimed well beyond the gubernatorial chair itself. One of the papers published, on "International Security: the Military Aspect," was, in part, an abbreviated version of *Nuclear Weapons*. Sold separately as a paperback,[23] it was also praised by Henry Luce, one of the panelists and incidentally the publisher of *Time* and *Life*. Its views represented the hard-line position of both Kissinger and Rockefeller, whose future nuclear bomb shelter program was supposed to give support to the concept of limited nuclear warfare.[24]

The end of the special studies project marked a hiatus of sorts in Kissinger's relations to Rockefeller. He remained as a consultant to Rockefeller, averaging, according to one source, about $12,000 a year.[25] In the fall of 1957, however, Kissinger returned to Harvard. It was an ambiguous return: he who had consorted with the high and mighty of the world, dominating them with his intellect and presence, was clearly more of a prophet out of Harvard than in it. At Harvard he was offered a lectureship instead of an associate professorship. Though this allowed him to bypass the assistant professorship rank, and the dogfight over promotion, it still left him in an anomalous position. True, as we know, he was also appointed Associate Director of the Center for International Affairs (ignoring the advice of a Council staffer, whose judgment he had sought, about the difficulty of working for Bowie), and Director of Harvard's Defense Studies Program.

It is not clear why Kissinger chose to return to Harvard. Was he expecting to return in triumph to a scene of former humiliation? Such an expectation would show how little he knew about Harvard. Was it because Harvard, in spite of its drawbacks, offered an excellent base for Kissinger's ever-expanding connections between academia and the world of power, with his directorships being the key element here? Was Harvard's simply the best offer he could get? Whatever the answer, Kissinger did return to Harvard and by 1962 had worked his way to tenure and a full professorship.

In the interval he was doing a lot of other things, pointing away from the classroom at Harvard. Some of his activities were in terms of the mountain and Mohammed. Thus, Kissinger brought to his classes and his seminars on arms control a continuous array of high-level politicos and bureaucrats from the Departments of Defense and State to mix with the cognoscenti on defense matters of the Cambridge community. But Kissinger also kept his hand in outside of Cambridge, serving as secretary of an arms control panel at the Council on Foreign Relations in 1958–1959. Thus he was poised for an entrance on the Washington stage when John F. Kennedy was elected President in 1960. In this golden age of service for Cambridge academics, Kissinger was ready to play his part, advising a Democratic President, just as he was ready to advise a Republican one (hopefully, Rockefeller at some point). The publication of his second book[26] in January 1961, coinciding with John F. Kennedy's inauguration, embodying Kissinger's repudiation of limited nuclear war as our preferred strategy, and espousing strengthened conventional forces instead, was his intellectual calling card. More important, however, was his introduction to Kennedy by Arthur Schlesinger, Jr. The result was that Kissinger was named consultant to three important groups: the National Security Council, under McGeorge Bundy; the Arms Control and Disarmament Agency; and the Rand Corporation. Kissinger, it seems, was on his way in Washington.

Kennedy

The most important thing to say about Kissinger's drive for power and position under John F. Kennedy is that it was a failure. The failure, in turn, points up how important it was for Kissinger to find a patron with whom, for reasons of personality and political ideological conviction, he could get along, in both senses of that phrase. If Kennedy had remained President until 1964, and then been reelected to serve till 1968, Kissinger's career, as well as America's political life, presumably would have taken very different turns. The assassination of John F. Kennedy eventually gave not only Nixon his chance, but Kissinger his opportunity to be Special Assistant to the President on Foreign Affairs, and Director of the National Security Council. Chance, as well as character, was obviously necessary to leave Kissinger's imprint in history. (To paraphrase Freud a bit: Character is Destiny, but Destiny is Chance.)

The next thing to say about Kissinger's effort to serve in John F. Kennedy's administration is that it illustrates his "nonpolitical" willingness to go to Washington for either party. Now in this regard Kissinger was hardly unique. Foreign policy types are a peculiar group (with apologies to those who do not resemble the description that follows). Typically, they are very power-oriented, and tend to be hawkish in their advocacy of the use of power. To a large extent they are intellectual "guns for hire"; in 1968, for example, many of them were as willing to work for Humphrey as for Nixon (this was Kissinger's position, as it finally turned out). Justification for this attitude is at hand in the doctrine of bipartisanship in foreign policy matters, a doctrine widely preached in the post-World War II atmosphere. Moreover, the mark of a *policy* adviser is that he must always have a policy to recommend, no matter what the topic or the area. Ideally, he must never seem indecisive or unknowledgeable (he can always change his recommendation later, when he has briefed himself on the subject, as long as his second recommendation is stated in the same certain and dogmatic tones as his first). Thus, the foreign policy adviser should be willing to advise *any* states-man on *any* issue.

Kissinger came close to the ideal. From his earliest days he had shown a marked disinterest in domestic politics, thereby echoing his German-Jewish heritage with its center-party in-clination (if any). Although he apparently voted for Kennedy in 1960, he seems not to have bothered to mark the rest of his ballot for Massachusetts Senator, Governor, and so on. He was, as we have noted, filled with confidence and dogmatic certainty. He was prepared to take on any subject, and, in a short time, to pontificate, e.g., on nuclear warfare, at the Council. (This trait becomes extremely important when we view, for example, his diplomatic efforts vis-à-vis China, an area about which he originally knew nothing.) As a quick learner and a master synthesizer he was extremely apt in this area. All in all, then, Kissinger seemed a likely prospect to suc-ceed under Kennedy.

Yet he failed, and knew he had failed. At first, things seemed to go well. Kissinger initially found John F. Kennedy attractive, partly because of the aura of power around him. The two men seemed equally hawkish, equally committed to maintaining America's power in the world. Kissinger now spent much of his time in Washington, flying there frequently from Cambridge. Even when in Cambridge, however, he was wired in directly to the CIA, and his office, to Bowie's apparent chagrin, was the only one at the Center with a top secret safe. In 1961, for the first time, he was too busy personally to pick the members of his International Seminar.

Alas, the honeymoon was soon over, and Kissinger removed from the round table of power. Perhaps it was because, as most critics suggest, Kissinger seemed oafish in Camelot, his pom-posity and pretentiousness hardly calculated to appeal to

John F. Kennedy. Kissinger showed none of his future sense of humor; it may be that he learned the use of self-deprecating humor from John F. Kennedy, but too late. Perhaps it was because, at bottom, Kissinger had trouble working with or for someone close to his own age; all his other patrons were clearly older figures.

There were other, more objective reasons besides those of personality. Kissinger's policies revealed themselves increasingly as divergent from Kennedy's. Taken on as a general adviser on European affairs, Kissinger found himself especially involved in the critical issue of the Berlin wall in August 1961, on a crisis basis. Kissinger's advice was to take a tough line: the wall was an act of aggression which must be checked immediately. He advocated force and the use of troops to tear it down. When Kennedy took less drastic and ultimately ineffective, steps, Kissinger was shaken. The gunning down of an East German refugee thereafter, without our reacting, left Kissinger dismayed. All in all, he was extremely disturbed and annoyed at Kennedy's overly "passive" attitudes.

Was Kissinger overreacting? Were his feelings in some way connected with his German past? In any event, Kissinger felt that he wasn't getting his point of view across effectively enough to Kennedy. He tried end-running around Bundy, and that seems to have been the beginning of the end for Kissinger. In February 1962 Kissinger was advised to resign. He had overvalued his position and prestige and lost out badly in the power policy struggle. As he later complained bitterly to a friend, he had discovered that there were "ball games" about which he did not know, and whose rules he was not sure he could learn. Connections, we might say with hindsight, were one thing; converting such connections into actual power in Washington was another matter. A presence at the Council in New York, Kissinger was merely an irritating consultant in the nation's capital.

Rejected by the Kennedys, Kissinger was equally harsh

in his condemnation of them. It seems the disillusionment on both sides had grown apace. Kissinger now viewed John F. Kennedy as "light," a glamour-boy not deserving or capable of greatness. He was a poseur, a man who really didn't have the necessary guts. His policy was too unsophisticated and romantic. The whole Kennedy crowd, and apparently he now included even men such as Schlesinger and Galbraith, appalled Kissinger by their confusion and ineptness. The Kennedy entourage itself was "pretty puerile"; Bobby Kennedy was especially singled out, as sitting in the back of meetings and blowing bubble gum. As a measure of Kissinger's reaction, we must note the fact, if an insider's story can be trusted, that when John F. Kennedy was assassinated Kissinger did not express himself as unhappy. To the contrary, he injudiciously admitted in front of some of the Center staff that Kennedy had been "leading the country to disaster." Hell hath no fury, it may be said, as a policy adviser scorned.

In fact, the whole episode according to one of Kissinger's close colleagues at the time, was a "traumatic experience" for him. Kissinger himself confessed years later that he had "blown it, messed up a good opportunity."[27] It does seem as if he overreacted badly to this initial failure. Of course, it was his second professional failure, so to speak, for, as we know, his relation with Bowie at the Center had also soured after an auspicious start. In that first episode, however, Kissinger had retrieved his dignity and suffered little loss of power. In this second instance much more was at stake, and in his self-estimation he had lost a great deal more. There was another factor involved, of a less public nature. As we shall see shortly, Kissinger's marriage was also in the incipient stages of breaking up. Thus, Kissinger was having to face himself as a failure in both the personal and professional areas of his life.

Failure aside, the whole Kennedy episode shows that Kissinger's style of operating needed a patron of a very special sort: a Kraemer, an Elliott, or a Rockefeller. Undoubtedly,

Kissinger learned from his experience of 1961. When he came back to Washington in 1968 he was a sensationally successful bureaucratic infighter. Again he demonstrated his enormous adaptability in *certain circumstances*. Between 1961 and 1968 he was learning additional political lessons, and most of them, though not all, were at the side or in the shadow of Nelson Rockefeller.

A Varied Service

In 1964 Nelson Rockefeller made his bid for the presidency, seeking the Republican Party's nomination against Barry Goldwater. Kissinger was his foreign policy adviser, involved for the first time in the hurly-burly of a domestic political campaign. It was not a pleasant experience. Rockefeller, a staunch anticommunist and a conservative, was pictured by the Goldwater forces as a wild-eyed liberal out to destroy America's traditions and institutions. (The right's hatred for Rockefeller is one of the weirder, more paranoiac episodes of our time.) Rockefeller's recent divorce did not help. The convention, in a frightening outburst, tried to prevent his speaking by booing.

Kissinger's job was to serve as Rockefeller's chief adviser and to help prepare position papers on foreign affairs. By the summer of 1964 he was also involved in working on a book[28] and was clearly spread too thin. His secretaries noted that he was beginning to blow his cool. Kissinger became increasingly frustrated during the campaign, especially over the way many of his papers got lost in the Rockefeller bureaucracy. By the end of the campaign, Kissinger felt his time and energy had been wasted.

Rockefeller's defeat, and the way it occurred, hit Kissinger hard. Having invested so much in Nelson—victory would have meant the realization of so many of Kissinger's ambitions, as well as his "friend's"—the loss to Goldwater had an overwhelming effect on him. As one close observer put it, Kissinger cried like a baby at the news of Goldwater's nomination. The campaign of 1964 became a lesson to Kissinger, for what had happened both to Rockefeller and to himself.

With the election of Lyndon Johnson in 1964, Kissinger was able to place his technical abilities at the service of another Democratic President. This time it concerned an area about which he knew very little and with which he was not personally involved: Vietnam. It would, of course, be an area in which he would eventually become almost as much involved personally as he was with Germany. Henry Cabot Lodge, Johnson's ambassador to Saigon, seeking outside advice, appointed his son, George Lodge, and Kissinger as consultants to the State Department.

The way Kissinger came to this appointment has its own interest. Back in 1963–1964, Kissinger had been looking for someone from the Harvard Business School to participate in the International Seminar. What he had in mind, apparently, was for the right person to give classes on what was happening socially and politically in America. He settled on George Cabot Lodge. Lodge was quite taken with Kissinger's wit and self-denigrating humor, and was impressed by Kissinger's deep concern over the lack of a moral purpose and consensus in America. They discussed the matter over several lunches, and then Kissinger introduced Lodge to Father John Courtney Maury, of Fordham University, and the three had a number of lunches at the Century Club in New York, talking over their common interests in moral problems. Kissinger apparently had come to know Maury as part of his Rockefeller connections.

When Kissinger suggested that Lodge join him and Maury in getting a group together to revitalize America, Lodge did not manifest great interest. However, when his father, then ambassador to South Vietnam, appointed young George as a

Henry as a child (left) with his younger brother, Walter. (UPI)

Henry's mother, Paula, and father, Louis. Picture was taken in November 1973 after they had received the Charles Evans Hughes Award for their son. (UPI)

A Fürth high school class of the Israelitische Realschule. Kissinger is at bottom left. (© 1974, New York Post Corporation)

Henry's first wife, Ann Fleischer, in a picture taken in 1946 while Henry was still in service overseas.
(© 1974, New York Post Corporation)

Kissinger on leave with Ann Fleischer and K. Oppenheim, a boyhood friend from Fürth. The Army was a crucial influence on the Americanization of the future Secretary of State.
(© 1974, New York Post Corporation)

Kissinger with his daughter, Elizabeth, and son, David.
(© 1974, New York Post Corporation)

Henry Kissinger at Harvard.
The picture was taken in 1957
at a time when Kissinger
was establishing a reputation as
an expert in national
security policies. (UPI)

Henry Kissinger
and Nelson Rockefeller.
Rockefeller played an
important role in launching
Kissinger onto the
national scene.
(WIDE WORLD)

Kissinger with his second wife,
Nancy Maginnes. (UPI)

With President Nixon,
Kissinger's most
important patron. (UPI)

The Diplomat at Work

With Hanoi's Le Duc Tho. (UPI)

With Leonid Brezhnev of the Soviet Union. (UPI)

With Chou En-lai (UPI)

consultant—the younger Lodge had had a good deal of experience with social and economic development in Latin America and was expected to carry this expertise into a survey of the Vietnamese situation—he did recommend his father get Kissinger over there also to look at things and give a report.

Kissinger prepared himself by spending a good deal of time getting briefed by various academics. He talked especially to Paul Mus, at Yale. Though now quite old, Mus, a Frenchman, had worked with Ho Chi Minh during World War II and knew him and the Vietnamese scene well. Kissinger apparently also talked to a lot of people elsewhere in the United States to whom the State Department was not talking, and thus got a rather independent assessment of the situation.

In short, he was not entirely ignorant, though obviously not a scholar in the field, when he visited Vietnam in October 1965. According to the friendly account of the Kalbs, for example, Kissinger exposed himself there not only to the official version of what was happening, but went outside these circles, asking more pointed questions and emerging with a "brilliant analysis of the war."[29] Another observer is reported as saying, "His mind was open. He wasn't carrying a lot of ideological baggage around."[30]

Whatever Kissinger's verbal comments may have been, his article in *Look* in 1966[31] took mainly the official position, and rocked no boats. He believed that American withdrawal would be disastrous, because "a demonstration of American *impotence* in Asia cannot fail to lessen the *credibility* of American pledges in other fields." In Vietnam, he claimed, we were not only fighting for the Vietnamese and ourselves, but "for international *stability*" [my italics]. The way to achieve our goals, however, was not through military means, but by negotiations. Here Kissinger was in his favorite milieu. As he concluded, "The primary issue in Vietnam is political and psychological, not military."[32]

Kissinger had other assignments in Vietnam under Johnson:

another visit in October 1966 and a role in secret exchanges of messages between Washington and Hanoi through a French intermediary. Though the latter came to nothing, it was useful experience for Kissinger's later efforts at covert negotiation with the North Vietnamese. His service under Johnson also established his reliability: although a known Rockefeller man, his discretion and loyalty to whatever person he worked for had been proven.

The 1968 presidential campaign returned Kissinger to Rockefeller's side. Earlier, Kissinger had been asked to serve as a consultant to George Romney (who was, of course, Rockefeller's candidate at the time). Kissinger flew out to Mackinac Island, and apparently handled Romney beautifully. Instead of being distracted by Romney's incompetence, he praised his integrity, honesty, and general high moral standards. Obviously, Kissinger was hedging his bets in case Romney were to win.

After New Hampshire it was clear that Romney was out. Kissinger now devoted his full talents to Rockefeller's campaign against Nixon, recruiting to the cause at least one of Romney's top advisers. Again he tapped his connections, getting friends and colleagues to write position papers and telling them, "You should get to know Rockefeller." Kissinger himself threw all his energies into the campaign, as if his foreign policy positions would make or break Rockefeller's candidacy. Kissinger even began to be interested on the domestic side. In the end he concluded that the pros, like Leonard Hall, were all wrong in their belief that Americans were not interested in issues. After the campaign, in fact, Kissinger regaled friends with a long diatribe on how he would have done it better. He had come to the conclusion that the so-called pros, or experts, were not to be trusted in domestic politics.

Whatever the faults in the campaign strategy, it was apparently clear to all but Kissinger that Rockefeller had no chance of winning. Nixon was a sure thing at Miami Beach. Kissinger's only hope, paradoxically, was for Humphrey to win the election itself. As everyone now knows, Kissinger expressed himself avidly and incautiously on the subject of Nixon's deficiencies. He is recorded as having called him a "disaster," an "asshole."[33] With Humphrey, on the other hand, he had good connections through his service to Johnson on the Vietnam negotiations. Whether or not he would have been named National Security Adviser, as Humphrey later claimed was his intention (others thought *they* were to be given that post), it was clear that his lines to the Humphrey camp were open and strong.

It was Nixon, of course, who emerged victorious on Election Day in 1968. Kissinger's connection to Rockefeller seemed to have led to a dead end. As with Elliott at Harvard, his powerful patron seemed unable to deliver the goods, in this case, foreign policy adviser to the President instead of an assistant professorship at Harvard. Then, out of the blue, President-elect Nixon invited Kissinger to a meeting at the Hotel Pierre—and the rest is public history, which we shall examine later in Chapters 10 and 11. In defeat, rather than victory, as it turned out, Nelson Rockefeller had in fact been able to carry Kissinger to the top of the foreign policy tree.

Nelson Rockefeller

Nelson Rockefeller is like Kissinger's previous patrons and yet unlike them in key ways. He is like Kraemer and Elliott in being hard-line in foreign affairs and conservative in domestic matters. All three of them were regarded by Kissinger as "strong men," of "seigneurial" presence. In common, they all helped Kissinger with their patronage: Kraemer primarily in the army, Elliott at Harvard, and Rockefeller in the world at large. And all three were older than Kissinger, Christian, and became his friends as well as his patrons.

Rockefeller, however, was never Kissinger's model in the

formative way that Kraemer and Elliott had been. Kissinger was already largely formed by the time he met Rockefeller. What Rockefeller could supply that the earlier two couldn't was extraordinary wealth, and the potential power that went with it. He was "a great gentleman," as Kissinger described him, with power and a feeling for style of life. Rockefeller was Kissinger's quintessential patron: a Renaissance man who was also a Prince.

For such a Prince, Kissinger saw himself as a fitting councilor. He had the brains, developed under the tutelage of Kraemer and Elliott, to supplement his patron's wealth and power. As Kissinger indiscreetly said about Rockefeller: "He has a second-rate mind but a first-rate intuition about people."[34] In the eyes of many of Kissinger's friends (incidentally, mainly Jewish), Kissinger became a "court Jew" to his new Prince. (Ironically, other friends joke about Kissinger's tendency to supply himself with a chosen gentile as his personal "court WASP.")

The fact that Kissinger was Jewish may well have enhanced his position in Nelson Rockefeller's eyes, at least unconsciously. In his statement to the Senate Rules Committee, considering his nomination as Vice President, Rockefeller submitted an extraordinarily revealing letter from his mother to him and two of his brothers:

> Out of my experience and observation has grown the earnest conviction that one of the greatest causes of evil in the world is race hatred or race prejudice; in other words, the feeling of dislike that a person or a nation has against another person or nation without just cause, an unreasoning aversion is another way to express it. The two people or races who suffer most from this treatment are the Jews and the Negroes. . . . I want to make an appeal to your sense of fair play and to beseech you to begin your lives as young men by giving the other fellow, be he Jew or Negro or of whatever race, a fair chance and a square deal. . . . The social ostracism of the Jew is less brutal [than lynchings and race riots], and yet it often causes cruel injustice and must engender in the Jews a

smoldering fire of resentment. Put yourself in the place of an honest, poor man who happens to belong to one of the so-called "despised" races. Think of having no friendly hand held out to you, no kindly look, no pleasant encouraging word spoken to you. What I would like you always to do is what I try humbly to do myself: that is, never to say or to do anything which would wound the feelings or the self-respect of any human being, and to give special consideration to all who are in any way repressed.[35]

Did Rockefeller see in Kissinger "an honest, poor man" who happened to be of the so-called " 'despised' race," to whom he could hold out the helping hand of friendship? One suspects that the attraction of Christians for Kissinger was matched by the appeal of Jews for the religiously and ethically motivated Nelson Rockefeller.

There were, of course, other less subtle bonds between the two men. Rockefeller clearly valued Kissinger's intellectual brilliance, his conceptual and synthesizing abilities, and his knowledge of foreign policy issues. He was impressed, as was everyone else, with Kissinger's stamina and energy, his ability for hard work. Kissinger's academic connections were a useful adjunct to Rockefeller's usual entourage. According to one source, Nelson felt he had made a great discovery, perceiving early on a major national figure in Kissinger. Impressed personally by Kissinger, he was flattered when others were similarly impressed.

The relationship, apparently, quickly became a friendship, as well as a consultantship. Whatever Kissinger's views on Rockefeller's intellectual abilities, the two shared similar opinions on the cold war and all related problems. It was not simply a matter of Kissinger's deferring to his patron, but rather a meeting of minds (though Rockefeller, in fact, may have been more hard-line and inflexible than Kissinger in his anticommunism). Moreover, Kissinger found that, where necessary, he could disagree with Rockefeller without offending him. In personal terms, the two men exhibited mutual respect, showing deference to each other in different areas. Though arrogant with fellow academics, Kissinger, not surprisingly, did not demonstrate this trait with Rockefeller.

One can assume limits to the friendship, which was bound to be one-sided, especially at first. As one colleague put it, Kissinger was "very respectful to Rockefeller," "deferential," and "smoothly serviceable." It was not, in the nature of things, a relationship that could be buddy-buddy, and it goes against all we know of Kissinger even to assume he would have wanted it to be.

In fact, of course, while Kissinger gave much to Rockefeller, it was primarily a dependency relationship for Kissinger, fitting in with the whole pattern of his life. Kissinger, the "honest, poor man" who had had to go to work in a shaving brush factory and had always worried about his job or his fellowship, suddenly found himself, as he put it, attached "for the first time in my life to someone to whom money is never a consideration." There was "money for whatever you wanted to do." On the Rockefeller expense account, Kissinger could now set up a lunch at the St. Regis or take a suite at the Hotel Pierre (where Nixon also chose to have his suite in 1968). Did he need a private plane? There was always Rockefeller's jet, in "better shape" than Air Force One, the presidential plane, according to an informed estimate.[36] Later there would be a $50,000 trust fund for Kissinger's children, a mammoth wedding party (celebrating Kissinger's marriage to Nancy Maginnes) for 350 guests at Nelson's Pocantico Hills 3,000-acre estate, and almost anything else of which one could dream.

Henry's brother Walter had become the family millionaire through shrewd business enterprises and investments. Henry's interest had become power; he appeared to have little direct interest in money itself. Now, almost accidentally, he too could live like a millionaire because of his Rockefeller connection.

As we know, however, while always seeking a dependency relationship, Kissinger had only scorn for those who sought to have any dependence on him. Ignoring his own pattern of dependency, he publicly extolled the virtues of independence—and, in fact, maintained a credible degree of it, as in his work at the Council. When Rockefeller suggested in the late 1950s and early 1960s that Kissinger leave Harvard and come to work full time for him, Kissinger was scared by the blatant nature of the dependency involved in such a move. Though it would have meant great financial gain, and even enhanced social status, and though Kissinger at first was fearful of rejecting Rockefeller's offer, he finally declined, gracefully asserting his independence. Harvard, as we can now see, gave Kissinger an "independent" base from which to operate.

Yet he could still serve Rockefeller whenever needed and enjoy his need to be dependent under adequate cover. In return, Rockefeller afforded Kissinger not only access to wealth itself, but more importantly to social status, to an upper-class way of life—and to power. Kissinger's rise is a classic success story, though he went about it in a very special way, with special consequences for his adopted nation. In that rise, patrons, as we have seen, played a key role. Rockefeller is the culminating, constant patron, establishing once and for all Kissinger's style of life and the "human environment" in which he wished to live. Although Kissinger, in his growth and Americanization, shed many other segments of his life, Rockefeller, and the Rockefeller people, have become a constant. We can see now that in marrying Nancy Maginnes, Kissinger was marrying into the family.

On to Nixon

Power and patronage are indissolubly linked in the story of Kissinger's life. He has been one of modern history's great "followers," almost inadvertently rising to a position of leadership as accidental "President for foreign affairs." Brilliantly seizing the tactical opportunity offered to him by the position of Study Director at the Council of Foreign Relations—which on the surface seemed a demotion, or at least a sidetrack to his academic career—he exploited his chance to the maximum. On one side, he used it to establish his intellectual credentials in the field where thought and power met, on the key issue of nuclear weapons. On the other side, he widened immeasurably his connections with the so-called Eastern foreign policy establishment.

The key connection, of course, was with Nelson Rockefeller and his entourage. Starting as Director of the Special Studies Project, Kissinger moved rapidly into the position of continuing consultant to Rockefeller, and became a key figure on foreign policy issues in his presidential campaigns. Though preserving his status as a bipartisan technician, willing to serve Democratic Presidents Kennedy and Johnson, Kissinger was clearly a Rockefeller man. Thus, bitterly upset by his fiasco as an adviser to Kennedy, Kissinger could still retreat to Harvard and to his consulting duties for Rockefeller. In the process he could also learn about bureaucratic infighting and political campaigns.

If luck favors those who are prepared, Kissinger had prepared with a keen eye for the possibilities, by means of hard work and dedicated attention to building up a network of contacts and connections. When the possibility came from an unexpected quarter—Richard Nixon—Kissinger was ready, willing (allowing for a bit of coquettishness), and able. From Harvard and academia to Washington and power had been his dream and his destiny. Here, finally, the line that had started in Germany could end. In Germany he had seen men of goodwill, such as his teacher father, lose all status and stability through lack of power. Now, in Washington, he could seek to bring intellect and power together in the service of international order and stability, as mediated through American national interests. Or such at least, we can confidently surmise, were Kissinger's unconscious thoughts and dreams.

Nixon, too, as we know, had a dream. In Chapter 10 we shall study the way these two men, and their dreams, interacted. At this point we need to turn back from the fulfillment of Kissinger's political ambitions to a more personal aspect of his life: his relations to women, marriage, and sex. As we shall see, these subjects too have their political significance, and are part of Kissinger's rise to political power.

Chapter 6

WOMEN, MARRIAGE, AND SEX

Sex

KISSINGER himself has told us that "power is the ultimate aphrodisiac."[1] As stated, this suggests merely his wry acknowledgment that he might be attractive to women for his power, not his personal attributes. Might it also hint at the fact that one might seek power, in part, out of sublimated sexual desires? That power and sexuality are tied more intimately than suggested at first glance? That one can be converted into the other? That the involvement of a political figure with such subjects as sex, women, and marriage is not solely a private, personal matter, but has public, political consequences?

In many ways these questions are the most difficult, and delicate, with which to deal. Sexuality, if one is to believe the Freudians, is the basis on which an individual's entire psychic life is built. How, then, can we neglect this element in studying a figure such as Kissinger? Attitudes to women, with all that they imply of feelings about masculinity and femininity, activity and passivity, cry out for attention. We know that marriage is a major involvement of the most important and intimate personal nature. A "mate" is just that, telling us of one-half a person's life. Children reawaken feelings about one's earlier family, and about authority, dependency, and related matters. Divorce can be traumatic, either in the sense of relief it brings, or the sense of failure, or, more usually, of both. How can any serious study of a personality bypass such subjects?

On the other hand, there are serious objections that must cause us to pause. Exactly because such subjects are so personal, perhaps privacy ought not to be invaded. Being so private, data about them may be less obviously at hand or obtainable. If obtainable, they may be unusable because of discretion. We must also meet more directly the argument that such subjects can have little to do with grand matters of state: thus, the Kalbs in their book on Kissinger devote two lines to his marriage, less than three lines to his divorce, and mention his wife otherwise only once in their 549 pages;[2] Stephen R. Graubard, taking his subtitle "Portrait of a Mind" literally and obviously believing the mind totally detached from wife, women, and sexuality, never even mentions Ann Fleischer Kissinger.[3] On the other hand, where attention, and indeed sometimes exploitive and voyeuristic attention, is given to Kissinger's "sex" life,[4] it is treated as pure bedroom farce, not seriously related to matters of state.

It is our contention, however, that a consideration of Henry Kissinger's personality and policies which completely ignores these critical elements of his life takes the easy way out, and, by avoiding these threatening depths, opts for a comfortable shallowness. In our view it *is* important, in every way, that, for example, Henry Kissinger married earlier than his fellow students at Harvard and that that marriage further removed him from the usual circle of his classmates. The fact that, at first, there were no children, but that eventually he and Ann did have children, involves issues of creativity and generativity that are crucial. His divorce, we shall assert, coincided with a midlife crisis in which his career also seemed to have reached a depressing point of failure. It was from that "crisis," however, that Henry Kissinger emerged as a new man of sorts, gradually taking on the image of a "swinger" which he used to great political advantage. It made him, above all, a "culture hero," a "super-man," an image created by himself and the media in collusion. At the end, his remarriage, to Nancy Maginnes, took him off the swing and gave him a new image, the results of which are not yet entirely clear.

These are subjects that cannot be neglected. We shall try to treat them responsibly and discreetly. Our thesis, in short, is that sexuality and its energies are a critical part of Kissinger's personality, and that the breakup of his marriage, around 1962–1965, marked a critical turning point in his life. From our perspective, Kissinger's midlife crisis must be viewed as a major feature of his midlife portrait.

Ann: Marriage and Divorce

As we have seen, at least according to one of Henry's close childhood friends, Henry had been very interested in girls at an early age. Arrival in America, and adolescence, appears to have led to withdrawal of overt interest in the opposite sex. Sexuality was sublimated in work and hidden under shyness. One girl, whose family had come to America from Nürnberg in 1937, eventually attracted Henry and in turn found him attractive. Anneliese Fleischer, who became Ann (and sometimes Anne) in the new world, was the daughter of Conservative, but not Orthodox, Jews who had been well-to-do shoe merchants in Bavaria. One uncle had been a well-known gynecologist in Nürnberg. Socially and financially the Fleischers were a step above the Kissingers. Religiously, they were more emancipated, though obviously Jewish.

As a young girl Ann Fleischer was pretty—some say beautiful—and shy and retiring. Her interests were apparently music and poetry. She was not an intellectual and had some academic difficulties at school. We simply do not have any public evidence as to why she and Henry Kissinger found one another of special interest, what "chemistry" was at work between them.

In any case, when Henry went into the Army, they continued to stay in touch by writing to each other. Henry, as we know, now gave overt vent to his sexuality by taking German mistresses. Returning to America and entering Harvard, however, meant a renewed sublimation of sexuality in work, intellectual in this case. We see again Henry Kissinger's ability to alternate between overt sexuality and its complete repression. Though he saw Ann Fleischer during his college years, we can assume that the relationship was quite "proper." Then, as we know, in his last year at Harvard (1949–1950) he and Ann were married.

Why did Henry Kissinger marry? Ann apparently was interested in children, but there is no evidence that this was a strong drive in Henry. His career was just beginning: Was a wife a help or a hindrance? Could it be strong sexual needs, which he now wished to satisfy and with a minimum of distraction? Was it overwhelming love? Did Ann give him a sense of security, an anchor to his past, while he was about to launch out on a new future? We can only raise such questions here.

At the beginning, Ann helped financially by working outside the home. It is a picture more familiar today than it was in the 1950s. They lived modestly in an apartment near Harvard. As we have seen, when Henry was turned down for promotion at Harvard, but secured the job of writing the results of the Council on Foreign Relations' study on nuclear weapons, they moved to New York and another apartment (at first a garden apartment in Westchester, then one in Manhattan), with Ann again taking a job. Return to Harvard in 1957 meant a better life. When Henry Kissinger reached Associate Professor, and security, in 1958, he and Ann bought a house in a fashionable section of Belmont. The Kissingers seemed to be a successful family who had moved up the social and financial ladder a number of notches. The only thing missing was children, and these came soon now: Elizabeth in 1960, and David in 1962.

Within a year of his son's birth, however, Henry Kissinger was separated from his wife, and a year later, in 1964, they were divorced. What had gone wrong? On one level, it is a typical American "success" story. The bright student marries the girl next door or the secretary at his university. Together they struggle upward, held close by adversity and the simple pleasures of life. Then the husband, changing and developing, inhabiting a wider world of professional work, discovers he has outgrown his loyal but staid wife. Usually, "another woman" enters as the spark that blows up the marriage (and provides a convenient explanation for what has gone wrong). At about this time, too, the man has entered the now familiar midlife crisis, seeking reassurance that he is still young and vigorous, with his best years ahead of him. (Today, of course, not only many men but women too are acting out this marital drama.)

On another level, the marriage and divorce of Ann and Henry Kissinger is not just a sociological fact, but a personal tragedy. This is the level that interests us particularly. The two levels interact, of course, when we realize that the praiseworthy ability of Henry Kissinger to change and develop, his capacity for "growth," is one of the basic causes of the sad breakdown of his marriage. As in all other areas, "growth" itself has a price attached to it, one which is usually paid by innocent people (such as children).

Almost everyone agrees that Ann was "nice." She was the one for whom their friends really had affection, the one the neighbors in Belmont really liked. Her interests were in gardening, in the simple things of life. She seemed content with the life of a suburban housewife, married to a respected academic, and in no way eager to climb any higher or to a more powerful

138

perch. Unfortunately, she seems also to have allowed herself to fall into the position of letting her husband treat her as a maidservant (Henry Kissinger, incidentally, was notoriously untidy), a "Hausfrau," who never stood up to him.[5] As he became more secure, she became more dependent, a position which, as we have seen, was hardly calculated to win her husband's respect.

There are dozens of awful stories of how Henry, to the distress even of his closest friends, mistreated Ann, publicly and privately. He ignored her at their dinner parties or interrupted her savagely. He was openly nasty to her. He humiliated her in front of friends. He built a lavish study for himself while consigning her to a dilapidated kitchen in their Belmont house. And so on.

While these stories are not always true, or have other explanations (the lavish study seems definitely to fall into this category), enough persist to set the general tone of the marriage in the late 1950s and early 1960s. By his increasing "inhumanity" toward his wife, we can surmise that Henry Kissinger was trying to "distance" himself from her and her dependency on him—as well as from complicated feelings in himself with which he could not otherwise grapple.

There is, of course, another side to the divorce (how could it be otherwise?). In this view, Ann's passivity deliberately invited Henry's cruelty. The result was a classic sadomasochistic pattern. At least one careful and informed observer also sees Ann as not just passive, which she certainly was, but manipulative in her own manner. In various subtle ways, she got her own back. On this account, Ann was a fairly disturbed person, depressed and difficult. Alas, Henry was just the person whom she had sought out, who was calculated to make her the "victim" which a part of her wished to be.

From Henry Kissinger's side, something deeper and stronger was perhaps also operating. What follows is obviously only speculation, but I believe it touches a fundamental part of the truth. One must note that the marriage was already in difficulty before the children were born. Did Ann and Henry Kissinger hope that children would bring them closer again and hold the marriage together? What would lead Henry Kissinger to leave his wife with a one-year-old child? The evidence suggests strongly that Ann did not want either the separation or the divorce but was brought to the former and then the latter by her awareness that her husband had become involved with another woman in 1963. The evidence also suggests strongly that Henry Kissinger was deeply troubled about leaving his children, and therefore did not wish to dissolve the marriage, even though emotionally it was no longer acceptable to him. Only when professional advice convinced him that the children would probably be better off in a divorced than in an obviously disrupted and hate-filled family did he agree to the legal dissolution.[6]

But why had the marriage become so intolerable for him *after* the birth of the children? One can speculate that deep-lying reasons are involved, the exploration of which would violate the privacy of our subject without illuminating the political arena. But we can usefully identify one or two elements in the emotional equation that do relate to Henry Kissinger's general pattern of behavior. On the testimony of many of his friends, being a husband and father was something of an impediment for Henry Kissinger (and given his work schedule, we can see one obvious source of his difficulties). Though Henry seems to have been a devoted and indulgent father to his two children, especially after the divorce, they still seemed to have brought strongly to the fore all of his fears of dependency, of how he could give adequately to others dependent on him. He seems to have known this about himself, for neither before nor after the first marriage does he appear to have wanted children as part of his continuous, day-to-day life.

Something similar, and even prior to the children, was involved in his relations with his wife Ann. As we have already remarked, he seems to have had increasingly to "distance" himself from her, to spurn her dependency on him. Somehow, when she became mother as well as wife, the feelings finally became intolerable to Henry Kissinger. At this point, a second part of his pattern of behavior, his ability to become "inhuman," came into play. He simply closed off all feeling, and certainly all positive and empathic feeling, toward his wife. As one astute commentator remarked, it was the same "inhumanity" that he demonstrated in the Christmas bombing of Hanoi. In spite of the leap involved, the emotions in the personal and political situation were, in fact, of a piece. (One can argue, incidentally, that the ability to close off feelings in this way may be essential for certain necessary political acts.)

More objectively, of course, Kissinger's divorce meant cutting off segments of his old life. Ann represented the ties to Fürth, to the Jewish community, to all the refugee-associated past from which he had moved so far. The Rockefellers and others had opened a new world to Henry Kissinger. He had become "Americanized" ultimately in their terms. It is understandable that there was no room for Ann, with her apparently un-ambitious, backward-looking nature, in such a *novus orbis*.

A New Man

It would be pretentious for anyone on the outside to judge the people involved in a divorce. By its very nature, divorce generally touches such deep and intimate aspects in the lives of the two partners, held in secret not only from the public but usually from themselves, as to preclude any feeling by outsiders other than compassion—and sadness. One seeks, therefore, only to understand a bit, not to judge.

We can understand that the breakup of Kissinger's marriage was gathering momentum at the same time that his professional life, marked by the Kennedy debacle in 1961 and his exclusion from the Washington scene until 1964, was overwhelming him with a sense of failure. For most of his friends and colleagues, Kissinger demonstrated no, or few, signs of his difficulties; as we know, he was hardly one to hang his heart on his sleeve. But at least some of Kissinger's close confidants believe that in 1962 Kissinger was close to a nervous breakdown. He appeared, in one episode, almost "to go off his rocker." His usual paranoia looked as if it were on the verge of getting out of hand. Although professional assistance seemed recommended, Kissinger apparently rejected it.

We must note that in 1962 Kissinger was also about to have his second, and last, child, a son. In some culminating fashion, as we have suggested, the emotional pressures on Kissinger had become unbearable. The marriage, the deepest part of his emotional life, could no longer hold together. By 1963 Henry and his wife had separated, and by 1964 they were divorced.

Henry Kissinger emerged from this trauma a new man. He lost weight,[7] began to dress more carefully, and even tried to take up tennis. He seemed to those around him more relaxed, happier in his work; as one colleague commented sardonically, he could put in his 18-hour day without disturbance.

His life style changed. As a bachelor he took a fashionable apartment in Boston, decorating it tastefully in blue, with a few pieces in teak. Here he entertained in a sophisticated manner, his parties catered (one remembers his mother!), and with a bartender (though he himself, as we noted, did not drink). When the group was too small for a catered party, Kissinger would take them to a small room in an elegant nearby restaurant, Joseph's. Although he would occasionally joke about not being able to afford something because of his generous alimony settlement, he didn't seem to worry about money. Instead, he entertained as a lavish host, in an ample manner, amusing his guests with easy and polite conversation.

It appears that at first Ann wouldn't let the children visit him, but then relented. When they came, he played games with them. During at least one summer, and perhaps two, he took them with him to Martha's Vineyard, where he stayed at a hotel. The two children fitted in graciously with his new life, and his relations with them are described as relaxed and friendly. Outside the marriage, if not in (and there had been no chance for this, as we know), he apparently was a good father. As Kissinger himself admitted in an interview, "I'm much closer to my children now than when I was their mother's husband."[8]

All in all, Henry Kissinger rebounded well from the breakup of his marriage. Surmounting his midlife crisis, he emerged changed and strengthened, free to pursue his career unencumbered by hostages to the past. Interestingly enough, after a while Ann Kissinger also seemed to prosper. She was now freer to pursue her interest in the Ethical Culture movement (a secular version of religion) and even to work for Women's Liberation. Thus she, too, eventually expanded her life after the break, and her remarriage, to a Brandeis professor (of biochemistry), seems to have left her a happy, contented woman, raising her two children and tending her garden.[9] The divorce had liberated Ann as well as Henry Kissinger.

The Swinger

Free from Ann, Henry Kissinger could now proceed gradually toward becoming a swinger, a significant part of his image as a culture hero in the early 1970s. Opinions about Kissinger and women are wildly divergent. Some women find him courtly, fascinating, and attractive (made more so by his accent). Others find him uncouth, boorish, and even frightening. For one he's a "teddy bear"; for another, he's Dr. Strangelove. Such different reactions, of course, are not really surprising; what is unexpected is the vehemence with which I found them expressed.

More surprising are the divergent stories about Kissinger's

actual relations with women. I have been told by equally trustworthy sources both that Kissinger was a bottom pincher with his secretaries, and that he was painfully shy with them and could never have done such a thing. Verbal pinches, i.e., jokes, perhaps, but the other, impossible! From a number of unimpeachable sources, one is told that Henry Kissinger had an affair with at least one secretary, and perhaps two. Some of his closest friends are absolutely shocked at this notion, and vehemently deny its possibility: the Henry they know simply didn't behave that way.

Whatever the ultimate truth of these matters, and in my view they simply reveal two different sides of Henry Kissinger's personality, they do serve as necessary background to Kissinger's swinger image. That image emerged around 1970, seemingly by chance, when an apparently shy scholar-policy type, engrossed in American foreign affairs, suddenly blossomed as a "secret swinger."[10] For almost four years Henry the superlover tantalized the American imagination, a fascinating spot of color in the grey Nixon administration. A French journalist, Danielle Hunebelle—what a delicious name—wrote *Dear Henry*, a kiss and tell book,[11] surprisingly without any kissing. Pictures of Kissinger with a different beauty each week—a Jill St. John or a Marlo Thomas—appeared regularly in the newspapers and on TV.

Old friends were incredulous. Their typical reaction: "Henry a swinger! It just doesn't figure; he's too shy, and he couldn't possibly have time for such things." In fact, "such things" did not seem to include sexual liaisons, for all the available evidence points away from actual consummation. But that Henry Kissinger enjoyed being in the presence of beautiful women and enjoyed the notoriety involved is clear. Why not? Beautiful women were another of the trappings of wealth and power with which he liked to consort (a pattern whose beginnings we can see in his behavior in Germany in World War II). As a male chauvinist, he hardly minded fulfilling the fantasies of the American public concerning his presumed one-night stands. As he remarked, in heroic mood, to journalist Oriana Fallaci: "To me women are no more than a pastime, a hobby."[12]

Untrue in itself at the deepest level, for Henry Kissinger is more powerfully attracted to women and sexuality than he might care to admit, such an attitude apparently does allow him to treat most women as things, with whom he can be unemotional and "distanced," having only an aphrodisiacal rather than a meaningful human relation. It also allows him to use women and sex for political purposes.

On one obvious level, Kissinger used his swinger image to diplomatic advantage. As he remarked, "I believe my playboy reputation has been . . . useful, because it has helped and helps to reassure people, to show them I'm not a museum piece."[13] Like his admired predecessor, Metternich, Kissinger then went on to use his dalliances as a cover-up for serious diplomatic negotiations, pretending, for example, to be dating a beautiful TV producer in Paris while actually holding secret talks with Le Duc Tho.

On another level, Kissinger could use the swinger publicity to underline his image as a strong, masculine statesman. One wonders whether he learned this trick from John F. Kennedy. Kissinger, who had accused Kennedy of being a "glamour boy," now seemed to mimic his former boss and President. In tune with his male chauvinism, it was another way of conveying the idea that he was both a powerful person and statesman (Kissinger was aware of the attendant risk of seeming "light" and frivolous, and managed to walk a narrow tightrope, avoiding the snapping jaws of those in the Nixon administration who would have liked to bring him down).

Last, on yet another (and in my view the most important) level, Kissinger's swinging image gained him domestic support. His apparent love affairs were the materials out of which were woven much of his status as a culture hero. America's closest facsimiles to royalty are our Hollywood stars. By associating himself with such public celebrities, Kissinger took on the same aura. Indeed, he has joked, though half seriously, about himself acting in films, and he has been offered high administrative positions in the film industry.[14] In any event, without a political constituency of his own in Washington, he now developed a public following throughout the country. As the polls at the time showed, Kissinger was the best-known and most admired member of the Nixon administration. Such a hero-worshiping constituency brought with it its own power, which he could translate into immense leverage in the capital.

It is a commonplace that women and sexuality are transmuted by advertisers into economic gain. Pretty women sell products totally unrelated to them. Kissinger, with the connivance of the media, which of course wished to sell newspapers, magazines, and so on, ingeniously contrived to translate his supposed amours into political gain. Sexuality was now placed directly in the service of power, and the two made interchangeable. One must admire his feat in swinging back and forth from one to the other.

Remarriage: The Ultimate Assimilation

Kissinger's swinging image helped carry him to the position of Secretary of State, but once he was in that dignified office, it clearly became a disadvantage. As we all know, shortly after his appointment Kissinger married Nancy Sharon Maginnes. The two had first met back in 1965, almost immediately after Kissinger's divorce. Nancy Maginnes was part of the Rockefeller entourage, working for the Governor, keeping her independence, and enjoying a special ability to tell Rockefeller unpleasant truths when necessary. She had majored in history and political science at Mt. Holyoke (class of 1955) and was in her own way a competent intellectual. Bright, overly tall, out of place in some ways, she was, like Kissinger's first wife, a very private person (in contrast to the swinging starlets), but in this case a person in her own right.

All their close friends knew that, though in the background, Nancy was the one Henry Kissinger would marry. Perhaps it was because, unlike Ann, she apparently did not threaten him with dependency and children. Probably, most would say undoubtedly, she formed a fated part of Henry's assimilation, of his ultimate identification with the values and culture of waspish America. Earlier, Henry's brother Walter had married a blond, blue-eyed Christian girl. Now Henry's parents had to face, sadly, another marriage of a son with a gentile.

Kraemer and Elliott had given Kissinger a model, and Rockefeller, its perfect exemplar, had provided him with the possibility of realizing it. Nancy Maginnes was part of the pattern in which the realms of power, women, marriage, and sexuality all came successively and successfully together. In growing and changing, in becoming fully Americanized, we should not be surprised that Henry Kissinger exhibited an inward unity compounded from the apparent diversity of his life. As a political being, he remained a person; as a person he was also always a political being, seeking power.

PART II

An Intellectual

with a World View

Chapter 7

A CONSERVATIVE INTELLECTUAL AND ACTIVIST

A Professional Intellectual

WE HAVE NOW traced in some detail, though focusing on the broad outlines, Kissinger's personal development—his life history. We have asked: What are Kissinger's major character traits, his patterns of behavior, and how did he come to these consistencies in his life? Now we must ask: What are his mental attitudes? His ideological convictions? His basic concepts? In short, we must take Kissinger seriously as a special sort of person, an intellectual, addressing these questions independently and in their own right, while ultimately asking ourselves what is the link between character and ideology, and how do the union of these two elements affect Kissinger's policies? In doing so, we might bear in mind the comment of one longtime Kissinger observer that Kissinger "turned scholarship into projective biography."

No other Secretary of State has been a professional intellectual in the same sense as Kissinger. Of course, there have been other intellectuals connected with foreign affairs. Walt Rostow, for example, was an outstanding economic historian and academician before serving as adviser to President Johnson. George Kennan, one of the most admired of foreign policy thinkers, served as head of the Policy Planning staff under Secretaries of State Marshall and Acheson, but, unlike Kissinger, he was a career Foreign Affairs officer and never became Secretary of State. Dean Rusk, who did become Secretary of State, was at one point a law professor, but he authored no powerful, intellectual analyses of foreign affairs. None of these men had made a broad mark as an intellectual and theorist of international affairs, with a separate professional identity, before coming to Washington. Perhaps the figure closest to Kissinger would be Woodrow Wilson, who, as Professor of Government at Johns Hopkins and Princeton, made a substantial independent reputation for himself as a political scientist; but Wilson as an academic concentrated on domestic affairs, and he became President, not Secretary of State.

Kissinger, therefore, could well pride himself on his superior intellectualization, if not intellect, in his chosen area. And, as we have seen, much of his power over others lay in the impression of brilliance of mind and command of knowledge which he made. When, in his article "The Policymaker and the Intellectual,"[1] he poured scorn on the businessmen and lawyers usually entrusted with foreign policy formation, and extolled the superior potential abilities of the intellectual, he was deservedly and confidentially speaking of himself. Outside the usual State Department network of the old school tie— one need only read Acheson's memoirs to see how this functioned for others—Kissinger had been forced to construct his own network, his famed connections, on the basis of intellect instead of shared social background. It was an audacious and unique enterprise.

There is no need to summarize or paraphrase Kissinger's books, the best and most obvious source for his intellectual positions; others have done that at great length.[2] Rather, our task is to single out certain constant intellectual concerns, repeated themes in Kissinger's mental picture of the world. Such a construct is sometimes called a "world view," or an "ideology," or even an "operational code."[3] However called, there is an assumption of coherence, continuity, and unity among the ideas or views involved. To this assumption must be added an awareness that often the unity is made up of polarities, the continuity erratic, and the coherence a dialectical one. What part of the ideology or world view will come into play at any given moment, and with what force, is extremely difficult to predict.

Even more difficult, in practice, is relating the ideology to the personal development and the character traits of the individual involved. We *know* that Kraemer's injunction to the young Kissinger about goodwill not being enough on the docks of Marseilles is related to Kissinger's view of world policies (and in fact, we will try to show where and how it relates); but to trace the link in concrete detail is, in the nature of things, extremely difficult, for Kissinger is hardly likely to blurt out the connection for us. We must trust to our own sense of "fit," of how one piece of evidence coheres with another, and not be afraid to use inference and intuition as long as data, logic, and psychologic (with this last often contradicting everyday logic) support our leap.

Obviously, Kissinger developed personality traits and characteristic patterns of behavior before he became an intellectual with ideas on foreign policy. The problem of figuring out the relationship is compounded, however, because intellectualization, grounded in the character as a defense and an adaptation, takes on a life of its own. As a defense, Kissinger's intellectual work can become so effective a mechanism as to block from sight, both his and ours, any roots it may have in his emotional life. (We have already talked about the way Kissinger could "block" off human feelings in relation to individuals as well as political actions; intellectualization is another way of doing this: for example, "It is not I, but strategic doctrine that

153

requires this or that 'inhuman' action.") Consequently, his ideology must be interpreted first in its own terms, and only then in more psychological terms. So, too, as an adaptive mechanism, intellectual activity may be, in part, largely conflict-free, connected to the process of reality—the situation "out there"—and often subject to the constraint of extrapersonal interests and circumstances, to the virtual exclusion of intrapsychic dynamics.

Thus, neither too much nor too little must be aimed for in seeking to connect an individual's life history and his intellectual formulations. With this caution, let us see what emerges from a consideration of Kissinger's "world view," his "ideology," as we are able to extract it from the books on foreign affairs he has so willingly, and openly, written.

Conservatism

The most important overall comment to be made about Kissinger's world view, or ideology, is that it is conservative. The superiority of his thought rests on the fact that he has developed and enunciated a fully worked out and articulated conservative doctrine, especially in relation to foreign policy. He has formulated this world view in order to restore a world of stability. Right or wrong, its farsighted analysis, overly pretentious as it often is, provides a consistent, coherent perspective that supplies guidance to an operational code (if one can separate the view and the code in this way), and a sense of direction and certainty. There appears very little comparable to it on the "liberal" side,[4] and, at the risk of making it sound pretentious, one must look to the communist ideology to find its match in this sense.

Most scholars will disagree with me. They believe either that Kissinger's philosophical efforts are jejune, or that if he does have an ideology, he suspends it in the face of opportunism. In my view, this is to underestimate both the man and the seriousness of his intellectual and ideological commitment. Thus Kissinger sounds the keynote of his work when he says, "In the years ahead, the most profound challenge to American policy will be philosophical: to develop some concept of order. . . . But a philosophical deepening will not come easily to those brought up in the American tradition of foreign policy."[5]

Kissinger, of course, was not brought up in that tradition. His philosophical mentors were Kant, Hegel, and Spengler; his conservatism is more Hegelian than Burkean, more German than Anglo-Saxon, and more European than American.

Yet its applicability is to America. Kissinger is convinced that in our time we are faced with a new, revolutionary situation (comparable to the aftermath of the period of the French Revolution and Napoleon). The dilemma is how to conduct foreign affairs in such a context, in which the revolutionary forces have taken on new forms, such as communism and nuclear weapons. This time the major status quo power is the United States. As Kissinger describes us, we are the "satisfied power," the "status quo power."[6] In the definition of Hans Morgenthau, one of Kissinger's early guides, "The policy of the status quo aims at the maintenance of the distribution of power which exists at a particular moment in history."[7]

As we know, Kissinger has not been particularly interested in domestic affairs, except as they relate to the international arena. It is clear, however, that he postulates and assumes a conservative domestic policy as a sort of given, a necessary correlate to a conservative foreign policy. Again, he would agree with Morgenthau that "one might say that the policy of the status quo fulfills the same function for international politics that a conservative policy performs for domestic affairs."[8]

It would be a grave mistake to look at Kissinger as a conservative in terms of specific domestic policies: as pro or con welfare assistance or unemployment insurance extensions. His is a philosophical conservatism, a flexible willingness to take various actions in the name of preserving the basic status quo (while allowing, in theory, for some change).[9]

With this said, one must add that, for better or for worse, there is not a liberal bone in Kissinger's body.[10] At no point has he evinced the slightest convincing regard for the traditional liberties or values that undergird the American tradition of liberalism; or for the newer concerns of civil liberties and social welfare. In his mind, "liberal" is a kind of epithet. Thus, in the bibliography of his *World Restored*, he singles out two authors to condemn as typical of the "reaction of liberal historiography;"[11] one looks in vain for a similar sarcastic, negative statement about "conservative historiography."

Philosophically, Kissinger believes that American liberalism is based on a Newtonian view of reality as external to the observer (a description of American liberal epistemology incidentally, with which most scholars, including myself, would agree). Such a view, or at least its overemphasis, Kissinger asserts, "may produce a certain passivity and a tendency to adapt to circumstance rather than to master it."[12] What is crucial here is not that Kissinger is wrong—he is, for British and American history from the seventeenth century on, with their Newtonian view, have hardly shown passivity or a lack of mastery—but that he believes these traits to be the likely consequences of the epistemological foundations of Anglo-Saxon liberalism. As a result, he turns instead to praise "other cultures which escaped the early impact of Newtonian thinking" and which believe that "the real world is almost completely *internal* to the observer."[13] Initially a liability, insofar as this non-Newtonian view inhibited technological mastery, Kissinger clearly sees the emphasis on internal will, on *changing reality*, as an advantage today that is enjoyed by the communists. To anyone who has read Kissinger's undergraduate thesis, "The Meaning of History,"[14] it is clear that his epistemological heroes are not the empirical realists, Locke and Hume, but the metaphysical idealists, Kant and Hegel. Putting philosophy aside, merely reading Kissinger's later writings on foreign policy show his preference for "will" and for changing "external reality." As he remarked in *Troubled Partnership*, the last book written before joining Nixon, "There are two kinds of realists: those who use facts and those who create them. The West requires nothing so much as men able to create their own reality."[15] Kissinger obviously sees himself as such a man.

Kissinger's conservatism is fundamentally neither Burkean nor Metternichian, nor, indeed, a carefully delineated and defined set of statements. It is a personal compound of Burkean, Metternichian, Hegelian, and Clausewitzian elements, the result of which, however, is an all-pervasive coloring of the political world around him. In short, it is primarily an attitude, a sort of world view, rather than a set of dogmas. We shall try to grapple with it by analyzing the themes that constantly preoccupy Kissinger as he looks at international affairs.

Kissinger's own scholarly treatment of conservatism as a historical phenomenon is both vague and heavy-footed. It suffers badly in comparison with, say, Karl Mannheim's awesome, though difficult, article on "Conservative Thought."[16] In fact, what Kissinger has to say on the subject in *World Restored* tells us more about Kissinger than about historical conservatism. "The conservative in a revolutionary period," Kissinger announces, "is always somewhat of an anomaly."[17] What the conservative has taken for granted as unquestioned —spontaneous acceptance of order and authority as the basis of liberation and freedom—now must become a matter of self-conscious examination and affirmation. The conservative himself is thus forced to become self-conscious, which violates his principles; he must, in short, pick up one of the revolutionary's tools. He who wishes a quiet stability must now fight. As a result, Kissinger claims, "It is no accident that in revolutionary contests the conservative position comes to be dominated by its reactionary—that is counter-revolutionary—wing, the group which fights in terms of will and with an ethic of loyalty [which Kissinger equates with orthodoxy; I confess I find the idea of loyalty one of Kissinger's more garbled ideas]. *For the true conservative is not at home in social struggle. He will attempt to avoid unbridgeable schism, because he knows that a stable social structure thrives not on triumphs but on reconciliations"* [my italics].[18]

Here Kissinger has stressed two parts of his own "true conservatism," surrounded as it is by counter-revolutionary and revolutionary forces: stability and reconciliation. To one familiar with Kissinger's life, the overwhelming, unquestioned desirability of stability appears to coincide with his personal experiences; the desire for reconciliation seems to look back toward his identification with the enemy and ahead to his extraordinary negotiating abilities. Though hardly major pieces of intellectual dogma, stability and reconciliation are constant poles around which Kissinger's world rotates, or, rather, holds steady.

Burke and Metternich, Kissinger tells us, were both conservatives, but the difference between their positions is "fundamental."[19] Burke's conservatism was based on an appeal to history, Metternich's on an appeal to reason. For Kissinger, Metternich was the "last champion" of the Enlightenment in the nineteenth century. Much as Kissinger admired Metternich, it is clear that he did *not* take him as his complete ideal; one need only look at Kissinger's suspicion of abstract reason and his preference for history. (See, too, Chapter 9.) As for Burke, his limitation is implied when Kissinger seems (the passage is quite obscure) to relate him to Locke, claiming that Burke was merely making clear to the Continent what was taken for granted in Great Britain. On this view, Locke becomes only a conservative (most historians view Locke, *in his context*, as a liberal), and we are informed that "a society based on Locke's concept of freedom [i.e., freedom as the absence of restraint, where society and the state are considered separate] is always conservative, whatever form its political contests take."[20]

As we know, the American political system is based primarily on Lockean ideas. Thus, for Kissinger, America is naturally "conservative," and in his view to be conservative, happy coincidence, is also to be intensely American. The only problem is that, as we also know, Kissinger had grave doubts about the "will" and the ability to create facts and reality of the Newtonian-Lockean position. Thus, America's native conservatism needed to be given vitality by an infusion of Continental epistemology and conviction, in the form of Kantian and Hegelian notions. The implication is clear that Kissinger, with his dual identity, could serve as the "confluence" where these various streams of thought and consciousness could be made to meet and fuse.

Kissinger's old teacher, Carl Friedrich, was right when he said that his pupil was only average in his abilities as a political philosopher. When Kissinger writes on conservatism or similar topics, he is not trying to be an abstract or objective scholar per se. Rather he is seeking to construct and express the melange of ideas and emotionally charged perspectives that we are calling Kissinger's conservative "ideology" or "world view." Here we are in the presence of a personal statement rather than a systematic political philosophy. The fact that it is ponderous, and often pretentious, merely points to one of Kissinger's strengths: his ability to impress people with the "weightiness" of his arguments, frequently causing his listeners to neglect to examine critically the validity of his assertions.

Activism

The animating force in Kissinger's conservatism is that, while committed to stability, it is paradoxically based on the extolling of activism. Kissinger's conservatism is no ivory tower philosophy, but a fighting creed. As we have seen, Kissinger's evolution from shy, introverted youth to activist conservative took place during World War II, under the tutelage of Fritz Kraemer. It was confirmed, intellectually and emotionally, while at Harvard. Nevertheless, a certain amount of (deeply hidden) guilt, at the abandonment of his father's pacifism, passivity, and scholarly dedication, always underlay Kissinger's shift. Only in that most revealing of his articles, "The Policymaker and the Intellectual," does he allow a glimpse of some of his doubts to appear. Here Kissinger laments that the activist intellectual, under pressure to offer counsel, may be forced to sacrifice his true creativity: "Moreover, the pressure is not produced only by the organizations that ask for advice; some of it is generated by the image the intellectual has of himself. In a pragmatic society, it is almost inevitable that the pursuit of knowledge for its own sake should not only be lightly regarded by the community but also that it should engender feelings of insecurity or even guilt among some of those who have dedicated themselves to it. There are many who believe that their ultimate contribution as intellectuals depends on the degree of their participation in what is considered the 'active' life."[21] However, overcoming any guilt feelings he might have, Kissinger insists that "the intellectual should therefore not refuse to participate in policy making, for to do so confirms the stagnation of societies whose leadership groups have little substantive knowledge. But in co-operating the intellectual has two loyalties: to the organization that employs him and to values which transcend the bureaucratic framework and provide his basic motivation."[22]

What are these values in Kissinger which "transcend" his commitment to society and the policy-making organization? One needs to turn all the way back to Kissinger's undergraduate thesis, "The Meaning of History; Reflections on Spengler, Toynbee and Kant" (and originally intended to have included Hegel and Schweitzer) for the most open and naive expression of his values. Again, though much of the thesis is a paraphrase of his three thinkers, Kissinger is really less interested in a scholarly analysis of their ideas than in a working out of his own ideas, as suggested by the use in the subtitle of the word "reflections," with its echo of Burke's *Reflections on the French Revolution*. Thus, in spite of the murky prose, Kissinger's transcending values begin to emerge, both for himself, at age 27, and for us.

The overriding problem of the thesis, as well as of history, is how to reconcile necessity and freedom. Guided by Kant, Kissinger declares that "necessity is an attribute of the past."[23] What has happened is subject to the law of causality. The individual, however, has the experience of inward freedom. Thus, "law ever fights against the unique, against the personal experience, the inward bliss. . . . Yet every event is not only an effect but also an inward experience. As an effect it is ruled by necessity, as an experience it reveals the unique in the personality" [p. 2]. This view of necessity and freedom is applicable both to the individual's life history and to history at large. Kissinger applies it directly to his own awareness that "one's journey across the meadows [of life] has indeed followed a regular path. . . . The direction is set" [p. 1]; yet the future is a matter of choice. In history, this becomes the problem of "What is the meaning of a causality that accomplishes itself under the mode of freedom?" [p. 4], and this problem is addressed by the philosophy of history.

Kissinger's answer is rhapsodic and mystical. "The ultimate mysteries of life," he exclaims, "are perhaps not approachable by dissection, but may require the poet's view who grasps the unity of life" [p. 12], and here we hear echoes of both the romantics and Spengler. Kissinger's poet's view then tells him that the individual's life history and history itself are joined, and that the meaning of history—its only inner meaning—is the unfolding of the individual's personality. In his high-sounding prose, Kissinger announces that "the resolution of the dilemma of historical events serving as the condition for a transcendental experience or reality exhausting itself in phenomenal appearances discloses *the ethical predispositions of a personality* [my italics] not a property of historical data" [p. 12]. Then, invoking Kant again, Kissinger declares that "an act of self-transcendence . . . overcomes the inexorability of events by infusing them with its spirituality. The ultimate meaning of history—as of life—we can find only within ourselves" [p. 23]. If we recall Kissinger's two kinds of approaches to reality, the Newtonian externality and the internally oriented non-Newtonian which creates reality, we can now see more vividly how his philosophy disposes him to the latter.

Thus, history for Kissinger becomes the expression of personality. Such a view, of course, can tremble on the brink of megalomania, with all time merely the echo of oneself and one's "ethical" acts. Though Kissinger does also acknowledge a different empirical level of historical analysis, which will "perforce discover a cyclical pattern" [p. 24], he has little interest in this approach; we have already seen his scorn for "dissection." Later, he adds that "the frantic search for social solutions, for economic panaceas testifies to the emptiness of a soul to which necessity is an objective state, not an inward condition" [p. 333]. As such a statement shows, Kissinger is clearly not an *idéologue* in the usual sense, looking for "solutions" or particular social arrangements (and his lack of such concern fits in with his later disregard of economics).

Instead, Kissinger turns to a second, preferred level of historical analysis: "The ethical which views history as a key to action" [p. 24]. This is history's real meaning, and lesson. "Objective necessity," Kissinger repeats, "can never guide conduct" [p. 34]. Our concern, rather, is with "activity [which] reveals a personality" [p. 341], and history is merely the temporal field on which our activity takes place, thus realizing our personality. In short, history *is* personality, realizing itself by a freedom of choice and action that transcends the constraints of mundane necessity. (Later, as we shall see, there are "limits" to be considered; see Chapter 8.) Such transcendence, therefore, is an *active*, not a mere contemplative, one. Kissinger's conservative world view, as we have said, intrinsically requires activism irrespective of the given historical moment.

Goodwill

At the core of Kissinger's commitment to activism, both psychologically and intellectually, is his despair over the ability of "goodwill" by itself to effect anything in the real world. His father, that man of great goodness, had not been able to stop the Nazis from bringing his world crashing down. As Kraemer had taught young Henry, when one is stalked on the docks of Marseilles, "being reasonable or good doesn't matter" (see Chapter 2, p. 53). One must act, and act with power.

Kissinger sounds this theme compulsively in his intellectual work, where we see his personal concern with the weakness of mere goodwill reified into an analysis of foreign policy. *The Necessity for Choice*, for example, is filled with the subject. From the very first page, warning America that it may not always dominate, Kissinger reminds us that "for all the good will . . . we can go the way of other nations which to their citizens probably seemed just as invulnerable and eternal."[24] Our enemies, the communists, know this full well; for them " 'good will' and 'good faith' are meaningless abstractions," and only "objective factors" and the relation of forces count [p. 172]. We, however, are naive, and believe peace and the status quo can be maintained solely out of a good heart's desire; thus "we grow restless when good will goes unrewarded" [p. 175].

Kissinger reserves much of his sharpest criticism for Eisenhower (and Dulles). He mocks the prevalent view of the 1950s that Eisenhower could personally win over the Soviet leaders by flashing his warm smile at them, convincing them of his good intentions, and drawing them " 'into the circle of his good will' " [p. 182]. For Eisenhower's famed summit meetings, Kissinger has only scorn: "During his last two years in office President Eisenhower was at conferences, preparing for or recuperating from good will visits almost constantly. Such a diplomacy may suit a dictatorship or a state which wishes to demoralize its opponents by confusing all issues. It is not conducive to developing constructive long-range policies" [p. 189]. As Kissinger sums the matter up: "The quest for good will in the abstract has been . . . demoralizing and . . . fruitless" [p. 175].

The implications of Kissinger's view of goodwill are many. On a specific level, it leads him to reject the argument that a change of heart in the Soviet leaders, or a basic transformation of Soviet society, or both, are the prerequisites and guarantees of any successful negotiations with the Soviet Union [p. 191]. A change of heart—goodwill—will not change the Soviet's basic interests or power position, in Kissinger's view. (Incidentally, one can see how his policy of noninterference in "internal" Soviet affairs, such as emigration, follows logically and psychologically from such a view.)[25]

On another, more general and lofty level, Kissinger's view of goodwill leads directly into the major argument about American foreign policy, waged under the terms realism versus idealism. In this debate, America's policy is seen as guided too often by misplaced idealism, by goodwill projected outward as a universalistic, missionary impulse. Thus George Kennan, one of the most intelligent of the realists, laments "The congenital aversion of Americans to taking specific decisions on specific problems . . . their persistent urge to seek universal formulae or doctrines in which to clothe and justify particular actions."[26] For example, Kennan points out, Wilson at Versailles preached a principle of self-determination which ignored the realities of self-interest and history. Almost 30 years later, President Harry Truman gave to the "Truman Doctrine" what Kennan calls a "universalistic and pretentious note, appealing to the patriotic self-idealization which so often sets the tone of discussion about foreign policy in our public life, but which is actually unrealistic and pernicious. . . ."[27]

Goodwill and universalistic messages are not synonymous, but in America the first underlies the second and is tied directly to our tendency to idealism and neglect of hard realities in foreign affairs. Though Kissinger himself seems rarely, if ever, to argue in abstract terms of idealism versus realism, it is clear which side he is on. His commitment to realism is so strong that it does not even need to be explicitly articulated. Given his intense distrust of mere goodwill, how could it be otherwise? Needless to say, a belief in realism in foreign affairs, as with Kennan, can be based on reasons other than a suspicion as to the effectiveness of goodwill. With Kissinger, however, the connection is clear and strong.

Will

If goodwill is not enough, one must resort to active use of power: such was Kissinger's deeply rooted conviction. At the heart of action, nevertheless, must be *will*, even if not goodwill. This was the answer to the question of the meaning of history: it is the exercise of will, of choice, of freedom, in the face of external causality. Will, then, creates its own reality.

Thus, for example, in *Nuclear Weapons* Kissinger is constantly concerned with the way the very power and destructiveness of nuclear forces "may merely paralyze the will"; we must "develop weapons systems which do not paralyze our will."[28] He admires the communists precisely for their will, for their "greater moral toughness" [p. 59], for their "iron-nerved discipline" [p. 95], and quotes Lenin approvingly when the latter accuses the West of suffering from " 'a weak will' " [p. 48]. As Kissinger points out, the Soviet Union, although she lacked the atomic bomb from 1945 to 1949, nevertheless "demonstrated that in the relation among states, strength of will may be more important than power" [p. 95]. Kissinger's final message in the book is that democracy must be "able to find the moral certainty to act" [p. 251], i.e., to exercise will rather than respond passively to events and challenges.

So, too, the title of Kissinger's next book was *The Necessity for Choice*, and the emphasis is the same. "We can still shape our future,"[29] he tells us, in spite of our dire situation. We cannot do it, however, by relying on economic forces and solutions—"panaceas," he had scornfully said in his undergraduate thesis—if they "do not involve also an act of political construction."[30] Because of their own national development, Americans, in Kissinger's view, were all too prone "to believe that any sensible nation would prefer economic development to foreign adventures."[31] We rely "on an evolutionary theory in which the assumed forces of history have replaced purpose and action."[32]

Paradoxically, the evolutionary theory is also held by the communists. They, too, believe in economic determinism, though in different guise and to a different end. But, unlike us, as Kissinger recognized, the present-day communists, if not the earlier Marxists, believe in the absolute necessity of pushing history along in its predetermined direction by the exercise of will and, if a pun be allowed, determination.

In his famous interview with the Italian journalist, Oriana Fallaci, Kissinger spoke of how he was willing to talk to pacifists, but only "to tell them that they will be crushed by *the will of those that are strong* [my italics] and that their pacifism can lead to nothing but horrible suffering."[33] (Was Kissinger equating pacifism with passivity? Was he thinking of Gandhi's nonviolence as leading to "horrible suffering," in contrast, for example, to the war in Vietnam?) A little later, when asked to what extent he had been influenced by Machiavelli, Kissinger replied, "The one thing I find interesting in Machiavelli is his estimate of the Prince's will."[34] Even this, however, he immediately dismissed with the flip comment, "Interesting, but not such as to influence me." Perhaps he was more interested in and influenced by Machiavelli's observation that "a man who wishes to make a profession of goodness in everything must necessarily come to grief among so many who are not good. Therefore, it is necessary for a prince, who wishes to maintain himself, to learn how not to be good, and to use this knowledge and not use it, according to the necessity of the case."[35]

The Lonely Leader

What Machiavelli calls the prince, we today prefer to call the leader. Kissinger is open and constant in his elitism and in his praise of the willful, lonely, strong leader (though he hedges by reminding us that "a structure which can be preserved only if there is a great man in each generation is inherently fragile").[36] Again his position follows both logically and psychologically from his belief in history as the expression of personality, and politics as the reflection of will, not goodwill. We encounter his view everywhere in his work, as well as his action. Typically, in *The Necessity for Choice*, he speaks of the need for "heroic effort," of how "a democracy, to be vital, requires leaders willing to stand alone."[37] Such a leader must stand beyond the need for popular acclaim; he must even set aside the temptation to "personal humility which is one of the most attractive American traits" [p. 343]. Though attractive, such a trait must be forsworn because it leads to bureaucratic ways and "a penchant for policymaking by committee" [p. 343]. Beset by "incurable inner insecurity . . . even very eminent people are reluctant to stand alone" [p. 343].

On one side, Kissinger equates the need for a strong leader, standing alone, with America itself. "As the strongest and most cohesive nation in the free world we have an obligation to lead and not simply depend on the course of events. History will not hand us our deepest desires on a silver platter. A leader does not deserve the name unless he is willing to stand alone" [p. 339]. As a nation that leads, America, like the individual leader, must be prepared if necessary to be unloved "though we of course prefer to be popular" [p. 338].

On the other side, Kissinger obviously identifies the strong, lonely leader with himself. As he remarked in his extraordinary interview with Fallaci, "I've always acted alone. Americans admire that enormously. Americans admire the cowboy leading the caravan alone astride his horse, the cowboy entering a village or city alone on his horse. Without even a pistol, maybe, because he doesn't go in for shooting. He acts, that's all: aiming at the right spot at the right time. A Wild West tale, if you like."[38] Later, Kissinger was to exclaim, "How could I have given such an interview? Me, I can't even ride a horse" (we recall that his brother, Walter, was an expert horseman). It *is* a Wild West tale, an American fantasy assimilated by Kissinger, but nonetheless true and revealing for all that: fantasies do motivate, and express the motivations of people. As Kissinger concluded, "This romantic, surprising character suits me, because being alone has always been part of my style, or of my technique if you prefer."[39] It is a style, or technique, that he would put into action, for better or for worse, as head of the National Security Council and as Secretary of State.

Seemingly, the only constraints on such a leader are those imposed by self-limitation, and the need to work in terms of the available environment. Conservative policy, Kissinger explained in his doctoral dissertation, has always been a policy of self-restraint (in contrast to the revolutionary policy, which knows no bounds).[40] It is a theme we shall develop at great length later (see Chapter 8). In the published version of his thesis, *World Restored*, he pointed out that "a statesman must

168

work with the material at hand,"[41] and was so impressed with this formulation that he repeated it verbatim in *The Troubled Partnership,* applying it to de Gaulle and adding that "if the sweep of his conceptions exceeds the capacity of his environment to absorb them, he will fail regardless of the validity of his insights."[42]

Of domestic restraint, of checks and balances as a legitimate part of policy formation, there is no mention. Domestic politics appear important only as providing legitimacy to authority, without which there can be no stability.[43] Thus, Kissinger was clearly aware, for example, that "the acid test of a policy . . . is its ability to obtain domestic support."[44] Such support is difficult to obtain because there is an incommensurability between domestic and international experience. "Domestically, the most difficult problem is an agreement on the nature of 'justice.' But internationally, the domestic consensus inherent in the definition of a policy must often be compromised with a similar domestic consensus of other powers."[45] The result of this situation is that foreign policy must be more or less forced upon the domestic polity, whose major function therefore is to offer acquiescence and "legitimacy" as the basis for its government's external actions.

Kissinger seems to exhibit no sense of domestic politics, i.e., the values and beliefs of the people, shaping the foreign policy leader's actions, except as a constraint, a condition of the "environment," which he must take into account. The domestic polity is material to be worked on, more than a body of fellow citizens from whom one seeks guidance. Nor does Kissinger speak anywhere of domestic leadership. Unlike another realist, for example, George Kennan, who believed in the necessity of domestic social changes for America, changes which would put our own moral house in order, Kissinger implicitly rejects such changes, though often calling for "moral" ones.[46] And indeed, as we have seen in his attitude to Soviet internal politics, he was perfectly willing to divorce the domestic and international spheres in regard to other countries as well as his own.

Kissinger's leader, then, is a figure solely on the international stage, and history is the expression of a personality which transcends not only external causality but national boundaries as well. Kissinger, of course, could well say that his interests and expertise are limited to the international arena, and that there is no necessity to concern himself with domestic affairs. However valid this explanation, it is clear that in speaking of a Napoleon or a de Gaulle as a leader, Kissinger is concerned only with their effect on a "world restored," on international stability, and only in the most peripheral sense with their impact on more parochial, domestic matters. It is a strange mutation, a reversal of his own personal experiences, in which a domestic Nazi revolution first undermined his father's status, overturned the order and stability of his family's world, murdered his people, and only then launched outward on its career of world conquest and destruction.

Chapter 8

HOLOCAUST–NAZI AND NUCLEAR–AND THE PROBLEM OF LIMITS

A Displacement of Feeling

T OWARD the end of his undergraduate thesis, Kissinger mentioned one of the conditions under which a leader would have to labor in his effort to act creatively: "No person can choose his age or the condition of his time . . . the generation of Buchenwald and the Siberian labor-camps cannot talk with the same optimism as its fathers."[1] This is one of the few references to Nazism and the Holocaust that Kissinger has allowed himself to make in print. In his lectures, as well, he has avoided almost completely the subjects of the Nazi experience or Hitler, even as purely intellectual topics. In Israel, where a visit to the Holocaust museum is *de rigueur*, we are told only that Kissinger stood in silence, and seemed grim.

Outwardly, Kissinger appears to have blocked off all feeling about the destruction of the Jews (which could easily have included his own destruction), partly by repression and partly by the mechanisms of forgiving and then identifying with his former enemy. In my view, another mechanism is involved: displacement. Kissinger has dealt with much of his feeling about the Nazi Holocaust by displacing hostility toward the Nazis with hostility toward the communists—hence the equation of Buchenwald and the Siberian labor camps (I am not questioning the intellectual validity of this connection, only underlining the emotional ties). The fear and trembling surrounding the Nazi extermination of the Jews—the original experience—has now been shifted to the possible nuclear destruction of the human race.[2]

In the nature of things, these are difficult assertions to demonstrate, and the reader may well respond that many people are concerned with fears of a nuclear holocaust without ever having experienced the Nazi threat. The point, however, is not what lies behind other people's fears but specifically what lies behind Kissinger's. In lieu of the free association that might emerge on an analyst's couch, I must rely on my "feel" of the man and on a variety of subliminal clues which he has offered.

Improbable as it might seem at first glance, the very absence of Kissinger's direct comments on the Nazis and the Holocaust, in contrast to his compulsive attention to the communist threat, counts as part of the subliminal evidence. As Sherlock Holmes remarked to Watson, the absence of the dog's barking is the significant clue in the case. What requires explanation is Kissinger's deliberate omission of any serious attention to the Nazi experience, domestic and international. I am suggesting that the answer lies in the displacement of his very real feelings of fear and loathing onto other objects—nuclear and communist—prefigured intellectually by his antipathy to Napoleonic expansionism, as we shall see shortly, and that such displacement plays a very important part in shaping Kissinger's world view.

It is in the context of some such explanation that Kissinger's lack of overt identification of Nazis with communists, of Hitler with Stalin, must be weighed. It is clear, however, that he perceived both movements as set upon world conquest, and both men as willful individuals. From Kraemer he could learn that a true conservative opposed both the Nazi hoodlums and the Bolshevik thugs, and that communism was merely Red Fascism. (It is a measure of Kissinger's ability to grow, incidentally, that in the case of the communists he could go beyond these simplicities.) Over time, in fact, Kissinger came to identify with many of the traits of the communist enemy (as well as the German one), and one frequently feels—as for example, in *The Necessity for Choice*—that he is measuring himself against the Lenins and Stalins of the Soviet world, asking himself, and America, if we can muster the same amount of will, of deliberate "philosophy." Most importantly, Kissinger views our time as a revolutionary one in which the revolutionary forces of Hitlerism and communism have supplanted the nineteenth-century French revolutionaries and Napoleon.

As for the Holocaust, that now became the threat of nuclear annihilation rather than the ovens of Buchenwald. Discussing nuclear deterrence, Kissinger remarks that "any crisis . . . may set off a holocaust." As he concludes, the unstable situation "makes all-out war almost inevitable."[3] The psychology involved, I suggest, is that all-out nuclear war threatens to be a "final solution" for the world's population, not just the Jews.

Kissinger's fear is, of course, not solely his own; it is one that we all share. Youth especially sees the threat of genocide everywhere—in race relations, in Vietnam, in overpopulation, in overpollution, and, most dramatically; in nuclear extermination. In fact, Kissinger's absorption in the question of nuclear weapons and the possibility of a second "holocaust" ought to be seen in the context of America's refusal to take seriously, and to deal overtly with, its dropping of the atomic bombs on Hiroshima and Nagasaki. Unlike the Germans, who finally seem in large numbers to have come to terms with their part

limited domestic claims, and the frontiers which permitted adjustments are gone forever. A new concept of international order is essential; without it stability will prove elusive."[5]

Kissinger first attacked the problem of the new international order by indirection. He went back in history and studied the nineteenth-century international system at the moment its stability was "restored," in 1815 at the Congress of Vienna. The first paragraph of the published version of his dissertation informs us that "it is not surprising that an age faced with the threat of thermonuclear extinction should look nostalgically to periods when diplomacy carried with it less drastic penalties, when wars were limited and catastrophe almost inconceivable."[6] In the dissertation itself Kissinger went further, in a preface later left unpublished, and confessed that "I have chosen for my topic the period between 1812 and 1822, partly, I am frank to say, because its problems seem to me analogous to those of our day." In our period, too, we are "faced with the construction of a new international order, and, therefore, with all the dilemmas of foreign policy in their most immediate form: the relationship between domestic and international legitimacy, the role of the balance of power, the limits of statesmanship."[7]

When he came to write *Nuclear Weapons*, Kissinger was still prepared to draw the analogy, yet also aware that something new had been added: conceivable catastrophe. The similarity between 1815 and 1955 was that both were revolutionary periods in which the challenge was to construct a stable new international order; in 1955 the revolutionaries were perceived by Kissinger as the "Sino-Soviet bloc, which is determined to prevent the establishment of an equilibrium. . . ." The difference is the existence of nuclear weapons, which poses the prospect of mutual annihilation if a stable new order cannot be constructed. The task, Kissinger concluded, was complex, "different from any before in our history; for there is little experience to guide us."[8]

In spite of this disclaimer, we must conclude that Kissinger *was* guided by his study of 1815; it is hardly credible that he would disregard the "little experience" over which he had spent so much time and thought. John Newhouse, in writing about the Strategic Arms Limitation Talks (SALT), correctly sensed what was involved: "Thinking about SALT . . . is richly rewarding less because of its self-evident importance than because SALT is probably the most fascinating, episodic negotiation since the Congress of Vienna. SALT is likely to go on indefinitely. Thus, even though progress may be slow, the affair prone to bog down occasionally, SALT could develop a cumulative impact on the world system comparable to that of the Congress of Vienna, whose achievement was to spare Europe any major bloodletting for 100 years. Such is the hope."[9] Newhouse equates Castlereagh's hope that the Congress would establish "effectual provisions for the general security" with "stability . . . in the nuclear age."[10] When he adds that "all SALT issues arise from instabilities, real or potential,"[11] we recognize that we are in Kissinger's world, and dealing with one of the major themes that concerns him personally and professionally, and which he addressed both in *World Restored* and *Nuclear Weapons.*

Allowing for Newhouse's possible hyperbole in comparing the Congress of Vienna to the SALT negotiations, we can see that Kissinger, in moving from his doctoral dissertation on the events of 1812–1822 to the Council on Foreign Relations study group about nuclear weapons, was not taking as inexplicable a jump, intellectually, as it first seems. Untrained in the details of nuclear weaponry, Kissinger's world view on international affairs allowed him to enter the new field with a fully developed conceptual position: the conservative one we have been detailing. It also allowed him to come to terms with his strong and powerful feelings about the Holocaust, feelings now displaced, or projected, forward to the future and away from the past.

Limits

The problem for the great leader is how to act and use power so as to prevent nuclear holocaust or, indeed, instabilities of any sort, and yet not to succumb himself to the temptations of unlimited power. Looking over what Kissinger has said about his concept of the leader, one is struck with the significant appearance of the word "limits," or some variation thereof. Kissinger was, and is, obsessed with the notion of "limits." It is a major theme, both in his life and in his writings. Other scholars, of course, have also talked about limits: limited war, limited aims, and so on. What is special in Kissinger is the intensity and frequency with which he invokes the term and wrestles with the problem. His dilemma, of course, is that of the conservative who wishes to use power to preserve the status quo, and is aware that there may be no limits to his own use of power other than self-restraint. Acton's dictum that "power tends to corrupt; absolute power corrupts absolutely" haunts Kissinger too. As Kissinger admits, "to be meaningful, self-restraint must set limits even to the exercise of righteous power."[12]

The theme of limits manifests itself most succinctly in Kissinger's basic conservative interpretation of history. Kissinger's thesis is that modern history has been a time when revolutionary forces, such as those embodied in a Hitler or Napoleon, emerge limitless in their power-seeking ambitions, thereby enjoy an initial triumph over the tradition-bound status quo powers, and then eventually overreach themselves and plunge to their doom. Napoleon, for example, would not or could not legitimize his rule so that it rested on anything other than naked power. He could not, therefore, "seek his safety in self-limitation";[13] he was unable to accept "limits."[14] So, too, was the case with Hitler. As Kissinger remarks about the cause of Hitler's downfall in one of his rare references to the Nazi leader, "Was it the invasion of Russia, the declaration of war in 1939, the seizure of Prague or the Anschluss? Or perhaps was the fact of collapse immanent in a personality to whom the recognition of limits constituted an admission of defeat?"[15]

Kissinger's analysis is both psychological and structural. Napoleon's and Hitler's personalities were such that they could not accept limits, could not exercise self-restraint. Moreover, and here Kissinger borrows a notion from Max Weber, as charismatic leaders they were unable to institutionalize their power, to give "legitimacy" to their rule. Thus, they could never rest with what they had, or enjoy stability, but Faust-like had ever to strive forward. In the present-day version of this drama, a new note has entered: there is now the possibility that such revolutionary forces will destroy whole peoples and even the world (this is the communist threat in a nuclear age) unless opposed by intelligent activism which resorts to countervailing, and balancing, power.

In *Nuclear Weapons* Kissinger was obviously aware that the advent of nuclear power seemed to pose the threat of "limitless" destruction. Yet, the situation was filled with paradoxes and opportunities. In the eighteenth century, before the coming of revolution, wars were limited wars. Monarchs aimed at specific gains, and not the destruction of nations or peoples. Revolution and Napoleon changed all the rules of the game, and "total war" became the guiding principle into the mid-twentieth century. The paradox of nuclear weapons is, in principle, that it makes total war unthinkable. Leaders henceforth are presumably under the *necessity* of self-restraint (unless they are madmen, an idea we shall discuss shortly). Unexpectedly, then, nuclear weapons have become a "conservative" force.

In Kissinger's view, however, there was another paradox, an unfortunate side effect of this development. At least in 1955, when he was writing *Nuclear Weapons*, Kissinger believed that, by limiting the U.S. power to wage war with the weapons (atomic and hydrogen bombs) in which it had a superiority over the Soviet Union, nuclear power played into the hands of the latter, with its superiority in conventional arms. As a result, Kissinger advocated "limited" nuclear war as an acceptable strategy for America, even though most analysts were convinced that such war could not help but lead to unlimited nuclear destruction.

In 1955 Kissinger was willing to skirt the thin edge of holocaust in order to maintain America's power against the Soviet Union, and thus paradoxically contribute to international stability. But later he changed his mind on the issue. By 1961 he was willing to agree that the military could not be trusted to keep such a war limited; besides, the Soviet had by this time achieved parity, or near parity. Thus, Kissinger now disowned limited nuclear war and opted instead for the buildup of conventional forces with an eye to waging traditional limited wars. Our major concern here, however, is not so much with Kissinger's changing technical view on limited nuclear war as the fact that it continues to demonstrate his compelling interest in the problem of limits.

But lots of arms control people are concerned with limited warfare. What is so special about Kissinger's concern? We need to return to his first major work, "The Meaning of History," written when he was 26. At the very beginning Kissinger sounds the theme of limits in his life, marking its intensely personal note before extending it to the historical and international scene. In a passage reminiscent of Karl Marx's youthful essay on choosing a profession, Kissinger declares that, "in the life of every person there comes a point when he realizes that out of all the seemingly limitless possibilities of his youth he has in fact become an actuality. No longer is life a broad plain with forests and mountains beckoning all-around, but it becomes apparent that one's journey across the meadows has indeed followed a regular path, that one can no longer go this way or that, but that the direction is set, the *limits* defined . . ." [my italics].[16]

The context for Kissinger's *cri de coeur* is his discussion of necessity and freedom, and clearly the acceptance of limits is the acceptance of necessity, of the "inexorability of the road . . . of the directedness of our life."[17] Although we know that elsewhere Kissinger insists on the possibility of freedom, of being able to transcend necessity, in this particular mood he stresses instead the requirement of acceptance. "From the acceptance of limits derives the feeling of reverence which sees history not merely as an ordeal, or mankind as a tool but as a deep fulfillment."[18] Such an attitude, Kissinger insisted, was "not a kismetic resignation but an *active recognition of limits*" [my italics].[19] We must note, incidentally, that these views were delivered in an almost 400-page thesis, which exceeded the usual "limit" by a good deal and caused the Harvard government department to institute a new rule drastically limiting senior theses!

Intended or not, we might observe also that Kissinger's attempted resolution of the tension between necessity and freedom, acceptance and activism, limits and transcendence, could have the happy consequence of reconciling his father's tendency to passivity with his mother's activism. In any case, Kissinger remained compulsively concerned with the subject in his Ph.D. dissertation, which became his book, *A World Restored*. Indicating, as we have noted, that a key dilemma of foreign policy was "the limits of statesmanship," Kissinger reveals in the preface that his original intention to deal with Bismarck, and thus to analyze the disintegration of a legitimate order, had to be foregone because it was necessary "to stay within the limits of a Ph.D. thesis."[20] Restricting himself, therefore, to the policy of Metternich and Castlereagh, and the events surrounding the Congress of Vienna in 1815, Kissinger, as we have seen, analyzed the way in which Napoleon, a charismatic leader, was unable to accept "limits."

Intellectually, acceptance of limits became for Kissinger the touchstone of his conservatism. Personally, was he so threatened by his own feelings of aggression, of wanting to destroy others, that he felt a compelling need to "limit" his desires for domination and power? In the introduction to his dissertation, he remarked that "a conservative policy—conservative in the literal sense of the word—is therefore always a policy of *self-restraint*" [my italics].[21] Would it not be equally true that a conservative *personality* would pursue self-restraint? We must remember Kissinger's earlier statements, in his undergraduate thesis, that "the acceptance of limits" was a "deep fulfillment." Was the fulfillment the result of such a personality's mastering its overweening ambitions? We know only that later in his life Kissinger spoke jokingly, but frequently, of his own megalomania, his "Napoleon complex."

In any case, limits and self-restraint did not lead Kissinger to quietism, as might be expected. Instead, as we have noted, he preached an "active recognition of limits"; he saw in history "activity [revealing] a personality," not mere harmony and peace. In *Nuclear Weapons* and his other books, he continued to emphasize the absolute necessity of will, of voluntarism, in face of the deterministic and fated parts of history.

Powerfully influenced by Kraemer and Elliott, who preached a life of power and will, though limited by absolute values and a lofty morality, Kissinger also had before him in his historical studies the examples of Metternich and Castlereagh. Indeed, it is fashionable today to see Metternich as Kissinger's inspiration. However, such a view (while partially true) overlooks the fact that Metternich offered Kissinger only the stress on limits. Missing was the emphasis on creative activism. As Kissinger says in *World Restored*,

Lacking in Metternich is the attribute which has enabled the spirit to transcend an impasse at so many crises of history: the ability to contemplate an abyss, not with the detachment of a scientist, but as a challenge to overcome—or to perish in the process. Instead one finds a bittersweet resignation which was not without its own grandeur, but which doomed the statesman of the anachronistic Empire in his primary ambition: to become a symbol of conservatism for posterity. For men become myths, not by what they know, nor even by what they achieve, but by the tasks they set for themselves.[22]

Was Kissinger already thinking secretly of his own "myth?" As he recognized,

> Those statesmen who have achieved final greatness did not do so through resignation, however well founded. It was given to them not only to maintain the perfection of order, but to have the strength to contemplate chaos, there to find material for fresh creation.[23]

Bismarck, in fact, could have been such a statesman. Instead, he turned his talents in the direction of a "white revolution," nonetheless revolutionary for that, abandoned restraint, and transgressed the limits. Neither Bismarck nor Metternich, taken alone, then, can be said to have served as Kissinger's historical model. It was necessary to fuse the limiting spirit of the one and the will of the other to make the right combination.

Limits: acceptance and transcendence—a compelling theme in Kissinger's life and thought. Can one "demonstrate" the correctness of this interpretation, "verify" the fact that it does play the role attributed to it in Kissinger's personality and policies? One way is to analyze his past utterances, as we have done, and see if he is, in fact, constantly preoccupied with the subject, in the terms we have outlined. Another way is to seek validation in the future. Fortunately, one such "validation" has already occurred. In an earlier version of this chapter, I emphasized the theme of limits; thereafter, Kissinger had his long and weighty interview with James Reston. How delightful, then, to see him spontaneously confess,

> When one looks at the process of growing up, it is largely a process of learning one's limits, that one is not immortal, that one cannot achieve everything; and then to draw from that realization the strength to set great goals nevertheless. Now, I think that as a country we've gone through this. We were immature in the sense that we thought the definition of goals was almost the equivalent

of their realization. . . . When you get to the recognition of your limits, then the question becomes whether you transcend them or wallow in them. That is a choice that is up to us.[24]

Here we have all the opposing concepts made familiar to us in Kissinger's undergraduate thesis: limits, recognition of them (resignation), and yet transcendence of them, and thus choice. We also have a clear identification of Kissinger's personal development with that of America. The immaturity and then growth to maturity of the two are conflated. Both presumably have accepted their "limits," their conservative "deep fulfillment."

The Limit to Limits?

Kissinger's acceptance, as we have noted, was "an active recognition of limits." How far, in fact, could the "active" part carry him to the edge of "limits"? Might he unwittingly go too far? The "Dr. Strangelove" image attests to the fear of many that Kissinger may go over the brink and bring about the very holocaust which he consciously, obsessively seeks to avoid.

In 1962 Kissinger wrote, "On October 22, President Kennedy boldly seized an opportunity given few statesmen: to change the course of events by one dramatic move. His action achieved far more than the immediate goal of dismantling Soviet missile bases in Cuba. It exploded the myth that in every situation the Soviets were prepared to run greater risks than we."[25] Almost *exactly* 11 years later, on the night of October 24, 1973, Kissinger took a similar action. With President Nixon upstairs in the White House, preoccupied with his Watergate problems and brought into the Middle East crisis only to approve the actions taken by his new Secretary of State, Kissinger had in effect become the President for foreign affairs, the fortunate statesman able to "change the course of events by one dramatic move." Kissinger ordered an alert that, designed to prevent a unilateral Soviet move into the Israeli-Egyptian front, might well have ended in a nuclear war. Like Kennedy, Kissinger succeeded in the game of "chicken."

A dilemma of conservative foreign policy is that, dedicated as it is to limits and self-restraint, it must nevertheless impress its opponent, the revolutionary power, with its willingness to go beyond the limits, if necessary. In short, it may have to act "mad." Kissinger wrestled with this problem in abstract terms in *The Necessity for Choice*. His arguments there are rather tortuous and inconclusive. At first he argues that mutual deterrence makes any threat of nuclear war unbelievable. He dismisses the argument "that deterrence is achieved not so much by the certainty that we *will* strike but by the uncertainty that we *might*. No Communist leader will stake his hard-won industrial complex on the chance that we do not mean our threats." Kissinger declares instead that "if an overwhelming counterforce capability was insufficient to prevent Communist pressure during the period of our strategic preponderance [i.e., when we alone had the bomb], reliance on it will be sheer irresponsibility in the age of invulnerable retaliatory forces."[26]

But having dismissed the subject, Kissinger returns to it a few pages later. Now he warns that "in any crisis, rather than show our 'nervousness'—*which would be a wise course from the point of view of deterrence* [my italics]—we are much more likely to seek to demonstrate that we are 'calm,' 'rational,' 'calculating,' 'accommodating'—all qualities which, if taken seriously by the aggressor, may cause him to doubt our resolve to resort to all-out war. When President Eisenhower said with respect to Berlin that 'only a madman would start a nuclear war,' he may have intended to warn the Soviet leaders. In fact, he was merely illustrating our dilemma." Kissinger concludes his discussion by saying, "a great deal of Mr. Khrushchev's violence during the General Assembly of 1960 may have been designed as a warning of his capacity for irrationality if thwarted."[27]

To solve the "dilemma," Kissinger seems to have learned from his enemies. (Was he also identifying with them?) Like Khrushchev, apparently he has become willing, when necessary, to appear "irrational." One thinks of Adolf Hitler and the success of his technique of appearing (was he also in reality?) a madman. Thus, for example, Kissinger and Nixon in their mining of Haiphong harbor and their bombing of Hanoi seemed to be signaling to their enemies how unpredictable and irrational they could be. Another example is the Middle East crisis in Jordan of September 1970, where the Kalb brothers report that "Rabin [Israeli Ambassador to Washington at the time] was convinced the Russians were genuinely concerned about Nixon's next step. They seemed to feel that since he had behaved so outrageously in Cambodia, he might act outrageously in the Middle East too."[28] The clear message: don't push us too far, for we may transgress any and all limits.

An interesting light is thrown on this problem by Daniel Ellsberg. In 1970, according to Ellsberg, Kissinger in a last talk suddenly confided that he had learned more from Ellsberg "about bargaining than from any other person." As Ellsberg tells the story:

I was taken aback. I didn't know what he was referring to, although my academic specialty had been "bargaining theory." And suddenly I remembered that 11 years earlier when I had given a series of talks on "The Art of Coercion," I had also given a couple of those lectures to Kissinger's seminar at Harvard. "You have a very good memory," I said. And he replied, "They were good lectures."

When I rethought that incident later, it made the hair on the back of my neck stand up. The lectures I had given had to do with Hitler's blackmail of Austria and Czechoslovakia in the late Thirties, which had allowed him to take over those countries just by threatening their destruction. One of those lectures was "The Theory and Practice of Blackmail." And another was called, "The Political Uses of Madness."

New leaks about the Cambodian invasion, obviously coming from off-the-record backgrounders by Kissinger, had revealed a major motive of the invasion was to convince the Russians and the Chinese that our decision-making was unpredictable, and that since we could do something as apparently unpredictable and crazy as invade Cambodia, they could not count on our reasonableness or prudence in a crisis.

That was Hitler's conscious policy: The threat of unpredictability. I had described it in my lectures as being a possibly effective, but extremely dangerous strategy. It was a commitment to madness.[29]

Whatever one wishes to make of Ellsberg's highly motivated account, it is clear that Kissinger has played with the appearance of a "madman" as a part of his diplomatic activity. There are those who believe that Kissinger is, in fact, megalomanic and dangerous, whereas others read him merely as being "crazy like a fox." It is a delicate issue. In my view, Kissinger, although deeply threatened by his megalomania and "Napoleon complex" —hence, in part, his compulsive fascination with the question of limits and transcendence—has mastered these elements of his personality and placed them under control and in the service of conservative intentions.

In seeking to maintain limits, Kissinger, as we know, has embraced the necessity of power. To preserve order and stability, he has been willing to go to the brink of destruction. All this we can understand. We are left, however, with a disturbing question: Able to control his own personal megalomania, to exercise self-restraint, might his confident psychological and historical calculations about his and America's "enemies," i.e., the Soviet Union, continue to "limit" the possibility of war, or could one of his alerts some day meet an "irrational" response, the subtle signal misread? Only time and events will tell. It may be that Kissinger is convinced that the Soviet Union is no longer a revolutionary force, but, like the U.S., a "conservative" power. In this event, both will respect the "limits," and thus avoid the threatening holocaust.

Chapter 9

HISTORICAL
AND PSYCHOLOGICAL
APPROACH

Expected and Unexpected Approaches

KISSINGER'S basic approach to foreign affairs is historical and psychological. The emphasis on history should not surprise us in a conservative who prefers Burke to the overrational Metternich. Still, in the 1950s it set Kissinger off from the increasing tendency in political science toward the behavioral approach, and it made him unique among arms control specialists who lean toward the analytic and ahistoric.

The intensely psychological emphasis in Kissinger's world view, however, is somewhat unexpected. Given the way Kissinger represses personality and objects to the behavioral approach, the stress on the psychological at first glance seems alien to his central way of seeing the world. Yet the psychological approach turns out to be the essential counterpart to Kissinger's historical approach; the two are actually inseparable. Since the meaning of history, for Kissinger, is ultimately a theater for the discovery and expression of personality, the two tend to become one.

A Tragic Vision

For Kissinger perhaps the overriding meaning of history is that it is tragic, a dimension simply left out of all abstract approaches to foreign affairs. Interestingly, Kissinger does not sound this note, except implicitly, in the course of his undergraduate thesis, although at one point he does quote Alfred North Whitehead to the effect that "the inner feeling belonging to this grasp of the service of tragedy is Peace—the purification of emotions."[1]

By the time of *World Restored*, the idea of tragedy is very much to the fore in Kissinger's writing, and it remains so thereafter. He identifies it in all his work as a European perception that is completely lacking in Americans. In *World Restored* he places it in the context of "The Meaning of History" when he announces that "in any political situation there are factors which are not amenable to will and which cannot be changed in our time. [Here Kissinger seems to equate tragedy with the leader's need to accept his surrounding circumstances.] This is the guise Necessity assumes for the statesman, and in the struggle with it resides his tragic quality."[2] Kissinger also adds a personal note, though in rather backward fashion, when he continues, "Tragedy can be the fate of nations, no less than of individuals, and *its meaning may well reside in living in a world with which one is no longer familiar*" [my italics].[3]

As we know, Kissinger's own life was subject to events outside the control of his will, which forced him into living in a world with which he was unfamiliar. His life—and his family's and his people's—was "tragic" in this sense. One senses in Henry Kissinger a need to reenact, if only in historical imagination, his tragic experience, and thus to work through and control his feelings about that experience.

The reward of such a working through of tragedy is

creativity. This is true for nations as for individuals. Thus, Kissinger sees the history of the West as marked by periods where "each tragedy was followed by a new burst of creativity."[4] But the creative resolution of tragedy is itself the cause of a further tragedy. Thus, "as in Greek tragedy, the success of Clemens von Metternich made inevitable the ultimate collapse of the state he had fought so long to preserve."[5] "For the tragic aspect of history," Kissinger tells us, "is that creativity is constantly in danger of being destroyed by success. The more effectively the environment is mastered, the greater is the temptation to rest on one's oars."[6] Kissinger's tragic vision of history is clearly Sisyphean.

It is not a vision shared by Americans, and here Kissinger constantly takes us to task: "Nothing is more difficult for Americans to understand than the possibility of tragedy."[7] We are always seeking solutions, and are impatient with problems that do not have readily apparent answers. And at this point Kissinger relates our lack of the tragic vision to our conviction that goodwill can solve all problems.[8] We need the insight into history possessed by Europeans. Resuming his theme of "confluence," Kissinger declares, "Our idealism and impetuosity would gain depth if leavened by the European sense of tragedy." (And conversely, "The European consciousness of history could recover dynamism if bolstered by our hopefulness.")[9] Who better, of course, than Kissinger to unite goodwill and will, idealism and realism, solutions and tragedies, America and Europe, for he has experienced all these polarities in his own life and incorporated them into his personality. His message to the West, in which he now fuses America and Europe, is that, "free from the shackles of a doctrine of historical inevitability, the nations of the West can render a great service by demonstrating that whatever meaning history has is derived from the convictions and purpose of the generation which shapes it."[10]

"Whatever meaning history has!" We are back at the

beginning of Kissinger's experiences and writings. Kraemer understood that young Kissinger yearned to understand what had overwhelmed all those whom he held dear, and whose status, stability, and sometimes lives had been destroyed. The answer emerges from the conflict of necessity and freedom, with the latter, in the form of will, of "convictions and purposes," giving history its inner meaning. Yet, like a nightmare that had constantly to be dreamed again so as to come to grips with the horrible images, and perhaps this time resolved, history for Kissinger is a tragic affair, a recurring alternation of challenges and creative responses. In the end, however, the experience of tragedy itself becomes the means, as Whitehead said, to peace, to "the purification [should we add purgation?] of emotion."

A Historical Ear

The historical themes announced in *World Restored* persist throughout all of Kissinger's later work. They form the ground plan of interpretation from which he never deviated. They are placed constantly in contrast to the use of mere pragmatism or of abstract models. In *World Restored,* Kissinger said, "To plan policy on the assumption of the equal possibility of all contingencies is to confuse statesmanship with mathematics [and we must remember that Kissinger was fairly adept at mathematics]. Since it is impossible to be prepared for all eventualities, the assumption of the opponent's perfect flexibility leads to paralysis of action."[11] In *The Troubled Partnership,* Kissinger announced that "our European Allies think of themselves not simply as components of security schemes but as expressions of a historical experience."[12] Nations, like individuals, are not abstractions or interchangeable parts. They are the result of past actions and historical aspirations (a fact Kissinger would know intimately from his own life). Thus,

Kissinger advises, "The memories of our Allies should be factors as real in the discussions of our policymakers as the analysis of weapon systems."[13]

Kissinger, in fact, did not ignore completely the usefulness of analysis and abstract models. Instead, he subordinated them to the needs of history and policy. Discussing de Gaulle and French policy, Kissinger declared, "Involved, ultimately, are differing conceptions of truth. The United States, with its technical, pragmatic approach, often has analytic truth on its side. De Gaulle, with his consciousness of the trials of France for the past generation, is frequently closer to the historical truth." The weakness of the expert is that "he may confuse creativity with a projection of the present into the future."[14] The implicit message is that Kissinger has both abilities—the creative and the analytic—and can correctly place them in the service of policy.

Yet, though Kissinger commands both skills, it is clear which has priority. History allows for creativity—freedom—whereas the abstract, analytic approach allows for mere projection—necessity. Speaking of de Gaulle, Kissinger is obviously also describing himself: "The art of statesmanship is to understand the nature of the world and the trend of history. A great leader is not so much clever as lucid and clear-sighted."[15] In short, the great leader understands "The Meaning of History."

The Lessons of History

If history has a grand lesson, it is that it is tragic, without final solutions (except a holocaust, which is the end of history, leaving it devoid of meaning). There are contingent lessons, however. The lessons are contingent because history is a matter of flux and movement. Structures, such as nations, change, and unfolding events leave behind them new memories. As Kissinger explained in *World Restored,* history differs from the physical sciences because it "teaches by analogy, not identity. This means that the lessons of history are never automatic, that they can be apprehended only by a standard which admits the significance of a range of experience. . . . [A state] achieves identity through the consciousness of a common history. This is the only 'experience' nations have, their only possibility of learning from themselves. History is the memory of states."[16]

History offers the *possibility* of learning, but not the guarantee. In fact, states tend to forget, or to misread, or to draw the wrong conclusions from their experiences. Kissinger goes on, "For the lessons of historical experience, as of personal experience, are contingent. They teach the consequences of certain actions, but they cannot force a recognition of comparable situations."[17] This is a statement he repeats more or less verbatim in *Nuclear Weapons,* underlining for us thereby how important he believes his assertion to be, and how continuous Kissinger's view of the world remains.[18] In that same book he makes his general statement applicable to the specific situation of the 1950s and the threat of nuclear war when he asks, "Do any of the factors apply today which in the past made possible a diplomacy of limited objectives and a military policy of limited wars?"[19] It is a rhetorical question, for Kissinger's entire book is one long exercise in examining the analogy between the conditions of 1815 and those of 1955.

Kissinger's strength (or weakness, depending on one's estimation of his views) is that he brings to bear on all current questions a fully articulated historical conception. At the same time he is aware, at least consciously, of the dangers of drawing too strict an analogy, without allowing for changes in the boundary conditions. Thus, he reminds us that "the truths of one decade become the obstacle to the understanding of another."[20] (Was he thinking unconsciously of his father, who could not recognize that things had changed in Germany and refused to face the new facts?) Examining the Atlantic Alliance almost 20 years after its inception, he warns that "perhaps the deepest danger we face is that, as with all great achievements, nostalgia for the patterns of action that were appropriate when America was predominant and Europe impotent may become an obstacle to the creativity needed to deal with an entirely new situation."[21]

Kissinger had experienced much change in his own life, and he had coped in part by changing himself. He was aware, therefore, in a very personal way that states might also change; in fact, *had* to change. On the loftiest level, this was the idea of tragedy; on a more mundane level it led to an awareness that today's enemies might be tomorrow's allies. Even the communists had to be expected to change. The question was always: In what direction? Thus, Kissinger insisted that evolution in communist societies "is inevitable. No system of government is immune to change. No country has ever maintained an unaltered social structure. But the nature of the transformation is by no means foreordained. It can move toward liberalization; but it can also produce the gray nightmare of 1984."[22]

The problem for the statesman, of course, was to ensure, if possible, orderly change rather than revolutionary transformation that undermined all stability. In a sense, the statesman is an educator, a teacher of his people, explaining to them the real relationship of forces. But this role, as we know from Kissinger's own academic life, was too restricted. The statesman had also to be a hero. In Kissinger's words, "the statesman is therefore like one of the *heroes* [my italics] in classical drama who has had a vision of the future but who cannot transmit it directly to his fellow-men and who cannot validate its 'truth.' Nations learn only by experience; they 'know' only when it is too late to act. But statesmen must act *as if* their intuition were already experience, as if their aspiration were truth."[23]

In Kissinger's conception, obviously, foreign affairs is more a matter of freedom than of historical necessity, that is, science, and the statesman is therefore an actor, not a political scientist.

At the very end of *World Restored* Kissinger returns to his first image of the "crucial" experiment in the political and physical sciences and announces the difference between the two: "Each generation is permitted only one effort of abstraction; it can attempt only one interpretation and a single experiment, *for it is its own subject.* This is the challenge of history and its *tragedy,* it is the shape 'destiny' assumes on the earth. And its solution, even its recognition, is perhaps the most difficult task of statesmanship" [my italics].[24]

Just as obviously, we can see that Kissinger, even as a graduate student, felt himself called to be one of those who would recognize the trends of history. Only destiny would tell whether he might also be an actor, offering solutions; we have seen how Kissinger helped destiny along by his efforts to enter the world of power and foreign policy making. By the time of his interview with Oriana Fallaci, he recognized himself as a "hero," though the setting was America's wild west rather than a classical drama.

A Psychiatrist *Manqué*

For Kissinger, international relations are based to an overwhelming extent (aside from being derived from) on two factors: power "realities" and psychological "relations." Kissinger, it must be emphasized, is the most psychologically minded of all foreign policy thinkers and actors. The most cursory glance at *World Restored* (or indeed any of his other works) confirms this fact. Speaking of Castlereagh, Kissinger writes, "Psychologists may well ponder how it came about that this Irish peer . . . should become the most European of British statesmen."[25] A few pages later, we are told that Metternich "prided himself on his knowledge of Napoleon's character," with Metternich himself confessing that "the whole policy of Austria is founded on Napoleon's character."[26] At the end Kissinger concludes,

"Metternich's diplomacy had eventually depended on the correct evaluation of two personalities, the Emperor [Alexander I] and Napoleon. Its success proved the reality of intangibles."[27]

The Congress of Vienna was a perfect setting for Kissinger to exhibit his skills at analyzing the "reality of intangibles." It was a supreme instance of a few key personalities—Napoleon, Metternich, Castlereagh, Alexander I—shaping all decisions, and interacting with one another. Here international relations was almost reduced to a classic example of interpersonal relations.[28] And here Kissinger, with his unique ability to "think into" the minds and intentions of divergent statesmen, to "identify" with them as historical actors, came into his element. It is an ability that underlies all his other intellectual work and, perhaps more importantly, forms the basis of his extraordinary negotiating skills.

Knowing about Kissinger's service as a consultant to the Psychological Warfare Board in Washington, we should not be surprised at his intense psychological interest. What has partly obscured it for the public, or led observers to underestimate it, I believe, is the particular psychology that Kissinger has used and his disclaimers about the psychological effect on him of his own experiences.

Kissinger's psychology is neither behavioral—one recalls his distrust of positive science—nor psychoanalytic (which, among other reasons, is tarred by its claim to be, in some sense, scientific). His psychology is purely intuitive and empathic, along the lines of Spengler's "history-as-intuition," i.e., "seeing" into the heart of events, and the hearts of men. Thus, it hardly seems "psychology" at all, but rather poetic insight as to the intentions and motives of great historical actors and nations.

A Personality Revealed

How personally involved has Kissinger been with the psychological understanding he uses so skillfully and unobtrusively? Has he, himself, ever had psychological training or psychotherapeutic assistance? In the course of my research, I came across the assertion that Kissinger had somehow been involved with a group therapy training effort, derived in some fashion from the Tavistock Institute in England. Further research was unable to substantiate this lead, and it remains a tantalizing but unsupported suggestion. Nor are there data about any possible training Kissinger may have had in connection with his work for the Psychological Warfare Board.

Kissinger himself, as we know, dismissed the effort to understand his German childhood psychologically by saying, "It is fashionable now to explain everything psychoanalytically,"[29] and he is obviously leary of all such efforts. So, too, in his undergraduate thesis, he declared " 'Know thyself'—was the motto of the oracle of Delphi. This was not meant psychoanalytically but implied: 'Know that you are a man and not God,' "[30] and showed no further interest in things Freudian. Yet it is interesting to note that later in life a number of Kissinger's reasonably close acquaintances in Cambridge were psychoanalysts, and they report no overt hostility to their profession on his part. (Perhaps we ought also to remember the assertion by his college roommate that Kissinger at one point had thought of becoming a psychiatrist; note, too, that the female member of the couple with whom he was closest at Harvard, the Springers, was a social worker, working at the time with a psychoanalyst.)

The evidence is also strong that at the time his marriage broke up, Kissinger sought professional counsel. Such counsel, however, though it *may* have touched on Kissinger's own personality to some extent, seems to have been concerned mainly with the effect of divorce on his children, and to have been relatively brief. An odd confirmation of the allegation that Kissinger had professional therapeutic attention at the time of his divorce occurs in his book, *The Troubled Partnership*, written between 1964 and 1965, in other words at about the same time as his marital difficulties were pressing upon him. Speaking of communist negotiators, Kissinger says, "Their attitude toward Western negotiators is very similar to that of Western psychiatrists toward their patients: no matter what is said, they think that they understand their Western counterpart better than he understands himself." (Why, one must ask, the shift from the plural "they," used for both the communist negotiators and Western psychiatrists, as well as for "patients," to the singular "he," a single patient, unless Kissinger is thinking of himself?) Kissinger speaks also of the U.S. dealing with its Western allies "almost psychotherapeutically," and of Germany possibly having "a subconscious desire" for nuclear weapons.[31] To my knowledge, this is the only book in which Kissinger uses such terms.[32] They seem to point to an unusual absorption at the time with therapeutic relations.

In any event, whatever he may have experienced and learned at this time has never been publicly acknowledged. Rather, Kissinger has seemed to scorn the usefulness of the psycho-analytic approach.[33] The irony is that Kissinger clearly has the knack of psychoanalytic "knowing." He listens to his negotiating partners with what has been called the "third ear." He is, in many ways then, a psychiatrist *manqué*, a psychological historian, interpreting international relations instead of intra-personal dynamics.

As for his own intrapersonal dynamics, he would obviously like to hide these from public gaze, at least consciously. In the interview with Oriana Fallaci, she said to him,

QUESTION: I've never interviewed anyone that evaded close questions and definitions like you, anyone that defended themselves as strenuously as you from attempts to penetrate their personality. Are you shy, by any chance, Dr. Kissinger?

ANSWER: Yes, I am rather. On the other hand, however, I believe I'm fairly well balanced. You see, there are those that describe me as a mysterious, tormented character, and others who see me as a merry guy always smiling, always laughing. Both these images are untrue. I'm neither the one nor the other. I'm . . . No, I won't tell you what I am. I'll never tell anyone.[34]

But in fact, as we have tried to show, Kissinger has told us about himself, difficult as it is to read the message. And he has told us about himself through his analysis of history, as well as his own activity in history, which, of necessity, must, to use his own term, "reveal a personality."

Psychology and Credibility

If Clausewitz said, "War is only a continuation of policy by other means," Kissinger might equally well say, "Diplomacy is only psychology translated into political realities." In fact, in *World Restored*, he does say exactly this at greater length: "A military victory always has two components, its physical reality and its psychological impact, and it is the task of diplomacy to translate the latter into political terms."[35] Even the war itself is largely a psychological matter, and certainly military policy is. As Kissinger tells us, "The success of military policy depends on essentially psychological criteria. Deterrence seeks to prevent a given course by making it seem less attractive than all possible alternatives. It therefore ultimately depends on an intangible quality: the state of mind of the potential aggressor."[36]

The preeminent potential aggressor is the Soviet Union. Thus, Kissinger has been at great pains to study its "state of mind," to understand its intentions. He admires the way *they* understand the "intangibles," the psychological aspect of foreign affairs. Admiringly, he concedes that "the task of psychological warfare is to hamstring the opponent through his own preconceptions, and this has been precisely the Soviet strategy with respect to nuclear weapons."[37] As in so many other instances, Kissinger admonishes us to imitate our adversary: "The U.S. must study the psychology of its opponents as carefully as they have studied ours."[38] In similar vein, he cautions us that "mastery of the challenges of the nuclear age will depend on our ability to combine physical and psychological factors, to develop weapons systems which do not paralyze our will. . . ."[39]

In his psychological analysis of nuclear warfare and strategic policies, Kissinger manifests what is best called a Talmudic mind. Erik Erikson tells a joke about a Jew who met another Jew in a Polish railroad station. "Where are you going?" asked the first. "To Minsk," said the other. "To Minsk!" exclaimed the first, "you say you go to Minsk so that I should believe you go to Pinsk! You are going to Minsk anyway—so why do you lie?"[40]

Kissinger resembles the first Jew on the train when he argues,

A strategy of limited war adds to deterrence for the very reason usually invoked against it. The danger that a limited war may expand after all works both ways. An aggressor may not credit our threat of massive retaliation because it would force us to *initiate* a course of action which will inevitably involve enormous devastation. He may calculate, however, that once engaged in war on any scale neither he nor we would know how to limit it, whatever the intentions of the two sides. The stronger the limited war forces of the free world, the larger will have to be the Communist effort designed to overcome them. The more the scale of conflict required for victory approaches that of all-out war the greater will be the inhibitions against initiating hostilities. In this sense a capability of limited war is necessary in order to enhance the deterrent power of the retaliatory force.[41]

Such Talmudic finesse must also be invoked to understand Kissinger's seemingly contradictory statements on memories and illusions. At a number of places Kissinger emphasizes how the statesmen must take into consideration the memories of nations. A typical statement is, "The memories of our Allies should be factors as real in the discussions of our policymakers as the analysis of weapons systems."[42] Yet at another moment he is advising us that "the countries of Western Europe and the United States must wrench themselves loose from their memories."[43] The apparent paradox is resolved if we recall that for Kissinger, "history is the memory of states." To understand a people, one must understand their memories; it is part of reality. To transcend reality, however, is also one of Kissinger's aims, and therefore one must let go of memories.

So, too, with illusions. At one moment Kissinger is opposed to them. Thus in *The Necessity for Choice,* for example, he declares, "Negotiations are important. But it is essential to conduct them without illusions,"[44] while in *The Troubled Partnership* he says, "Above all, the West must conduct its policy without illusions."[45] One might conclude from such statements that Kissinger was against illusions in foreign affairs. Not at all! In another place in *The Troubled Partnership* Kissinger praises Adenauer for his clever use of illusions: "Chancellor Adenauer's great achievement—just as de Gaulle's —was that he understood the psychological needs of his country. . . . Perhaps Chancellor Adenauer's most notable achievement was to bring about the optical illusion that conditions in the Federal Republic were as firm and stable as his own policy."[46]

As with memories, the paradox of Kissinger's position on illusions is resolved if we realize that, as as statesman, he must not allow himself illusions, but equally, as a statesman, he must foster illusions in the minds of his opponents and even his countrymen. Hence he commends Metternich for fostering the "illusion of sincerity" and the "illusion of independence" while himself gazing with icy realism on the character and action of his opponents.[47]

The aim in all diplomacy becomes credibility. In fact, this is the greatest illusion that must be maintained. "The side which is willing to run greater risks—or which can make its opponent believe that it is prepared to do so—gains a psychological advantage."[48] Kissinger then (in 1961) takes America to task for its performance in Korea, where our bitter domestic debate and seeming resolve not to engage in similar wars in the future undermined our whole diplomatic posture in that part of the world. His praise is reserved for the Soviets who, though in a position strategically inferior to ours, nevertheless enjoyed a psychological advantage. "From the Berlin blockade [one recalls Kissinger's hard-nosed advice to John F. Kennedy] to Korea, to Indo-China, to Suez, to Hungary, to the Congo and Cuba, the combination of reputation for ruthlessness, willingness to run risks . . . enabled the Soviet Union to blackmail the free world. The dilemma of our post-war strategy has been that the power which was available to us has also produced the greatest inhibitions, while we have had no confidence in the kind of forces which might have redressed the psychological balance."[49]

The theory of credibility, or what in pre-Nixon days Kissinger generally referred to as illusions, leads quickly to the theory of linkage.[50] Weakness or indecision in one area, such as Berlin or Korea, is linked to the enemy's expectations of how one will behave elsewhere. Ours is, psychologically (if not politically), one world. As early as 1961 Kissinger was writing that "the precarious peace which is being maintained between the Arab states and Israel in part by the fear of Western intervention against aggressive acts might not long survive a demonstration of Western impotence in Europe."[51]

There is nothing really original in this conception. We are all aware, on reflection, that events and forces are linked, and that illusions become realities if believed in. What Kissinger has done is to synthesize very consciously these various ideas and to place them at the center of his world view, and to do so with his usual "weightiness."

A Consummate Negotiator

Kissinger is not only a theorist, offering sage observations on the nature of history and the importance of psychology; he is also a practitioner who, as we all know, has the reputation of being a superb negotiator and, in this sense, a practicing psychologist. (I say "reputation" because a few keen observers believe his negotiating skills to be a legend created by the media. Such critics point to what they see as the absence of real results. For example, he didn't actually end the war in Vietnam. In my view, these critics underestimate Kissinger's achievements as a negotiator, even if the achievements are only "illusions.")

Kissinger's negotiating skills proceed directly from his historical and psychological approaches to foreign affairs. Well could he say of himself what he wrote of Metternich: "Metternich was aided by an extraordinary ability to grasp the fundamentals of a situation and a profound psychological insight which enabled him to dominate his adversaries."[52] In fact, as we know, the realization of Kissinger's negotiating abilities came late—they were invisible at Harvard and only faintly visible at the Council on Foreign Relations—and it may be that he learned from his relations with Nelson Rockefeller and his experience with John F. Kennedy. It is also probable that he needed to gain the confidence provided by his increasing scholarly reputation and his growing mastery of connections. Most likely, he needed the actual experience of power negotiations, an experience only gained under Nixon, to display his unique talents.

In any event, once empowered as Nixon's negotiator, he astonished everyone by his skills. We shall try to analyze them here, in general terms, indicating their conceptual basis and leaving consideration of specific negotiations for Chapter 11. Though Kissinger behaves differently with different opponents, or opposite numbers, and in different situations, we can discern certain general features in his negotiating behavior.[53]

First, however, we must note the optimal conditions he needs to succeed. The most favorable negotiating situation is one that is most "personalistic"; that is, where the issues can be determined by the participants involved and do not depend on long-term economic and social trends and policies.[54] In such a situation, it is better to deal with authoritarian governments than with democracies, the negotiators for which may be constrained by having to consult parliamentary bodies or domestic constituencies, and hence do not act with full power. Ironically, though Kissinger as negotiator is most concerned with the personalities of his opposite numbers, he depersonalizes the situation, and its outcome, by numbing himself to the actual human beings involved in the solutions, e.g., Bangladesh or Cyprus. The other side of Kissinger's "personalizing" of foreign affairs is that he, one of the most personally highly motivated statesmen, "depersonalizes" himself as well as the situation, i.e., seeks to hide or disguise his own personality.

The second condition for Kissinger's successful pursuit of negotiations is that diplomacy—talk—be combined with force, or the threat of force. Kissinger attacks sharply the Eisenhower-Dulles notion that the process of negotiation is a "legal process in which force played a small role, if any," or that "military strategy and diplomacy represent successive phases of national policy."[55] We have noted Kissinger's scorn for legal types in foreign policy making, and here we can see the reason for it from another angle. We can also see how the Eisenhower-Dulles approach tended to rely on "goodwill," and how useless Kissinger felt that reliance to be without the support of power. Thus, citing the Korean War as one specific instance, Kissinger pointed out that "by stopping military operations we removed the only Chinese incentive for a settlement; we produced the frustration of two years of inconclusive negotiations. In short, our insistence on divorcing force from diplomacy caused our power to lack purpose and our negotiations to lack force."[56] In the light of such statements, we can see how true to his intellectual formulations Kissinger has been in the bombing of

Hanoi and the calling of a nuclear alert in the Middle East. (As for the threat to use armed force against the Arab nations during the oil crisis, that move ran counter to Kissinger's own injunction about credibility, and was a mark of frustration.)

A third and related, though less important, condition is a previous reputation for "irrationality," or "madness" (see Chapter 8, p. 185), which lends credibility to the threatened use of force if negotiations were to be broken off in an unsatisfactory manner. Clearly, however, this maneuver applies only to a small number of actual negotiations and is only a reserve condition.

Given these conditions, Kissinger's famed abilities have room to show themselves. Negotiation is the art of persuasion; it is intended to achieve policy by means other than the use of force, though force is an element in the persuasion, i.e., as a last resort.[57] Kissinger's unique genius in persuading others seems to lie in his ability to convince them that he understands and sympathizes with their point of view.[58] This ability, I believe, is based mainly on Kissinger's basic trait of identifying with his opponent, manifested first with the Germans, and subsequently with innumerable other holders of power.[59] It is this identification that enables him to make others believe in his sincerity. As we have seen him confess to Oriana Fallaci, "I am always convinced of the necessity of what I am doing. And people feel that, believe in it. And I attach great importance to being believed: when one persuades or conquers someone, one mustn't deceive them."[60] Kissinger's opponents could, indeed, believe in him because he had actually identified with them more than even he knew.[61]

In fact, Kissinger's identification is limited; that is, he seeks to keep in mind and contend for his own country's interests and purposes. Kissinger, I believe, is aware of the dangers of his empathic approach. Thus, at one point he warns that "too often the laudable tendency to see the other point of view is carried to the extreme of refusing to make any moral distinctions."[62]

Referring to Foreign Minister Macmillan's comment that the Geneva spirit " 'meant seeing the other man's point of view. It meant, above all, the human note . . . ,' " Kissinger called the statement moving but also "fatuous."[63] Some of Kissinger's former admirers feel that, especially in the Middle East, he has gone too far in seeing the other point of view. Others believe this to be untrue, that Kissinger always retains a large conceptual framework, never losing sight of his central objectives (though these may be hidden from other observers as he juggles numerous balls at once), and that this ability goes hand in hand with his empathic approach.

On balance, the evidence is very strong that Kissinger does give the persons with whom he is negotiating the feeling that he "understands" them. He appears also to have the remarkable capacity of giving his hearer the impression that they share a common view, and that both Kissinger and his interlocutor are smarter and more intelligent than the "others." Kissinger seems to achieve this effect in part by snide remarks about the mighty and powerful, in which he joins with his opponent in a common conspiracy of understanding. (This is undoubtedly what happened in his discussions with the Israeli leaders, and underlay the censorship of the book by Matti Golan, the Israeli author, reporting such remarks about Gerald Ford and others, and, more lately, in Kissinger's remarks in Canada, which were inadvertently overheard.) In the course of my interviewing I picked up many examples of this kind of indiscreet, but effective, usage on Kissinger's part, including derogatory remarks about Nixon, and even Rockefeller. Denigration thus becomes the other side of Kissinger's mode of ingratiation.

Part of Kissinger's effectiveness comes from the quality of "weightiness" we discussed earlier. As a negotiator he impresses with his intellect, his mastery of the issues, his seriousness. He seems able to give an "objective" stance to the negotiations by his ability (really an academic one) to analyze the issues, thus adding to his depersonalization of the most personal of negotiations. He appeals also to the concept of "honor" and the need to act as a responsible statesman. The introduction of humor at the right moment oddly enough supports this portrait, suggesting that, though serious statesmen, the participants are also men of affairs who do not take themselves too seriously, except at the right moments.

To all this one must add Kissinger's tenacity, his memory, and his ability to seek out the vulnerabilities in his opponent. He also has the gift of flattery, including the flattery of seeing his opponent's side, and this borders on the art of seduction. In many of his negotiating situations Kissinger is able to invoke an almost sexual note. He woos and courts the people whom he hopes to win over. Like a lover, he tells those with whom he negotiates what they want to hear. He is not blatantly duplicitous, for that would be self-defeating—as he remarked to King Faisal, "I do not deceive your majesty because in two months time you would know that I have deceived you"—but he so phrases things as to say them in the way the other person wishes to hear them. In this he is like a good confidence man playing the role of a lover.

Kissinger, it should be clear by now, has an astonishing repertoire of negotiating skills. He uses different methods with different opponents, and changes his style to suit his partner (see, for example, his behavior with Sadat and Faisal, pp. 250–251). The aim is always, however, to reach a mutually acceptable outcome. Unless both parties, having moderated their absolute positions, benefit, there can be no reason to expect the negotiated arrangement to remain stable. True to his own conservative world view, Kissinger uses confidence tricks in order to win real confidence and thus stability.

Looked at in this positive light, Kissinger's negotiating technique is a form of what Erik Erikson has called mutuality and has attributed to Mahatma Gandhi in the political field.[64] It is a situation in which two parties mutually gain and come to trust one another. At Kissinger's best, this is what he aims at.

Overidentification with his opponent, a misunderstanding of the objective situation, a misreading of the personalities involved, his own included, a loss of confidence through his own over-cleverness: all these are the dangers inherent in Kissinger's personalism of foreign affairs. Such is the greatness and the weakness—the constant paradox—of this most psychological of modern negotiators.

PART III

Kissinger in Power:

Policies and Procedures

Chapter 10

KISSINGER AND NIXON: A"SPECIAL RELATIONSHIP"

A Patron, Not a Model

KISSINGER came to power through, and at the same time as, Nixon. That is a central fact in Kissinger's success story. In a sense, Nixon became Kissinger's last real patron (though Rockefeller, of course, remained one constantly; as for President Ford, that is a different sort of relationship, with the roles partly reversed). True, Kissinger outlasted Nixon—a sign of his genius—but his major achievements in foreign policy from 1968 to 1973 are inexorably intermixed with the President, and sorting out the credit (or debit) is a complicated matter. In any case, the real issue is not so much who gets what credits, but how the two men related to one another, and in what ways their personalities and politics meshed so as to bring about a kind of revolution in American foreign policy.

This time, Kissinger's relations with his patron were purely formal and intellectual. The two men never became friends, and to the end their attitudes were cool and correct, with Kissinger calling Nixon "Mr. President." As Kissinger replied when asked if he were fond of Nixon, "I have great respect for him."[1] In that sense, it might almost be better to view the relationship as one between business associates rather than patron and patronized. In any case, the two men were made for one another, as if destiny had decided to play a joke by bringing them together, as we shall see, in an unlikely way. If Nixon had not chosen him out of the blue—and this time Kissinger had nothing to do with choosing his own patron— Kissinger, the master negotiator and extraordinary culture hero, would surely have never come into being as a reality, whatever his potential.

As Kissinger himself acknowledged in 1972,

I . . . am not at all so sure I could have done what I've done with him with another president. Such a special relationship, I mean the relationship between the President and me, always depends on the style of both men. In other words, I don't know many leaders, and I've met several, who would have the courage to send their aide to Peking without telling anyone. I don't know many leaders who would entrust to their aide the task of negotiating with the North Vietnamese, informing only a tiny group of people of the initiative. Really, some things depend on the type of president. What I've done was achieved because he made it possible for me to do it.[2]

History has recorded other such intense relations between a President and his adviser—classic examples are Woodrow Wilson and Colonel House and perhaps Franklin D. Roosevelt and Harry Hopkins. Unlike the others, however, the Nixon-Kissinger relationship changed in unusual fashion, with the adviser growing stronger as the President weakened and eventually exercising seemingly independent power, as well as surviving his leader's loss of office and power.

In getting along with Nixon, Kissinger once again showed his ability to "fit" with different types of men. He also showed his "diplomat for hire" attire, and his drive for a power that would allow him to put his world view and policies into play.

As we know, however, though Kissinger was a man for most seasons, he was not one for all. Bowie and Kennedy were failed relations, touching on nerves in both parties that could not respond sympathetically. Such was not the case with Nixon. Although by no means identical in all their personal traits, or even in their views and policies, the two men resonated together in a very special way. Nixon was the happy chance that allowed Kissinger's destiny to unfold itself in a world-shaping fashion.

Who Manipulates Whom?

Kissinger and Nixon first met at a party on December 10, 1967, arranged by Claire Boothe Luce. The hostess was significant: a right-wing Republican and China-lobby supporter, Mrs. Luce "thought they would hit it off. I told Nixon, 'I think you'll admire Henry.' I knew that if Henry spent an hour talking with Nixon the two men would get along famously."[3] Although Nixon's reaction to Kissinger seemed relatively favorable, Kissinger recalled that Nixon had been stiff, and he himself aloof. "Neither of us is very good at cocktail party conversation," he commented.[4]

Kissinger was still very much Rockefeller's man, looking ahead to the convention at Miami Beach. The inability at small talk, which later would be one of many similar traits to draw the two men together, served only to make the first meeting stiff and formal, and to leave Kissinger confirmed in his low estimate of Nixon: "That man Nixon is not fit to be President" was one of his gentler remarks.[5] In Kissinger's eyes, Nixon was a *parvenu*, lacking in culture. Kissinger shared the general view prevailing at the Council on Foreign Relations, where Nixon was disliked and distrusted. In fact, Nixon's policies were basically the same as Rockefeller's; it was his entourage and his style that seemed so different, so unestablishment.

Kissinger admitted his disparaging remarks about Nixon and explained his shift in retrospect. "I didn't know him, that's all. My attitude towards him was the conventional highbrow one, that's all. I was wrong."[6] It took Nixon's election and an invitation to meet the President-elect at the Hotel Pierre on November 25, 1968, to begin the reeducation of Kissinger on the subject of Nixon. Rockefeller had been hoping he would be named Secretary of Defense, if not State, but it was Kissinger who was offered a job, as special assistant to Nixon on foreign affairs. After consulting with Rockefeller and others, Kissinger accepted the post from the man whose integrity and abilities he had distrusted, but who was, after all, something Rockefeller wasn't: President of the United States as of January 20, 1969.

Knowing Kissinger's general attitudes and patterns of behavior, it is easy to see why he accepted Nixon's offer. As he remarked later to one of his dubious assistants, "I'm here because I'm working for the presidency, not for Richard Nixon personally."[7] Indeed, a refusal on Kissinger's part would have been a surprising action.

What requires special explanation is Nixon's behavior. Why did he hire Kissinger? Kissinger was clearly a non-Nixon man whose view that there was a possible difference between Nixon and the presidency could only be heretical to the true believers in the White House and to Nixon himself. And then there were Kissinger's disparaging remarks. And last, he was a Rockefeller man.

The latter fact, ironically, worked in Kissinger's favor. Nixon was obviously delighted to take him away from Rockefeller, an added insult to the refusal to give Rockefeller a place in the Cabinet. Kissinger was also a Harvard intellectual who himself made snide remarks about academia; thus, Nixon could have his cake—an in-house intellectual—and eat it, so to speak.

Moreover, Nixon wanted to run foreign policy himself, to be his own Secretary of State, and Kissinger, unrepresentative of any constituency and seemingly totally dependent on Nixon, could be the perfect tool to help him (it is noteworthy that Kissinger was appointed before the Secretary of State, Rogers, was selected, an important signal in the fervid Washington atmosphere of power).

Kissinger, needless to say, brought real abilities to his position. Nixon admired Kissinger's analytic abilities, made manifest in his books. His hard-line views on foreign policy were highly congenial with those of the President. Kissinger also had the advantage of appearing bipartisan. Had he not also served the Democratic Presidents, Kennedy and Johnson? Nixon wanted a National Security Council system which would present him with options, rather than a single recommendation. Who better than Kissinger, with his wide net of connections, to recruit the right people to work up divergent positions and to present them in orderly and impartial fashion?

As for Kissinger's early views of Nixon, the old politician allowed these to roll off his back in proverbial ducklike fashion. He well knew what strange bedfellows politics made of people, with partners exchanged at the opportune moment.[8] His acceptance of this fact would manifest itself daringly in the international arena with China and Russia.

There are those who say that Kissinger's greatest diplomatic feat was getting Nixon to trust him. I do not agree. Nixon had already decided to choose Kissinger as his special assistant before he was really exposed to Kissinger's persuasive skills. Kissinger's great feat was to survive in the bureaucratic struggle in the White House without being irretrievably knifed. Here, for once at least, his reputed paranoia stood him in good stead as he guarded himself against the Haldemans, Erlichmans, and Mitchells of the Nixon administration.

Once a member of Nixon's administration, if not his team, Kissinger proved himself exceedingly loyal. He not only accepted Nixon's decisions—he really had no choice—but went out of his way generally to identify with them, except for occasional propagandistic overtures to the liberals. For such deceptions Nixon would have nothing but praise, as this was one of the assets Kissinger brought with him to his job.

Kissinger has described the relationship, at least pre-Watergate, a number of times. "There is no 'Kissinger policy' on questions of substance," he said. "My task is to convey the full range of policy options to the President."[9] This description was literally quite accurate, though we shall see later, when we discuss the National Security Council itself, whether covertly Kissinger's work bore a greater resemblance to his staff performance for Rockefeller's special committees, where he provided "guidance" and not mere options. In a 1970 interview, Kissinger added, "it would be preposterous to say that somebody in my position is not asked which course he prefers. And of course, I have convictions. And when the President asks me what I think, and he often does, I tell him. And then, the last thing that usually happens is that he withdraws for a day or two with all the papers, and then makes his decision."[10] And in an interview four years later, Kissinger was still repeating: "It almost never reaches the point where he says I order you to do this. He'll ask my opinion . . . and I'll give it to him. But finally he makes the decision of what needs to be done."[11]

One need not go as far as William Safire, who likens Nixon to a puppet master and Kissinger to a marionette, to believe that Nixon made the final decisions. The real question is: How were these decisions arrived at? How did Kissinger influence Nixon, assuming he did? Here the matter is more complicated, and Safire glimpses the truth, although in a one-sided manner, when he writes, "Nixon, who constantly thought of himself not as he was but as he wished to be, could use Kissinger as a marionette, and then place himself in his own marionette's hands; the President understood in his assistant the needs [of his ego] he refused to examine in himself (Reston is right; perhaps all this is better left to the psychological novelists)."[12]

On the record as it now stands, it is clear that on most issues, at least till Watergate, Nixon called the tune. Thus, for example, the Kalbs tell us that after the April 1969 shooting down of an American spy plane by the North Koreans, "Kissinger sensed that Nixon seemed inclined to reject all recommendations for a swift retaliatory strike against North Korean bases, and he quickly shifted position."[13] We are told of similar "shifts" on an ABM system, as well as on the final negotiations with Hanoi and Saigon.[14] On China, the Kalbs admit this about their hero: "For the first six months of 1969, Kissinger was a mere passenger on the Administration's China train. The President was clearly its sole engineer."[15]

It is, therefore, in the realm of Safire's "psychological novelists" that additional information might be forthcoming concerning the relations of the two men. Was it only campaign oratory that led Kissinger to say of Nixon, "There's a certain, you know, it's a big word, but it's a certain heroic quality about how he conducts his business . . . !"[16] Did Kissinger really see Nixon as a "hero"? Or did he also see him, as he later is alleged to have said, as "unstable" and "paranoid"?[17] Was Kissinger the secret hero in the relationship, publicly eating humble pie when necessary, but exerting psychological control over his presumed master? Kissinger had studied Metternich's manipulation of his own Emperor, Francis I, as well as of Tsar Alexander; were these his models? Could Kissinger apply to himself what he said about Austria: that it must "strive to save its national substance by adaptation to the victor. This is not necessarily a heroic policy, *although in certain circumstances it may be the most heroic of all* [my italics]. To cooperate, without losing one's soul, to assist without sacrificing one's identity . . . what harder task of moral toughness exists?"[18]

We do not as yet have Nixon's reflective views on Kissinger.

Perhaps when both men write and publish their memoirs, we shall have a better account; or, rather, we shall at least have the story as they both perceive it.[19] Until then, and perhaps even then, we can only indulge in an analysis based on assumptions about the two men's characters: their similarities and differences and how they have apparently related, one to another, as persons as well as policies.

A Comparison: Nixon and Kissinger

By now, the Watergate tapes and various other accounts have made many of Nixon's character traits familiar to us.[20] It is, of course, the synthesis of these traits in him, not their mere existence as a list, that offers us the possibility of a dynamic insight into his actual personality. Thus, to compare various traits in Kissinger and Nixon is only to give the bare bones of each man's character, and, even then, little sense of how they rattle against one another.

Still, such a comparison is a useful beginning. Even a cursory glance shows how much Kissinger and Nixon seemed to have in common, a fact that would make their relations with one another potentially comfortable, if not friendly.

Both men were self-made success stories, apparently coming from nowhere to unexpected great power. Neither, therefore, had much social "background," and in choosing Kissinger, Nixon set himself off from most previous Presidents, who chose foreign policy advisers or Secretaries of State with "aristocratic" connections, such as an Acheson or a Dulles.[21] Thus, Nixon rejected a Dulles-type, such as chosen by Eisenhower (the President under whom Nixon had served as Vice President) and selected a Kissinger, whose "connections" were of a very different sort, achieved by hard work rather than blood lines.

Both Kissinger and Nixon had pronounced traits of shyness and insecurity, though they matched them with differing degrees of arrogance. We have already noted their lack of small talk. Both have been known to give way to tears in distressing situations. Both are notorious for their "loner" qualities and share the conviction that the leader should make his decisions in isolation, scorning the ephemeral applause of the populace. Thus, their basic conception of the style in which foreign policy should be conceived and carried out was alike. And both had a penchant for secrecy that bordered on a paranoiac suspicion of others.

Both were much concerned with the assertion of their masculinity. It was not only Nixon who admired General Patton and went to see the movie *Patton* innumerable times (forcing Kissinger to see it, too). Patton was also Kissinger's hero during World War II; one of Kissinger's army buddies recalls his saying, "Patton's a dashing man, he has guts," and Kissinger preferred him to Eisenhower and Montgomery. (This army friend also reports Kissinger as having admired Chiang Kai-shek, and even praising Stalin as a good guy.) Both Kissinger and Nixon also saw themselves as strong men, and were loud in their praise of others whom they perceived as strong men. If Nixon admired Connolly and Agnew as strong men, Kissinger matched these likes by his own praise of Le Duc Tho, "very strong," and of Nixon, "great strength . . . a strong character."[22]

For both Kissinger and Nixon, the Vietnamese war was a test of our strength and character as a people (and by implication of their own strength and character as leaders). Where Nixon, for example, defended the Cambodian invasion as a test of "our" character, Kissinger was still saying in 1975, with the fall of South Vietnam imminent, that our conduct at that moment (he wished us to continue supporting South Vietnam) would answer the question of "what kind of people we are."[23] As for the Mayaguez incident, Kissinger unnecessarily declared that our reaction was not to demonstrate our masculinity—thereby convincing almost all observers that that was exactly what it was calculated to do. Kissinger's aides tell stories of how he insisted on lots of "manly" phrases and assertions in the statements they prepared for him.

Both Kissinger and Nixon are given to pronounced alternations of depression and euphoria, or what some, for example, have called highs and lows. According to a number of observers, Kissinger became happy and inspired at hearing good news and rather irritated, even furious, upon being informed about plans not working out. In comparison, Nixon has been described as behaving best in the face of adversity and worst when he is confronted with success.[24] Whether these descriptions are correct or not (see our discussion of the role of depression in Kissinger in Chapter 4), both Kissinger and Nixon emphatically understood the other's manic-depressive phases, and this understanding helped them to get along with one another.

On a more lofty level, both Kissinger and Nixon had an acute sense of history and their role in it. Nixon had majored in history at Whittier College, and he was constantly concerned with how history would record his actions. (The Watergate tapes were one way he conceived of helping history along.) We have seen for ourselves how Kissinger's thought is permeated by a concern for history. He wishes not only to understand its "meaning" but, as his aides abundantly report, is worried about his own reputation and the legacy that he will leave.

Both Kissinger and Nixon see themselves, in part, as "white revolutionaries," i.e., as conservatives stealing revolutionary thunder and espousing revolutionary acts for stabilizing purposes. Thus, Nixon fancied himself as a twentieth-century Disraeli, and Kissinger has professed admiration for Bismarck, writing about him as a "White Revolutionary."[25] When not fantasizing themselves as white revolutionaries, Kissinger and

Nixon both have the identical fantasy of retiring to Oxford to write their historical memoirs!

One could go on at great length about the similarities, momentous and trivial, between Kissinger and Nixon. The fact is that, basically, their "styles," as Kissinger remarked, fitted one another. This "fit" made it easier for them to work together, and provided the day-to-day lubrication which made smooth the foreign policy actions on which they were intellectually agreed.

Naturally, the two men also had different characteristics. Nixon, as we know, was in no way a ladies' man; Kissinger pretended to other aspirations in this direction. Nixon was much given to foul language; this is totally absent in Kissinger. (Nixon's anti-Semitic remarks, incidentally, were known to Kissinger, who ignored them as he had Elliott's and would King Faisal's.) Other such minor divergencies could be listed.

What is most important is not the absence of a particular trait in one man and its presence in the other so much as a different valence placed on traits shared in common. Kissinger was duplicitous, as we have seen, but he did not indulge in mammoth denial, both of his own impulses and of reality, as did Nixon. Kissinger, like all of us, indulged in a certain amount of projection, but again not to the extent of Nixon's systematically constructed world of enemies. Kissinger could joke about his admitted paranoia; he did see a particular enemy lurking here or there behind some specific incident, but his environment was not infested with them. One need only compare Kissinger's and Nixon's attitudes to the press to see the difference (even bearing in mind Kissinger's extravagant reaction to criticism). Kissinger also did a certain amount of role-playing—his lone cowboy role will always haunt him—but unlike Nixon his role-playing rested on a secure sense of self. Beneath all his duplicities, projections, and roles, Kissinger has an abiding sense of who he is as a creative, independent individual, and it is this inner conviction that serves as the bedrock of his character.

Kissinger has something else denied to Nixon: an authentic claim to intellectual and scholarly abilities. This, too, reassures him and gives him confidence and an ultimate sense of security missing in Nixon. Both men disdain the academic establishment, but Kissinger does it with the knowledge that he was able "to cut the mustard," a sense lacking in Nixon. So, too, as conservatives, Nixon is a mere opportunist and visceral exponent, whereas Kissinger's tendencies are rooted not only in his life experiences, but in high-level metaphysical speculations. While they share a sense of history, Kissinger's is relatively precise, knowledgeable, and wide in its grasp of Western thought and action, whereas Nixon's is at best parochial, and at worst vapid, a matter of sheer invocation of the word "history."

In short, sharing many common traits of character, as we have seen, Kissinger goes well beyond Nixon in the integrity and synthetic healthiness of much of his personality. To this fact we must add the extremely important ability of Kissinger to change and grow in a way Nixon failed to demonstrate. Taken all together, Kissinger's fundamental character strengths, in spite of the serious flaws and warts that disfigure them, when added to his capacity for personal development, make him a much greater person (if not statesman) than Nixon, and explain in large part why he has survived the latter's fall. Nixon's historical importance comes solely from his role as President. Kissinger's comes from the fact that, like Metternich and Bismarck, he is a true authentic "hero" of sorts, a conservative statesman who has now become a prototype of what such a person might be: like "Machiavellian," we shall in the future speak of someone who is "Kissingerian."

The National Security Council

The mechanism through which Kissinger exercised his power over foreign affairs was the National Security Council. We will offer neither a structural analysis nor a history of Kissinger's stewardship but rather single out some themes that reflect some of the personality and policy concerns that have previously occupied our attention.[26]

The National Security Council had originally been set up in 1947 "to advise the President with respect to the integration of domestic, foreign and military policies to the national security. . . ."[27] Each President, from Truman on, used it in a different way, relying on the Secretary of State, or Defense, or a special assistant, according to his personal preference.[28] Under Kennedy, McGeorge Bundy ran it as a special assistant, with Rusk the titular leader as Secretary of State.

Kissinger now had Bundy's job. It surely gave him great delight to take over the position of the colleague who had forced him to resign back in 1962. Kissinger vowed he would avoid Bundy's error of getting involved in short-term crises; he would restrict himself to long-range planning. Alas, this plan was quickly put aside as events and Kissinger's style of managing the National Security Council combined to enmesh him in particular situation after situation. Indeed, Kissinger seemed to enjoy the detailed minutiae, and a number of reports tell how delighted he was, for example, consulting the Vietnam war maps in the basement room of the White House. "Like a child with a game of war" is how one observer described Kissinger's rapture as he moved flags about on the maps.

Kissinger quickly recruited his own staff, people loyal to him alone. A number were from the State Department; Kissinger simply raided it for bright young men. Some were old friends, such as Helmut Sonnenfeldt. Some were recommended by old friends, such as Colonel Alexander Haig, Jr., about whom Fritz Kraemer had good feelings, as he had had about young Henry Kissinger. The aim of Kissinger's team was to work up a wide range of options for President Nixon on specific issues, as well as long-range policies, and to free him from bureaucratic restraints, such as the Secretary of State. In short, foreign policy moved directly into the White House.

Kissinger tuned the National Security Council into an exquisite instrument for his, and presumably Nixon's, solo performance. Dominating the Council, Kissinger also made sure he was involved with all the other important foreign policy-making groups around the White House: the Washington Special Actions Group (WSAG), the 40 Committee, and numerous other such esoteric bodies. Here one could see Kissinger's style in sharp outline, coinciding with some of his strongest personality traits. He was the loner, controlling the whole decision-recommending apparatus as it worked its way up to Nixon. Though Nixon made the final decision, it was only on the basis of the options presented to him by Kissinger, and in terms of the way Kissinger presented them. Kissinger disliked bureaucracies; with the National Security Council he undercut Rogers and the whole State Department apparatus, while giving it the appearance of participation. Moreover, as the President's special assistant, Kissinger was not even accountable to Congress. Kissinger was convinced that force was part of diplomacy, and military problems interwoven with foreign policy issues; in the National Security Council he could weave the international warp and woof on one shuttle. Kissinger was a teacher; in the National Security Council he educated his assistants, indoctrinating them with his world view as well as his analyses of particular crises. Such training was in line with Kissinger's view that policy decisions were not to be made on the basis of competing interests or advocacy groups, but by intuitionists who understood the ultimate meaning of history.

As was to be expected, Kissinger was a hard taskmaster.

As at the Harvard Center for International Affairs, he warned his assistants how difficult he was to work for, how they would rarely see their families, and so on, and set the example himself. In addition to inspiring many of his young aides with a sense of the special responsibility and rigor of their jobs, such a warning served Kissinger as a blank check for abusing them: "After all, I've told you ahead of time" was the message. Some of his assistants got sick—Eagleburger, for example, had to resign for a while—and others found their marriages in trouble as a result, but Kissinger got his options worked up for Nixon on every conceivable subject. His aides either remained devoted to him or quit over the working conditions or, more usually, the policies.

The Cambodian invasion, of course, was a touchstone. Many of Kissinger's brightest young men were stunned at the callousness and secrecy of the operation, and eventually resigned out of moral indignation. An Anthony Lake, a Daniel Davidson, a Roger Morris, all resigned in great bitterness over Kissinger's Vietnam policy. Kissinger shielded himself philosophically from these defections, intoning, according to a member of his staff, as one who knew that history was filled with tragedies: "You have never seen the dissolution of a society." His, he believed, was the price the lonely leader had to pay; only history would redeem and reveal his true value.

As special assistant to the President and director of the National Security Council, Kissinger also revealed his obsessive concern with secrecy and with unauthorized leaks. This concern, as well as a need to protect himself from the sniping of the Haldeman-Erlichman group, which accused him of having brought in untrustworthy, liberal assistants, led Kissinger into the wiretapping affair which has sullied his reputation and led to his own threat to resign at Salzburg.

The wiretaps were placed from May 1969 to February 1971. They were originally inspired by the story leaked to the *New York Times* on the Cambodian bombing, to which the publication of the Pentagon Papers then added fuel. Kissinger admitted to being disturbed by such leaks, especially of the Pentagon Papers, and was clearly in favor of the wiretaps, which he believed to be legal (there was nothing in his makeup, as we know, to give him any qualms as to the civil rights involved; these rights became acute when the tap was kept on Morton Halperin even after he left the National Security Council.)[29] Kissinger's fears dovetailed at this point with his strongly held belief that a key factor in foreign affairs is credibility; how, he argued, could other governments trust the United States in negotiations if we could not keep our own most intimate secrets? The whole issue became personalized when Kissinger defended his actions and declared it impossible "to conduct the foreign policy of the United States under these circumstances *when the character and credibility of the Secretary of State* [Kissinger had been appointed in August 1973] *is at issue*" [my italics], and threatened to resign.[30]

Although obsessive, Kissinger's concern with secrecy, leaks, and bureaucratic back stabbing was grounded in some reality. Negotiations cannot be totally open, some leaks may be disastrous for national security, and Kissinger did have enemies in the White House. As the ancient Greeks so well knew, of course, everything is a matter of degree. What interests us in all of this as much as Kissinger's direct feelings on the matter is his alternating behavior and ambivalence on the issues of suspicion and trust. Thus, talking to William Safire in 1970, he spoke of "one wrong step, and he was finished, all the vultures would eat him up."[31] It was the same refrain about the effect of the Cambodian invasion and student reactions to it, such as at Kent State. "I'm dead," Kissinger is reported to have said, forgetting the actual students and thinking of how his White House enemies would now destroy him.

How ironic, in the light of his general suspicions, is the evidence for Henry Kissinger's overtrusting nature. He seems, for example, to have been innocent about the French journalist,

Danielle Hunebelle. Similarly, in an interview with Bernard Law Collier, after making an indiscreet remark about Nelson Rockefeller, Kissinger then said, with a defenseless smile, "I seem to trust people I shouldn't trust. . . . I hope I can trust you."[32] So, too, there is his "trusting" interview with Oriana Fallaci—"I'm not a person that usually confides in journalists."[33] On a more important level, there is Kissinger's comment that after two hours with Sadat, he knew he could trust him.[34]

Now some of these may be shrewd moves to take the other person in—see how defenseless I am; don't hurt me—while lulling the other person into a false trust. Another part is the obverse of suspicion: I *want* to trust people, though I know I shouldn't. Most of the time, Kissinger has behaved as one who has learned from bitter experience not to trust others: to be suspicious, lonely, and devious in turn. These were traits he exhibited in full bloom in his directorship of the National Security Council. They were hardly traits that would incur disfavor in the eyes of Henry Kissinger's fellow statesman, President Nixon.

Secretary of State

On August 23, 1973, President Nixon nominated Kissinger to be Secretary of State. It was an effort to lend credibility to an administration from which Haldeman and Erlichman had had to be dismissed a few months earlier. In his new post the State Department bureaucracy was now Kissinger's own, and not just someone else's to be run around. By retaining his National Security Council post, moreover, Kissinger carefully protected his flank from someone trying to do to him what he had done to Rogers. Effectively, all of American foreign policy-making apparatus, except for the President, was under Kissinger's control; with Watergate increasingly absorbing

Nixon's attention and reducing his power, Kissinger became in reality the President for Foreign Affairs.[35]

Before looking at the way Kissinger ran the State Department, we should consider three theories about foreign policy formation. The first may be called the rational model. It assumes that a particular nation's foreign policy is, or ought to be, the product of one central, national guiding intelligence. It presumes that there is a clear national interest, independent of particular individuals holding office or bureaucratic infighting, and that a single decision maker (the President, in the American case) makes a rational judgment. The second theory, espoused by such scholars as Graham Allison, Morton Halperin, and I. M. Destler, may be called the bureaucratic model. As Destler explains it,

> What results from this bureaucratic political system is, of course, foreign policy. But it is not necessarily "policy" in the rational sense of embodying the decisions made and actions ordered by a controlling intelligence focusing primarily on our foreign policy problems. Instead it is the "outcome" of the political process, the government actions resulting from all the arguments, the building of coalitions and countercoalitions, and the decisions by high officials and compromises among them. Often it may be a "policy" that no participant fully favors, when "different groups pulling in different directions yield a resultant different from what anyone intended."[36]

Such a policy may result in the lack of a clear signal to other countries. Indeed, "Foreign bureaucrats in turn receive and interpret these signals selectively since they are looking for evidence to support them in their own internal bureaucratic battles. Thus 'communications' between nations tend to become dialogues between the largely deaf and dumb."[37]

Here we can see an additional reason for Kissinger's dislike of bureaucratic policy making. With his fondness for "signals," Kissinger is distressed by the random noise of departmental politics. As for the third theory of policy formation, in John F.

Kennedy's words, "The essence of ultimate decision remains impenetrable to the observer—often, indeed, to the decider himself. . . . There will always be the dark entangled stretches in the decision-making process—mysterious even to those who may be most intimately involved." And George Reedy, reflecting on Lyndon B. Johnson, comments that "He [the decision maker, in this case the President] decides what he wants to decide, and any student of the White House who believes that he is making a contribution to political thought when he analyzes the process is sadly mistaken."[38] We can call the theory that describes this form of policy making the personal-actor model; clearly, it links strongly with a psychological analysis.

All these models, it appears to me, describe parts of the reality of foreign policy formation, and each comes more or less prominently into play depending on the particular President (to take the United States example) and how he operates. In turn, given a particular President, we can then make the same comments about a particular Secretary of State. In Kissinger's case, we can see that he would spurn the second, the bureaucratic model, and envision some sort of combination of one and three: a personal actor whose central intelligence is guided not so much by a "rational" idea of national policy, but by an intuitive, historical insight into international purpose and destiny.

With this view Kissinger would approach the State Department. He brought with him, or appointed, a small group of trusted assistants. As the *New York Times* tried to summarize the situation in a positive and favorable light seven months after Kissinger took office, "He has replaced almost all ranking officials with a highly motivated, individualistic team of people who are loyal to him but are prepared to speak their minds." Kissinger also promised to reorganize the Department itself and involve it more in the formation of foreign policy, but this was mere rhetoric. As the *Times* admitted, "Because of his extraordinary foreign travel, Mr. Kissinger has not been able to find the time to carry out his promise to 'institutionalize' foreign politics and to involve the 11,000-man department and foreign service fully in its execution." Further, as the *Times* says, "On occasion the Secretary's working habits have slowed the Administration's decision-making process in foreign policy. No action can be taken on major matters without his consent even if it means delaying a decision until he can study it. His desire to be fully informed extends to the furnishings of his offices and the menus of his meals; more than most Secretaries of State, he has involved himself even in minor matters." (Incidentally, this is a similar trait in Nixon, as Alexander Butterfield has informed us.)[39]

More intimate accounts of Kissinger's style in running the State Department substantiate and add color to the description just given. Kissinger, in choosing his top aides, sometimes tells them he is looking for "unconventional excellence"; that he wishes bright, vigorous men and not "old fogies." In the event, however, unconventional excellence means hard work as defined by Kissinger and in the directions he alone determines; independence of thought must be subservient to Kissinger's directives (not unexpectedly). As for bright young men, Kissinger is obviously more comfortable with those not of his age group, as well as those who are not blatantly dependent on him while at the same time they do not stretch their autonomy very far.

Kissinger's staff meetings (e.g., of the Regional Assistant Secretaries) are erratic. Although he has insisted on having such meetings, he has frequently not showed up, inevitably canceling them a half hour or so after he has not shown up. Rescheduled from the afternoon to early morning, once a week, even then, when Kissinger is in town, they have been described as being a waste of time, with Kissinger asking for discussion, then interrupting and dominating the presentations. Much forced laughter is in evidence, and anyone trying to stand up to Kissinger becomes subject to his wit.

Interestingly, Kissinger has had a verbatim stenographic

record made of these meetings. Although apparently only one copy is made, available in the Secretariat, Kissinger's remarks will presumably one day be available to historians. Many of these remarks, it is reported, are scathing, vitriolic comments on public figures—ministers, ambassadors—such as "the stupidest person whom I know." (As we noted earlier, the Israeli journalist, Matti Golan, apparently has many such comments in his book, which is partly why it was censored.) Why, one wonders, has Kissinger insisted that these remarks be recorded? Are we faced with another similarity to Nixon?

Kissinger, clearly, holds all the really important decisions close to his vest. He does not, in effect, trust anyone else, or feel able to delegate authority or power. With all decisions secretly linked in his own mind—and here we have another aspect of the theory of linkage—his associates are often in the awkward position of being slapped down for unwittingly interfering with some plan or action about which they know nothing. Ideally, only Kissinger knows everything that is going on. Thus, to take a relatively trivial example, all Assistant Secretaries must send in a daily report about how they have spent that day. If nothing else, such a requirement keeps the bureaucracy busy. Since many of them are afraid that Kissinger will shoot from the hip if they tell unpleasant truths, increasingly they avoid reporting disturbing facts. Reciprocally, according to one of the quips going the rounds of the State Department, "Henry Kissinger's chief lieutenants are like mushrooms—they're kept in the dark, get a lot of manure piled on them, and then get canned."

One can, of course, pour much scorn on Kissinger's way of running the State Department. In truth, many Secretaries of State have been suspicious of their aides and of the bureaucracy. The latter does tend to bog down in minutiae. It is hardly unnatural to surround oneself with people one trusts—up to a point. A strong Secretary does make his own decisions. Added to these truisms is the fact that, philosophically, Kissinger has

Chapter 11

KISSINGER AND NIXON: WHOSE POLICIES?

The Professor and the Secretary of State

THERE IS a definite gap between what Kissinger the academic wrote and what Kissinger the adviser to the President did. As Theodore Draper puts it, there is "the curious difference between Professor Kissinger and Presidential Assistant Secretary of State Kissinger," and Draper goes on to speak of the struggle between "the philosopher and the fixer . . . for the mind and soul of Henry Kissinger."[1] The Kalbs offer a specific instance when they write, "It would be madness, Kissinger warned, for the United States to negotiate with North Vietnam concerning the terms of a political settlement for South Vietnam—a warning Kissinger himself began to ignore within his first year in office."[2] And we can see that Kissinger, the disciple of Clausewitz, was violating the precepts of his mentor when he maintained the advantages of a two-track negotiating scheme against the North Vietnamese, separating the military from the political.

There is a further problem when we realize that most of

Kissinger's writings were on Europe, and most of his foreign policy actions in non-European areas. Then and now, Kissinger has had little interest in the so-called underdeveloped nations. In power, he could still ignore most of the countries in these areas, although eventually Cuba, Chile, South Africa, Algeria, China, India, Pakistan, and others came to call for attention either intermittently or continuously; but we have no recognition of or reflection on them by Kissinger prior to his becoming Nixon's special assistant.

To say all this is not necessarily to fault Kissinger. Once in power, many of his theories would have to give way to the exigencies of practical politics, while others would have to accommodate themselves to the desires of the President, Richard Nixon (and now Ford). Required by his position to offer assistance in all areas, Kissinger would quite obviously have to become involved with countries and social systems about which he had little expertise.

Bearing these factors in mind, we shall nevertheless look at some key areas and problems in policy formation and execution, with an eye to discerning how Kissinger's concepts, negotiating style, and personality traits interrelate. Needless to say, we shall not deal with all his policy positions, and shall only examine those we deal with in terms of certain themes.

The overriding theme here is Kissinger's constant concern with the Soviet Union. For him, only the Soviets are a realistic threat to international stability, and a potential source of holocaust. Kissinger admires the Soviets in many ways, frequently models his behavior on communist thought and action, and advocates, that America do the same. This, most emphatically, is not to say that he wishes America to be communist; rather, one must recall the efforts of the German patriots—Clausewitz, Scharnhorst, and Gneisenau—to imitate aspects of the French revolutionaries and Napoleon in order to defeat them. Kissinger has also evolved in his view of the Soviet Union. At first he saw it as a purely revolutionary force, necessarily transgressing the limits and irreconcilably threatening international stability. More lately he has seen it as becoming, like the United States, a status quo power.

Kissinger's initial conception of the Soviet Union, as a revolutionary adversary of the United States and international stability, coincides with his theory of linkage: political and psychological changes in one area affect developments in all other areas, especially when the revolutionary force has world-wide aspirations. Kissinger persists in his linkage theory, in respect especially to the Soviet Union. In the last few years, however, he has joined to the linkage theory the notion of détente. The two superpowers must each realize that their great power cancels out vis-à-vis one another, and imposes a limit to its actions relative to smaller powers, actions which may draw the United States and Soviet Union into perilous and concatenating confrontation with one another. Détente, therefore, is in the best interests of both powers. It is, simply, the updated and benign form of linkage.

SALT

Kissinger's first major public achievement was his book, *Nuclear Weapons and Foreign Policy*. It should not be surprising, therefore, that he would devote much of his personal energies to the effort to bring about an agreement with the Soviet Union, limiting strategic nuclear arms. In Kissinger's opinion, conveyed to the Kalbs, none of his efforts was more meaningful than the launching of SALT, the Strategic Arms Limitation Talks, culminating in an agreement reached in Moscow on May 26, 1972.[3]

Note that on the issue of SALT it seems to have been, as one knowledgeable student puts it, Kissinger who moved Nixon around to favoring it. Yet it was also Kissinger who counseled holding off from negotiations on SALT, which the Russians desired, until they were prepared to "give" elsewhere, e.g., in Vietnam. Thus Kissinger approached SALT as a part of an overall linkage, and strongly influenced Nixon in taking this same stand.

In coming to SALT, Kissinger also exhibited his ability to change with changed conditions. Thus, he accepted a shift in the objective of American nuclear policy from one of superiority over the Soviets to one of "sufficiency," i.e., enough to deter the Soviets from launching a first strike. Though Nixon, as a candidate in 1968, had advocated superiority, he was brought over to Kissinger's view. Kissinger also showed superb political skills in outmaneuvering the other bureaucracies. As one observer put it, "Only Kissinger by the force and strength of his personality, and the power of his position in the government, was able to hold the Pentagon at bay." Kissinger, in fact, was able to do this by never interfering with the actual weapons systems—he always knew how to throw the military a bone if he were putting something over on them elsewhere—but instead implementing his own conceptual position, and ignoring or undermining theirs. In more recent times, Kissinger's tactics brought him into overt conflict with former Secretary of Defense Schlesinger, and thus with the military hawks. This whole episode, incidentally, shows the reality elements surrounding Kissinger's need to "get along" with the far right.

Kissinger realized that in previous negotiations the American position had always been more constrained by debates within the American bureaucracy than by those with the Soviets. He now sought to circumvent this problem by coming to meetings with the Russians armed with a series of options rather than one proposal. As the Kalbs put it, "This novel approach eliminated the old bureaucratic hang-up that accounted for the loss of so much time—the need, first, to agree in advance on a specific proposal [one acceptable to all departments of the United States Government] and then, if it should be rejected by the Russians, the need to crank up the whole process again on another specific proposal."[4]

This novel negotiating style corresponded with Kissinger's style of presenting Nixon with options worked up by the National Security Council (which also worked them up for the SALT meetings). It is the Jacobovsky technique of there always being two possibilities, so suited to Kissinger's character. The options, moreover, were always devised with an eye to linkage, and each option had subtle links to other issues in an intriguing spiderweb fashion. The psychological possibilities and permutations were numerous, and, though Kissinger was not directly involved in all the face-to-face negotiations, he could feel that he alone held all the strings and might touch all the nerves involved. In this, potentially one of the least promising areas for personalization—arms limitation is highly "scientific"—we can still see present and active the elements of Kissinger's negotiating skills.

Vietnam

The key issue Kissinger sought to link with SALT was Vietnam. In this he was following his President, for Nixon, in a speech prepared for delivery in 1968 (though he never actually gave it), declared that "If the Soviets were disposed to see the war ended and a compromise settlement negotiated they have the means to move Ho Chi Minh to the conference table."[5] As perceived by Nixon and Kissinger, the problem, therefore, was to so dispose the Soviets, i.e., to put pressure on them elsewhere. Such a presumed solution, incidentally, coincided with the analysis of the Vietnamese struggle as an instance of communist aggression and part of a worldwide revolutionary effort.

Kissinger, of course, knew the Vietnam War was more complicated than that. He gave his own analysis in an article in *Foreign Affairs,* published a few weeks after he became Nixon's foreign policy assistant. As we recall, Kissinger had made trips to Vietnam in 1965 and 1966, for Henry Cabot Lodge, and had some on-the-ground knowledge of the situation. He knew, therefore, that the war was a "civil war," as well as a communist one.[6] In fact, Kissinger casually let it be known that he was not a hawk on Vietnam and disapproved of our initial involvement.

Kissinger made his overall position public in his 1969 *Foreign Affairs* article. In Kissinger's analysis, the United States was fighting a military war, and the North Vietnamese a political one. It was now essential to turn our military operations toward establishing a viable political position, i.e., a viable South Vietnamese political structure. Our task was to negotiate for the withdrawal of all "outside" military forces, to avoid a coalition government, and to let the South Vietnamese work out their own relations to the National Liberation Front and the North.

We could not afford to withdraw and let South Vietnam collapse. According to Kissinger, whether or not our initial involvement was right, "the commitment of five hundred thousand Americans has settled the issue of the importance of Vietnam." Here Kissinger reverted to one of his fundamental views: what was now involved was America's "credibility."[7]

Kissinger was also confident that, unable to force us out militarily, the North Vietnamese would have to negotiate. His analysis of the threats to North Vietnam independence from both the Chinese and Russians is perceptive, and his awareness of the complexity of the issues and the special quality of the North Vietnam negotiating style subtle and acute. The only trouble is that, as events proved, he was consistently wrong.

Kissinger himself recognized the one rock on which all his complicated, linked assumptions could founder. "If Hanoi insists on total victory, the war must continue."[8] Dismissing this unacceptable notion—for Nixon had pledged an end to the

war, and clearly America was not prepared to fight forever—
Kissinger concluded in a Nixonian style that "however we got
into Vietnam, whatever the judgment of our actions, ending
the war honorably is essential for the peace of the world."[9] It
is the position he maintained unceasingly for the next four
years—and more.

Ending the war honorably—that was the problem. Kissinger
thought he understood the Vietnamese, and he employed his
abilities at empathizing fully with his opponent. He even
consulted the work of an American psychologist on the
Vietnamese national character. "I understand Hanoi's point
of view," he proclaimed in his 1972 interview with Oriana
Fallaci.[10] With his historical and psychological understanding
of his opponent, Kissinger felt confident about bringing into
play his vaunted tandem act of combined force and negotiation.
He and Nixon sent "signals" to Hanoi and the Soviets: e.g., the
invasion of Cambodia, the mining at Haiphong.

Unfortunately, Kissinger was no more successful in actually
understanding the North Vietnamese than almost all other
Westerners. One need only look at the Kalbs' account—a
notoriously friendly one—to see how badly Kissinger failed.
Commenting on Nixon's initial withdrawal of 25,000 troops,
the Kalbs admit, "At this point, Kissinger actually believed that
the President's first withdrawal announcement could persuade
Hanoi to engage in serious negotiations. It wasn't the first time
that Kissinger would be wrong on Vietnam." And on the
March–April 1972 communist attack: "Kissinger reluctantly
concluded that the United States faced a full-scale invasion of
South Vietnam. Once again he had miscalculated the enemy's
intentions." In May, Kissinger made an offer to Le Duc Tho:
"Once again, though, Kissinger had misread his opponent.
Le Duc Tho disdainfully rejected Nixon's offer." Even more
revealing is an earlier comment by the Kalbs: "It was only in
the third year of his official negotiations with the North
Vietnamese that Kissinger finally stripped away the *veil of*

illusion [my italics] and grasped the central factor in Hanoi's calculation: the North Vietnamese really expected the United States to join them in displacing Thieu."[11]

We are faced here with an extraordinary paradox. Kissinger's greatest success, according to general acclaim, was the Vietnam negotiations. Yet on the record it is clear that he constantly misjudged and misunderstood his opponent. How ironic that Kissinger, who claimed statesmen must use illusions and not be subject to them (cf. Chapter 9, p. 200), was himself under serious illusions about Vietnam. Of course, the greatest paradox is that the American public (indeed, the world) suffered from the major illusion of them all, and came to believe Kissinger a hero for bringing peace to Vietnam, for which he received the Nobel Peace Prize.

Kissinger not only misunderstood the Vietnamese; to a certain extent he misunderstood his own American compatriots. Basically disinterested in domestic politics, he underestimated the damaging effects of the war on America and the erosion of confidence in the government and its policies by significant parts of the public. Through a good deal of duplicity, Kissinger tried to hide the real facts, especially of failure, from the American people. On innumerable occasions he shaded the truth. He gave misleading information to James Reston. In April 1970 Kissinger spoke of the South Vietnamese invasion of Cambodia, the Parrot's Beak operation, but revealed nothing of the Fishhook operation by American troops.[12]

Part of Kissinger's duplicity was also his affectation, as we have noted, of a "liberal" image, his effort to appear bipartisan. It was an image Kissinger could maintain for a while by hiring people such as Morton Halperin and Anthony Lake and encouraging them to argue the "dove" position. Kissinger also stayed in touch with the Cambridge intellectual community, soliciting their views on occasion. It took the Cambodian invasion to shatter the image of Kissinger as in some way a dove and a liberal.

The Cambodian invasion, and Kissinger's approval of it, was the real proving point, the litmus test of where Kissinger stood on the war and its conduct. A number of his aides—for example, Lake, Morris, and Watts—resigned over the issue. Most of Kissinger's former Harvard colleagues publicly ended their relation with him. When 12 of them came to Washington to argue with him, Kissinger bought them a steak lunch, only to be told that they "were fed up with him and his President," appropriate imagery for the occasion.

If the Cambodian invasion severed Kissinger's ties to the "liberal" community, it solidified his position with Nixon. As the Kalbs report, "it was his [Kissinger's] unstinting support for the President through the Cambodian crisis, when Nixon was being portrayed by his critics as having taken leave of his senses, that established the real bond between them."[13]

Kissinger was fundamentally more concerned with securing the support of the right wing than the left wing in America. He seemed almost obsessed by memories of the Weimar Republic and the legend of the stab in the back (when the liberals were accused of selling out Germany before she was militarily defeated). As if remembering the street fights of his youth, which he claimed had not affected him, Kissinger prophesied about the student demonstrations that "if political decisions were to be made in the streets the victors would not be upper-middle-class college kids, but some real tough guys."[14] (In fact, Kissinger's analogy is badly taken, for in Germany the students were generally on the side of the Nazis, differing in this respect from the American student radicals of the 1970s.)

It was, however, not only in the streets that Kissinger feared a right-wing reaction. In the White House itself he felt himself threatened by reactionary insiders as well as outsiders, with the likes of Haldeman, Erlichman, and Agnew likely to dominate if Kissinger were to go down. As he is reported to have told his Harvard friends at the time of the Cambodian troubles, "If you go after me, what will it look like? Agnew has been saying,

'Look, you [Kissinger] have been arguing for the Harvard students and liberal faculty against us for months, and who do they go after, you! The President will be delighted.' "

Kissinger appears to have seen himself as defender of humanist values against its Caesarian enemies, a lonely hero whose true worth would be acknowledged only by the judgment of history. At a later time, in Kissinger's view, we would see that the achievement of an honorable peace in Vietnam was what in fact prevented a right-wing reaction in America. Ironically, just before the actual takeover by the North of South Vietnam in 1975, Kissinger still maintained America's need to bolster the Thieu regime and accused the Democrats of stabbing America and its ally in the back, i.e., pulling the props out from under the military defense of South Vietnam.

If Kissinger had ever entertained doubts about the rightness of the Vietnam War, they were totally submerged by his fears of the right wing and his desire to maintain American credibility. Indeed, Kissinger's personal stake in Vietnam increased and he ended up, it appears, by completely personalizing the war and his role in it. His credibility, as much as America's, was involved, and even when South Vietnam was obviously lost, Kissinger persisted in trying to justify the fruits of his 1972 negotiations. Insisting that we must not engage in recriminations, he went to great lengths to show that the loss of South Vietnam was the fault of Congress. James Reston reported that "he is not worried by the rebukes of his old friends in the universities and the press, who condemn him for sticking too long with the battle in Saigon." According to Reston, "What does worry him is the prospect that he will be charged with negotiating a surrender in Paris, like Chamberlain at Munich."[15]

The settlement itself, in 1972, required a good deal of twisting of Thieu's arm. In fact, the settlement was a disguised surrender, and Thieu knew it. According to the best accounts now available, the Christmas bombing of Hanoi was not to bring North Vietnam back to the negotiating table but rather to get Thieu to go along with the agreement by showing to what irrational lengths we were prepared to go to support him if he were to sign.[16] It was the implied surrender over which Kissinger had a bad conscience, at least as much as over the conduct of the war itself.

Of course, the Vietnam negotiations were imposed on Kissinger partly by Nixon (needless to say, if he had been a dove, Kissinger would not have lasted long as Nixon's special assistant) and partly by Kissinger's own convictions. But however inspired, the dealings with Le Duc Tho then became the means by which Kissinger rose to fame as a negotiator, and became an American culture hero.

The whole affair abounds with a kind of mad logic. Though we shall deal with the question of Kissinger's morality in our next chapter, we can call attention here to his blocking of normal moral reaction to American deeds in Vietnam, as felt by opponents of the war, and point instead to his insistence that morality meant America's living up to its obligations, i.e., continued support of the war in Vietnam.

To this seemingly paradoxical definition of morality we can add a psychological paradox. It is that, in truth, Kissinger preferred his enemies to his allies. He admired Le Duc Tho and obviously disliked Thieu. He believed that, in fact, the North Vietnamese had been gulled in 1954 at Geneva. He felt that he could accept and understand their psychology, although he found them somewhat intractable. They were serious, dedicated people whom one could respect, whereas the South Vietnamese were corrupt and dependent. Yet destiny forced Kissinger into supporting the South Vietnamese and negotiating on their side. His feelings throughout the negotiations were undoubtedly curious and mixed, his identification with his opponent struggling against his own world view and his conception of America's national image and interest.

China

The model for Kissinger in the Vietnam settlement was Charles de Gaulle's withdrawal from Algeria. It may be that de Gaulle also gave Kissinger the hint that led him to seek an opening to Communist China. In 1965 Kissinger had analyzed the divergence of American and European interests. "The United States, with its global responsibilities, sees in Communist China an objective threat to its interests. De Gaulle, leading a country primarily concerned with European affairs, considers a Russia extending its power into the center of Europe as the principal danger. China, to him, is a distant country which could become useful in diverting Soviet energies."[17] What was needed was for Kissinger to realize that the use of China "in diverting Soviet energies" might serve American "global" interests as well as the more limited interests of Europe.

Prior to 1968, however, Kissinger showed little interest in and less knowledge of China. It figures almost nowhere in any of his writings or lectures. When he does mention China, it is in scarifying and stereotyped terms, as when in 1961 he wrote that "the prospect that China by 1975 might have the nuclear capability of the Soviet Union in 1960 is terrifying. Many of the notions of mutual deterrence may not apply with respect to a country which has shown so callous a disregard of human life."[18] In *Nuclear Weapons* he treated the Chinese and Russians as two identical faces of monolithic communism.[19] Though this view gradually changed, Kissinger was late to see the possibility of a Sino-Soviet rift.

It was Nixon, on the basis of all accounts, who moved faster in this area than Kissinger. A staunch anticommunist, a supporter of Nationalist China and the China lobby, Nixon, with his Pacific orientation, became aware by the late 1960s that his world of peace could hardly leave out the Chinese. His past record would defend him from the charge of being an appeaser or soft on communism, and Nixon, ever the pragmatist and opportunist, moved within a week of his inauguration to explore the possibility of a Chinese opening. He wrote a memo, asking Kissinger for a report on the possibilities.

Whatever Kissinger's earlier attitudes to China, he responded with his usual effectiveness. In Winston Lord he had a personal assistant with special interests in China, and there were excellently trained people on the National Security Council. It was Kissinger, however, who devised the tactics that moved the U.S. from 20 years of isolation to the first, secret meeting with Chou En-lai and Mao Tse-tung. It was a major diplomatic coup, marking a minor revolution in American foreign policy.

The strategy, however, was Nixon's. Kissinger was the ideal tool. As the President's special assistant, he could be sent to Peking and carry on discussions independent of the normal bureaucratic channels and the State Department. He could exercise his special negotiating talents; the highly personalized, secret, and lonely style was just what was called for by Nixon.

Kissinger began his relations with the Communist Chinese uninterested in them as such and concerned only with putting the screws on the Russians. The overture to China was part of the linkage: SALT with the Russians was to be used as pressure for a settlement in Vietnam, and now China might be brought in as counterweight threat to the Russians (and perhaps as pressure in Vietnam as well). The Chinese link, however, was not intended to threaten détente, and Kissinger and Nixon had to move carefully. They were aided in their efforts by the fact that China felt threatened by the Soviet Union and therefore was receptive to the idea of America as a counterweight to the Russians. America and China, it turned out, had common interests.

As Kissinger became more and more involved with the Chinese, he changed his views about their callousness and became enchanted with his new opponents. He was comfortable with them because they were stylized, yet tough and strong.

They were serious about power and politics, and yet one could joke with them. One of the first things Kissinger did, as he boned up on Chinese history and politics, was to ask the CIA for what the Kalbs call "a detailed biography of Chou," that is, a psychiatric profile.[20] When he met Chou, the two men got along famously: personalities and a clear idea of where power and interest lay all coincided. By the time Nixon entered the scene and made his famous trip to China, Kissinger seemed to be the key figure in the *rapprochement* with China, and Nixon had to keep assuring Chou that "it was really me," i.e., Nixon, who was to be credited. It speaks well for Nixon that, knowing Kissinger could negotiate and articulate America's Chinese policy best, he allowed him to monopolize most of the limelight. Kissinger, according to informed accounts, was less generous with his own aides.

China was, nevertheless, one of Kissinger's finest hours. He had negotiated with great style and finesse. Unlike the situation regarding Vietnam, Kissinger was not emotionally and personally involved. "You see," he told Fallaci, "approaching China was a difficult task from an intellectual point of view, but not emotionally difficult. Peace in Vietnam, on the other hand, has been an emotionally difficult task." (Note that earlier in the interview Kissinger had asserted, "I'm not one of those people that allow themselves to be swayed by their emotions. Emotions are of no use.")[21] Clearly Kissinger felt more comfortable with his enemies than with his friends; the Chinese (and the North Vietnamese), unlike the South Vietnamese, sat at the opposite side of the table rather than beside him. They could be negotiated with; one knew where one was in terms of the power game, and goodwill played no part.

We see the same pattern again and again in Kissinger's attitudes toward America's presumed allies. The Japanese, for example, were merely mercantile; Kissinger referred to them as "little Sony salesmen" and "small and petty bookkeepers" (what, one wonders, did he think of his father's position?).[22] For Kissinger, the Japanese were without any larger sense of purpose, and one could not play the power game with them. Further, they couldn't hold confidence (one thinks again of Kissinger's respect for credibility, and his reaction to the Pentagon Papers, which had just been published in the midst of his preparations for the China trip). All in all, Kissinger (like Nixon) had no respect for the Japanese.

Indians, in Kissinger's eyes, were pretentious, posturing in their pacifism. He disliked Indira Gandhi, and thought she and India were not serious about politics.[23] When the India-Pakistan war threatened to interfere with the opening to China, Kissinger's biases against India were such that he hardly needed Nixon's injunction to "tilt" toward Pakistan. Besides, for both Kissinger and Nixon the Pakistanis were "manly," whereas the Indians were feminine and generally passive.

We see, then, that Kissinger scorned America's presumed allies and fellow democracies, Japan and India (this was pre–1975 and Indira Gandhi's turn to authoritarianism), and admired her totalitarian enemies, North Vietnam, China, and Russia. Though Kissinger was shocked and annoyed by Russian negotiating tactics—they cheated you on nickel and dime issues, he said, thus unnecessarily eroding confidence in them—he recognized the strength and determination of the Soviet Union. Negotiating with them, he matched his own boorishness with theirs. With the Chinese Kissinger could employ a different style. Here it was a love affair, and one wooed one's opponent in courtly manner. The "secret swinger" could carry over his image from domestic dalliances to the international scene. Kissinger, in China, could become "superman."

The Middle East

After China, the scene of Kissinger's greatest diplomatic triumphs was the Middle East. Here, like a virtual superman, he seemed to be constantly flying through the air and saving one situation after another. Again, as with China, Kissinger had little prior knowledge of the area and its problems, and had written nothing on the subject. Before 1968 he had never been to an Arab country (though he had twice visited Israel).

Initially, Kissinger saw the Middle East as primarily and almost solely a problem in American-Soviet relations. Some observers feel he has shifted his viewpoint, and now sees the issue more as an intra-Middle East problem. However true this may be, the Soviet presence still colors all of Kissinger's reflections on the Middle East. Typically, he claims to see the Russian viewpoint and accepts their need for a stake in any settlement, but not their dominance in the area. With the Egyptian expulsion of the Soviets in 1972, and consequent developments in the Middle East, Kissinger could take pride in achieving one of his goals: the diminution of Soviet power there.

In terms of his linkage theory, of course, events in the Middle East were related to events elsewhere. One would have thought, therefore, that Kissinger's diplomatic approach would have been to emphasize linkage within the area, as well as outside. Yet, implicitly, his step-by-step diplomacy seems to separate issues rather than join them. This approach, he claimed, divided "the Middle East problem into individual and therefore manageable segments."[24] Thus, Kissinger opposed a Geneva meeting to deal with all of the problems at once, arguing that such a meeting would achieve nothing but inflammatory rhetoric and perhaps war. His own approach, he claimed, allowed for real negotiations, Kissinger's forte, with the linkages somehow known to Kissinger if not to the other parties in the disputes.[25]

Kissinger's negotiating stance in the Middle East has differed from that at SALT, Vietnam, and China. In those situations he was confronting acknowledged opponents. Here in the Middle East he could claim the role of honest broker, and others have accepted Kissinger's analogy and compared him to

Bismarck at the Congress of Berlin. Such a situation was optimal for Kissinger as negotiator, giving him the greatest scope for his varied abilities as we have described them. Perhaps his extended repertoire of roles in this case can be symbolized best by the widely published photo of him in Arab headdress.

The Middle East was also the most highly personalized of all political environments. Kissinger recognized this fact, deplored it in part, and then ultimately justified his own personalistic style. "The Middle East has a tendency to personalize issues. And therefore, in the Middle East, there has been a great tendency to throw me into the fray. At some point we have to turn it into more regular channels. On the other hand, I don't know if we could have moved so fast if it hadn't been for the personal participation."[26]

In fact, the Middle East negotiations came closest to duplicating the personalized nature of the Congress of Vienna. Kissinger's policy is viewed by most knowledgeable observers as not particularly new; it was simply that after 1973 the old policy could now be pursued effectively. But this is to oversimplify, and to ignore the fact that policy and persons are more closely intertwined in the Middle East than in most areas, and that emotions—the psychological factors so dear to Kissinger's heart —play a more obvious role there than elsewhere.

In negotiating with Arab and Israeli leaders, Kissinger changed his style frequently. He addressed himself differently to Sadat, Assad, Boumedienne, Faisal, and the Israelis, such as Meir and Rabin. But his central message—that the United States was dedicated to the preservation of Israel, but not its territorial conquests, and that it wished to help in bringing peace to the area as an honest broker (and, implicitly, thereby to avoid being dragged into war with the Soviet Union over a local conflict)—was unvaried. It took all of Kissinger's unique skills to tell each party what it wished to hear, in part, without ending up being deceitful and duplicitous.

Kissinger's relations with Sadat have really been the key personal encounter, the basis for his hopes of bringing a settlement to the area. Sadat was so eager to free himself from the Soviets that he was open to a deal with the least encouragement. In June 1972, however, Sadat's epochal expulsion of the Soviets from Egypt brought no response from Nixon, who did not wish to jeopardize the Jewish vote in the coming November election. To get things off dead center, Sadat opened a "limited" war in October 1973, the Yom Kippur War. It was a signal Kissinger could understand (although he had not recognized the signals of the war's approach ahead of time), and it paved the way for his meeting with Sadat in November.

The two men took to one another immediately. Kissinger had not been prepared for the man he met. Though he had surely read the psychological profile on Sadat beforehand, on its basis he had not anticipated the "changed" Sadat.[27] Most observers had misjudged Sadat, who had stood quietly in Nasser's shadow —and learned. When Nasser died, Sadat was seen as an interim figure, totally without talent, and shortly to be replaced. No one, it seems, recognized Sadat's abilities as a manipulator, or his exquisite sense of political power and timing. In some ways he was like Kissinger himself, a "follower" of a patron who then grew beyond all expectation as a leader.

At that first meeting, after a reported four to six hours of talk, Kissinger realized that Sadat was his man. Like Kissinger, Sadat was able to see the big picture, to take the long view. Both men also shared a common fascination with the exquisite diplomacy necessary to implement such a view. Their style was the same, with its attention to psychological nuances and its stress on the importance of emotions. Sadat, too, recognized a brother in Kissinger, and declared, "After two hours, I found I can trust this man. *We were lonely* [my italics] . . . both of us. And since that time . . . we worked together."[28] Not to understand the special relation of Kissinger and Sadat, I believe future history will show, is not to understand the extraordinary complicated maneuverings in the Middle East.

Something similar, though less deep and intimate, occurred in Kissinger's meeting with the Syrian strong man, Hafiz Assad. Again there was an initial session of about six hours. The two men engaged in a wide-ranging talk mostly about world history rather than the immediate problems. Assad showed great intellectual breadth, matched of course by Kissinger in a way probably not possible for any other American Secretary of State. At this point, apparently, Kissinger realized that Assad was also his man and that, in spite of the dismissal by Kissinger's advisers of Syria as impossibly radical and militant, Assad's support was obtainable and indispensable for a settlement in the Middle East.

Assad, however, had to bring his fellow officers along. In an extraordinary procedure he brought in his key cabinet men, one by one, and exposed them to Kissinger's person and message. Assad had Kissinger repeat what he had said earlier in order to convince them to share a common viewpoint. Kissinger was once again the teacher, as he had been at the International Seminar at Harvard, an experience now standing him in good stead.

Not all of Kissinger's personal encounters were as dramatic or effective as those with Sadat and Assad. With King Faisal of Saudi Arabia he had to listen to the standard anti-Communism-Zionism speech. As advised by Sadat, he made no effort to answer the diatribe, but quietly attempted to make his central points.[29] Kissinger seemed unaffected by Faisal's anti-Semitic remarks; as we have seen, he was prepared for this by his past experiences.

If relations with the likes of Faisal were cool and correct, those with the Israeli leaders were both more complicated and more changeable. Kissinger, after all, was a Jew who had been an anti-Zionist. After 1968, however, he had become a special assistant to the President on foreign affairs, and in 1973, American Secretary of State. At first he had made a special point of leaving the Middle East to Rogers, on the grounds that as a Jew his intervention would be suspect. Once he became

Secretary of State, however, Kissinger had no choice but to involve himself personally. The paradox is that, over the long haul, Kissinger won more acceptance and trust from the Arabs than from the Israelis.

Did the Israelis recognize too well the "court Jew"? Kissinger's relations with Golda Meir were warm and friendly. There was always much banter about Jewish mothers and cooking which seems genuinely affectionate. Gradually, however, the warmth and trust between Kissinger and the other Israeli leaders and public began to dissolve. Perhaps this was in the nature of things inevitable; Kissinger had to bring pressure on the Israelis for concessions, for he had little leverage on the Arabs. His view that he was working for the long-range interests of Israel in trying to negotiate piecemeal settlements, which traded territory for intangible prospects of friendlier Arab feelings and peace, did not convince the Israelis, to Kissinger's evident distress. With the replacement of Meir by Rabin, the mistrust continued to grow.

Did Kissinger's personal involvement, in spite of his disclaimers, play a significant role in the Middle East negotiations? Kissinger declared in 1974 that "I can't forget that it is my peculiar role in this negotiation to be the one party who is not . . . who does not have a personal stake in it and therefore if I'm going to make a contribution it must be in terms of the interests that unites these two sides."[30] Yet, as we know, Kissinger was of Jewish background. Did he really have no "personal stake" at any level of his being?

In the West Kissinger has been perceived, as we have noted, as a German, and hardly at all as a Jew (though, in fact, he had suffered one or two blatant anti-Semitic rebuffs in America, such as rejection at a "Christian" resort hotel, before becoming Nixon's special assistant). In the Middle East he was perceived differently. "Of course," one ambassador of an Arab country delightedly explained to me, "Kissinger is a semite, like us." The ambassador went on to explain how Kissinger understands the Arabs, and how he is unlike the rest of the Americans, who are cold and lacking in "personal" qualities. For the Arabs, also, Kissinger had the inestimable virtue of being able to negotiate with them and to force Israeli concessions without, presumably, being accused of anti-Semitism.

Had Kissinger, in fact, become more of a Jew in his later years? Was there a kind of "return of the repressed," a reversion to some of his earlier training? The evidence seems to suggest that, while Kissinger never returned to the orthodoxy of his youth, he did come to accept rather more fully his Jewish inheritance. Though many of Kissinger's acquaintances claim that he is still neither pro-Zionist nor emotionally involved as a Jew (and go so far as to say Kissinger gets more satisfaction from having Sadat embrace him than the Israelis applauding him), one close observer has reported that in the past few years Kissinger has made emotional statements about his Jewishness. The Kalbs report that, once he realized that Israel was a viable entity, Kissinger abandoned his anti-Zionism, and is today dedicated to preservation of the Israeli state.[31] As noted, at the Israeli monument for the Holocaust victims, Kissinger though quiet seemed profoundly moved.

Perhaps these are straws in the wind. At first, to please his parents Kissinger arranged in the early 1970s to have his children receive lessons in Hebrew and Jewish history. He opposed their being forced into any orthodoxy but wanted them to know about the historical origins of the rituals, to understand what it meant to be Jewish in the historical as well as the contemporary context, to be aware of the centrality of Israel in today's Jewish consciousness. Of special interest to us is that he wished them to have a feeling for the Holocaust, to know that they had lost many members of their own family in it. When his son David was Bar Mitzvahed (for the sake of his parents, again, Kissinger had insisted upon this in his divorce from his wife), Kissinger served as one of his three sponsors and renewed his own memory of the Hebrew phrases which he had once taught his brother.

Kraemer had said many years ago that Kissinger would come

to understand the historical currents that had overwhelmed his people. Although pursued in a circuitous and complex fashion, it should not come as a surprise that Kissinger might eventually return, and in a unique way, to his people (though not necessarily his religion) and to himself. Such a return, if one believes in its recurrence, is necessarily in terms of Kissinger's fully developed personality, as we have tried to see it, and in relation to his general policies.[32]

As a young man in the army, Kissinger started a conversation in a hayloft with his buddy, Antoun Mudarri, about Jews and Arabs. Mudarri was a Syrian—an Arab—but a Christian who had lived there with Muslims. Kissinger was then an anti-Zionist who advocated an intermixture of Jews and Palestinians in the area that would later become the Israeli state. Kissinger by conviction, and Mudarri by experience, were both agreed, therefore, on the rightness of an assimilationist position, and they talked on and on about "what can we do so as to live together as human beings."[33] As with the Germans, Kissinger was prepared to understand and enter into the viewpoint of the Arabs.

His discovery of the Israeli state as a fact, and the possible rediscovery of his own personal involvement with that fact, had necessarily to affect Kissinger's attitudes. But the effect could only be in terms of Kissinger's general world view and his stress on accommodation. He now had to add the Zionist and Jewish viewpoint to the Arab one and to balance the competing claims.

In the negotiations following the end of the Yom Kippur War, Kissinger declared, "There is justice on all sides." As the Kalbs report, "He spoke the Arabic words 'eli fat mat,' which means 'the past is dead'—and he quoted the Jewish sage Hillel, who had said, 'If I am not for myself, who is for me? But if I am for myself alone, who am I?' "[34] This is vintage Kissinger. In *World Restored* he had said, "For a 'right' is established by acquiescence, not by a claim, and a claim not generally accepted is merely the expression of an arbitrary will."[35]

Kissinger has stayed faithful to this view. He has realized that peace rests not only on a balance of power but of aspirations—the historical and psychological needs of a people— and that a stable international order must be one in which all countries are able to feel that their respective interests and desires can be accommodated.[36] As is obvious, it is a viewpoint that allows Kissinger, unlike John Foster Dulles, who refused even to shake Chou En-lai's hand, to negotiate with anyone. It is a stance which, though often honored only as an ideal, potentially allows Kissinger to participate in efforts which aim not only at preserving the status quo, but increasingly seek to bring the third world and the underdeveloped nations into a cooperative endeavor (thus meeting the objections of many of his critics).[37]

In practice, Kissinger has trimmed and tacked, often appearing rather devious in the process. To the Arabs he has said that Israel is part of America's national interest, not a matter of mere "goodwill" on our part, and thus a subject of our strongest support and commitment. To the Israelis he has sometimes said that America's support is weak and changeable, thus intimating that it is dependent on Kissinger's power and existence in office. In America he has worked hard to manipulate the Jewish community, seeing the presidents of various Jewish organizations every month. Thus, he has seemed to be all things to all men, partly as a consequence of his strongly held view that there is "justice on all sides." The intellectual position is highly defensible; the practical application is fraught with danger.

Some of the dangers came to the fore in Kissinger's handling of the Yom Kippur War. Like everyone else, he did not anticipate it. He refused to believe the Arabs would be so foolish as to start a losing battle. Convinced that true stability for Israel could only come from a negotiated, not a dictated, settlement, at first he feared another 1967. When he realized that, because of Israel's reluctance to take preemptive action, she was unexpectedly suffering reverses on the battlefield, he was not at all dismayed. Rather, he wished an initial Israeli setback so as to restore the Arabs' psychological position and thus prepare the way for true and equal negotiation. Timing and finesse were of the essence, and Kissinger's tightrope perform- ance has been the subject of competing explanations and in- terpretations. His own, given through the Kalbs, is that Kissinger rescued the Israelis in the nick of time by organizing a resupply of arms opposed by Schlesinger and the Defense Department. Other accounts suggest more persuasively that Kissinger delib- erately withheld the arms resupply until the last safe moment (and almost beyond), and then stepped in to prevent the Israelis from going further when they brilliantly and precariously recovered the initiative against Egypt.[38] Whatever the precise truth, one result was that Kissinger emerged as a prestidigator who had, however, lost much Israeli and American belief in him as anything other than untrustworthy and duplicitous. As Anthony Lewis remarked, "Mr. Kissinger's style is catching up with him. The oversell, the personal dramas, the Hairbreadth Harry escapes, the insistence that disaster will strike if he is not allowed to play the game by his own secret rules—it is all becoming too familiar to too many people."[39]

The other result disclosed by the Yom Kippur War was that Kissinger had effectively superseded Nixon in the forma- tion of American foreign policy. The Egyptian-Syrian attack on Israel began on October 6, 1973, exactly two weeks after Kissinger had become Secretary of State. On October 10 the Nixon administration was rocked by the resignation of Vice President Spiro Agnew. On October 20 the "Saturday Night Massacre" took place. Late on October 24, Kissinger, consulting Nixon only in the most pro forma way, if that, replied to Russian moves in Egypt by ordering a military alert.

The threat of force—a basic element in Kissinger's diplomacy, as we have seen—worked, just as the Egyptian use of force in starting the war seems to have unfrozen the Middle East stalemate, as Kissinger had wanted. The military alert also showed that Kissinger had become the President for foreign affairs and that domestic and international affairs were far more intertwined than he wished to admit. Indeed, in the eyes of many critics, the alert was first perceived as a ploy to exculpate the Nixon administration from the Watergate debacle. Though such was not the intention, it seems that the effect of the domestic development on international affairs was, nonetheless, great.

As we know, the alert did not save the Nixon administration. The administration fell, but Kissinger—a greater survivor even than Nixon—remained. He stayed on as Ford's Secretary of State, with Ford, a neophyte in foreign affairs, even more in need of him than Nixon. In the beginning some wondered if the moralistic Ford would accept the presumably amoral, or immoral, Kissinger. Such critics neither knew the real Ford nor remembered that he had been a guest lecturer in Kissinger's Seminars on a number of occasions in the 1950s. Nor did they understand how adroit Kissinger was at adapting to the personal needs and style of his new President. The result, as John Hersey has reported, at least until the upheaval following the resignation of Secretary of Defense James Schlesinger, was a special one-to-one relation to Ford, the glaring exception to Ford's canvassing of views on other issues.[40] The talents that served Kissinger here were the same ones he employed in his Middle East negotiations.

Economic Issues: The Broader World

The Middle East War unexpectedly also changed the terms of the foreign policy equations, its repercussions going far beyond the immediate geographical area of Israel and the Arab countries. The oil embargo was the vehicle for this change, in some ways having the same revolutionary effect on the international arena as had the atomic bomb. Now economics became as important a part of political decisions as the military factor Kissinger had learned to value from Clausewitz.

Kissinger at first was neither trained in economics nor sympathetic to its possible role in international affairs. We recall the scorn he poured on "economic panaceas" in his B.A. thesis, as testifying "to the emptiness of a soul to which necessity is an objective state."[41] Dean Acheson, mentioning the Congress of Vienna, is aware that "it permitted a century of international peace and of greater technology and economic development than in the whole period since the invention of the sail and wheel."[42] In *World Restored*, Kissinger has much to say about the stability of the international order resulting from the negotiations of 1815–1822 but not a word about the economic consequences. For a once-to-be bookkeeper (whose brother was a businessman), he has shown a surprising lack of interest in the world of commerce and technological change. But then, these were "mercantile" subjects which he seigneurially despised, at least at first.

Kissinger's critics have been quick to point out his deficiencies in this matter. As one critic succinctly put it, "He approaches economics with all the enthusiasm of a man making his twice-yearly visit to the dentist. 'I know I must go, but I wouldn't like it.' "[43]

When Kissinger did intervene in economic matters, he seemed to falter badly. On the wheat deal with the Soviet Union, even the Kalbs have to say that, though "Kissinger liked to consider himself a tough, unsentimental negotiator . . . these qualities were not reflected in the deal he negotiated with Brezhnev in Moscow . . . the American consumer, and the entire American economy, suffered because neither Nixon nor Kissinger appreciated the economic ramifications of the deal."[44] In first trying to deal with the oil problem, Kissinger exhibited his usual style of diplomacy. European diplomats resented, as one account puts it, "that Kissinger once more has figured out a proposal in the seclusion of his own tightly closed circle, and has tried to railroad his partners into acceptance by giving it his own big advance public relations buildup." A senior OPEC official is reported to have observed that Kissinger's views were "designed to serve only the interests of one side. A dialogue should solve problems, not create new ones."[45]

What Kissinger's numerous critics in this matter were saying was that he personalized economic issues when the very nature of the problems called for impersonal solutions. I believe this accurately describes Kissinger's early behavior vis-à-vis economic problems. It does not allow, however, for his capacity to change (though in this case the change was slow). While most of Kissinger's critics dismiss his present views on the economic factor as rhetoric, I am prepared to believe him, and for reasons that are rooted in his own personality, world views and policies.

Intellectually and personally, Kissinger was committed until very recently to the view that the interplay of human beings alone had importance, and that this was independent of social science-type analysis. But under the impact of his experiences in operating within the State Department and its complexities, added to his own capacity for intellectual growth, I believe that Kissinger has changed, and now recognizes the importance of the economic factor. He is now prepared to view the international arena as one not solely occupied by states operating as homogeneous factors, but as filled with economic, social, and technological problems transcending specific territorial units.

Thus, in his talks of May 1975 before ministerial meetings of the International Energy Agency and the Organization for Economic Cooperation and Development, Kissinger alluded to "The new problems of our era—insuring adequate supplies of food, energy, and raw materials—[which] require a world economy that accommodates the interests of developing as well as developed countries." I believe he was speaking of himself, as much as the current international scene, when he went on in classic Kissingerian philosophical tones, "Goethe said that 'the web of this world is woven of necessity and change.' We stand at a point where those strands intertwine. We must not regard necessity as capricious nor leave change to chance. Necessity impels us to where we are but summons us to choose where we go."[46]

I believe Kissinger's shift is real for a number of reasons. First, he is aware of the attacks on him by his critics, and has been cleverly moving to cut the ground from under his attackers. Second, Kissinger has himself become aware, as he remarked, that "economic issues are turning into central political issues."[47] Once he realized that, as one scholar puts it, "politics has never been about resources alone or even primarily, but about the accommodation of different values and different institutions for the production and use of resources,"[48] he was back in his element. At this point, my third reason enters. Kissinger, as we have seen, truly believed that a stable international order depended on the accommodation of divergent historical and psychological aspirations. What was latent in Kissinger's world view only needed to be provoked by necessity to emerge into a new choice.

To say all this is not, of course, to say that the change was easy, or complete, or that it supplanted his central commitment to personalism. Nevertheless, it was an effort that testifies to Kissinger's continuing capacity for change and growth.

It was a capacity missing in the man Kissinger first served, Richard Nixon. With Ford, of course, Kissinger entered into a new situation. Ford, before becoming an accidental President, had no knowledge of, and had evinced no earlier interest in, foreign affairs; he had not encountered the great leaders of the world and did not approach the international arena as one such strong personality himself. His forte was domestic politics, with the give and take of economic and social issues fought out in

Congress. Thus, conceptually and temperamentally, he was more sympathetic to Kissinger's taking an interest in such problems in the world at large. Given such vague and general encouragement, Kissinger could move more readily toward a greater concern with impersonal problems.

What, in fact, Kissinger's policies, successes, and failures will be in this larger context of international affairs has not yet been revealed. Of necessity, unlike his personal triumphs, the economic is a long, colorless process, the results of which only unfold over the long sweep of time (a time that may not be available to Kissinger).

Beyond Nixon and Ford

Kissinger served as Nixon's special assistant and then Secretary of State for five years. It was a long period in which the two men, together, would leave their mark on America's foreign policies. When Watergate surfaced and began to grow like a cancer on the Nixon presidency, Kissinger tried to treat it as a mere domestic issue, unrelated to foreign affairs, and important only as it undermined the authority of the President. The cancer, as we know, eventually touched Kissinger, and the disclosure of his role in the wiretapping, coming on the heels of knowledge about his connivance in the secret invasion of Cambodia, the mining of Haiphong, and the bombing of Hanoi, began gradually to destroy his superman image. Or rather it disclosed a superman with features unpleasantly reminiscent of Germans in the 1930 and 1940s, rather than Clark Kent, the all-American boy. The fact that Kissinger could survive the disclosures and, indeed, retain much of his popularity with the American public, though not the media, testifies to his durability and resiliency, his exquisite ability to survive.

When Watergate finally toppled Nixon, Kissinger regarded

it as a "human tragedy." He appealed for "compassion" and argued against an "orgy of recrimination,"[49] the exact terms he would use later, in 1975, to defend his own policies in trying to maintain South Vietnam in the face of the North Vietnam takeover. Kissinger seemed not really to exhibit any sensitivity to the profound political and moral issues involved in the Watergate affair. It was another instance of his disinterest in and lack of comprehension of domestic affairs.

At first Watergate made Kissinger the strongest figure in the Nixon administration, and thus the recipient of most of the credit for American foreign policy achievements. As Watergate ran its course, Kissinger, as we have seen, survived, but as a tainted figure. It is an irony of history that Ford, succeeding Nixon, has changed the image and style (although even that only in part), but not the policy, of the Nixon administration, thus reaffirming the "conservative" direction of American affairs, both domestic and foreign, as if Watergate had never taken place. Angola, and the Kissinger-Ford policy toward that troubled area, demonstrates this fact dramatically. By retaining Kissinger, and indeed strengthening him, Ford underlined the continuity of American foreign policy. It is the intellectual and conservative Kissinger, therefore, in power for at least eight years, and under two Presidents, who will be mainly identified with the "revolution" in American foreign policy of the late 1960s and early and mid-1970s. It is his personality, his style, and his world view that will color and permeate all future accounts of the policies America has pursued in the international arena during this time.

Chapter 12

POWER: TO WHAT END?

Power

By WHAT STANDARDS are we to evaluate Henry Kissinger? Should we regard him in his own terms, as a statesman, possessed of a superior world view, gifted with historical and psychological understanding of the meaning of foreign affairs, and courageously pursuing the goal of international stability? Or as a power-seeking individual, displacing his personal needs, the drama of his own inner life, onto the stage of world affairs? (And we recall his vision of history as the revelation of personality.)

In this book our response to such questions has been to fuse into one perception the various elements of Kissinger's life and work: his personality, world view, and policies. One major factor, however, has still not been given its due attention: the nature of the political arena in which any political figure must function—or, to put it another way, the nature of power, which the statesman seeks to gain and wield. Before we can come to conclusions about the character and worth of Henry Kissinger's achievements, we need greater insight into the meaning of power itself.

Power is, in fact, the central concept of political science. Thus, a typical definition of international politics is that, "like all politics, [it] is a struggle for power. Whatever the ultimate aims of international politics, power is always the immediate aim." As Hans Morgenthau continues, "The aspiration for power being the distinguishing element of international politics, as of all politics, international politics is of necessity power politics." The drive, or desire, to "dominate" is held to be "common to all men."[1]

Power equals domination. Is this what really drives Henry Kissinger and lies at the heart of his policies? For Morgenthau, power means "men's control over the minds and actions of other men." It is a "psychological relation between those who exercise it and those over whom it is exercised."[2] If physical violence is required, then military power usurps the role of political power; nevertheless, the *threat* of force is a key element of political power.

Bertrand de Jouvenal has dedicated a long and complicated book to the subject. He, too, announces that "power changes its appearances but not its reality. Politics are about power. . . ."[3] The extraordinary thing, as the eighteenth-century French statesman Necker pointed out, is that people do in fact obey. All politics turns on obedience; as Jouvenal proclaims, "Who knows the reasons for that obedience knows the inner nature of power."[4] The rest of his book explores the way power is related to fear, magic, partnership, force, habit, and so forth.

Such pronouncements as those quoted above are interesting, but ultimately vague, and thus unconvincing (even though the books that contain them are valid studies). They do not persuade us that we have learned very much. There is an imprecision about the concept of power that calls into question the whole scientific aspect of political science. Though power stands at the heart of political science, as value does in economic science, it does not allow us to manipulate the data and formulate other, related theories in the way Adam Smith and his successors have done in political economy.

One can measure value in monetary terms. How can one measure power? Values can be exchanged in a marketplace.

How can we measure the exchanges of power in a *polis* (for politics cannot exist, in the terms we are discussing, without the equivalent of a marketplace; international politics can only exist among political bodies)?

In economics, the actions of single individuals, no matter how powerful, are of little major consequence, for all are constrained by the market which exerts its pressures immediately on the individual; a J. P. Morgan, or even a General Motors, can exert only a minor perturbation in economics. Thus, the field is a fairly measurable and predictable one. In politics, on the other hand, an individual can, so to speak, change the whole system. A Napoleon or a Lenin simply dominates the scene, and we even talk of the Napoleonic period (who would speak of the Henry Ford period?).

The result is that any "science" of politics is made difficult, if not impossible. Thus politics, devoid of a measurable, calculable, and predictable meaning for its central concept of power, becomes largely a historical, psychological, and cultural study, rather than behavioral or scientific. In this sense, then, Kissinger was right in his approach to international affairs.

The anguishing thing about political science, therefore, is that there is so little real science to it. Mainly about power and power struggles, both internal and external, the struggle is amenable to descriptive approaches, to historical and psychological insight. Unlike history per se, however, political science is not primarily interested in conveying humanistic understanding or the historical context for the comprehension of human motives. Rather it seeks to offer guidance for action and advice on policies. The tragedy, and here again one must agree with Kissinger, is that little real advice is possible except perhaps for the very short-run problem, and that advice, in any case, is certainly not "scientific."

Historically, the effort at a political science came at about the same time as the emergence of an international system of nation-states, or of dynastic entities having some of the nation-state properties. It is closely connected with the scientific aspirations of the sixteenth and seventeenth centuries, which enjoyed such successful fulfillment in relation to the natural world. Machiavelli, for example, seeking to open a "new route," was one of the first to attempt to look at political material from a secular, scientific perspective.[5] In international relations, such thinkers as Grotius and Vattel sought to ground their work in natural law, which had now taken on the refracted tints of natural science. Thus, in the treaties influenced by their thinking, we find such phrases as were used by the Spanish king in renouncing any claims to the French crown: "It being to be believed, that by this perpetual and neverceasing Hope, the *Needle of the Ballance* may remain *invariable*, and all the Powers, wearied with the Toil and *Uncertainty* of Battles, may be amicably kept in an equal Poise; it not remaining in the Disposal of any of the Partys to alter this federal *Equilibrium* . . ." [my italics].[6]

Here, of course, we have the famous balance of power theory, with its assumption that power relations can be *calculated*, and thus studied scientifically. With the loss of faith in Christian morals as the force constraining the desire to dominate, the seventeenth century sought to replace it with magnetic or gravitational force, the *Needle of the Ballance*. It was an ambitious effort but, as we know, it failed, both in keeping anything more than an intermittent peace and in establishing a political *science*.

We are left, then, mainly with metaphors and vague notions about a mysterious entity called "power." And this conceptual deficiency persists at a time when the power of states has increased "immeasurably," internally and externally—and when the nuclear bomb has given leaders, and perhaps peoples, the power to destroy the world. In short, intellectually, we seem powerless to control power, because we have no scientific understanding of it. At best, there may be only some kind of practical art of politics available to deal with our situation.

Kissinger in Power

Kissinger has recognized aspects of this problem. "The nature of power has never been easy to assess," he tells us, and "even if the classic principles of strategy [i.e., balance of power politics] are not entirely outmoded, the statesman will inevitably be reluctant to put them to the test." With the coming of nuclear weapons, Kissinger recognized the paradox that "power has never been greater; it has also never been less useful."[7]

In his writings on nuclear weapons, however, Kissinger sought to derive the possibility of a new, rational calculation of power relations from the paradox. One could, potentially, measure megatons, and thus the actual power of the great powers, even though it was a power that negates itself. Here might be a true balance of power. Kissinger spells out one implication of such mutual balance: "As for the vulnerable side, where under conditions of mutual vulnerability it would win by striking first, this action can now only guarantee mutual suicide. The vulnerable country will have no motive whatever for surprise attack and a greatly reduced incentive for a pre-emptive strike —for *no reasonable purpose* [my italics] will be served by it. As a result, the credibility of its threat of all-out war is likely to diminish to the vanishing point."[8]

However, mutual deterrence requires as one of its conditions that "the opponent must be rational, i.e., he must respond to his self-interest in a manner which is predictable."[9] But this is exactly why politics is not a science, for its actors do not always (or even generally) behave in a purely rational, predictable fashion. History is the scene of the irrational not the rational. Moreover, as Kissinger himself recognizes, the threat, if not the reality, of irrational or mad behavior becomes a means of tilting the power balance in one's own favor. Thus, the ultimate paradox is that "rational calculation is likely to produce irrational behavior on both sides."[10] Is it any wonder that, intellectually as well as personally, Kissinger took a tragic attitude to history and politics?

Kissinger's dilemma, the feeling of powerlessness, is shared by many of his contemporaries, though in varying form. The theme of alienation, of being under the sway of forces out of our control, even though created by us, is a central theme of our time. The slogan, "Power to the People," is a reflection of this feeling, though on a parochial level that nowhere touches on the central issues of international politics.

The trouble with power is that, unlike value, it seems always to exist at someone else's expense. Economics quickly moved past its mercantile phase, with its balance-of-trade belief that one nation's gain was another nation's loss, and by the end of the eighteenth century realized that the expansion of production, through labor, held the possibility of gain for all. In practice, it is true, the reality has often been one of exploitation; nevertheless, the rising standard of living in much of the world testifies to the theoretical practicability of the ideal.[11]

In politics, as conceived in political science as we have described it, the ideal itself seems to be power, i.e., domination over others. The field has not been able to move beyond the mercantile conception.[12] Kissinger clearly accepts the world of power as a given, and seeks to work within its historical terms. Thus, intellectually he is wedded to the pursuit of power in a world of power relations.

Kissinger's "Power Drive"

What about Kissinger's personal relations to power? Most observers see him grasping at it, and some view him as seeking power for power's sake. His enemies would describe him as power hungry. Even his friends admit to his desire for power. As one top official exclaimed, "Henry adores power, absolutely adores it."[13]

Kissinger's own view is that "power as an instrument in its own right has no fascination for me. . . . What interests me is what one can achieve with power. Splendid things, believe me. . . ." To the question of why he chose to accept Nixon's offer, he responded, "It is not the craving for power that spurred me on to take this job," and cited his initial antipathetic remarks on the President as proof that "Nixon was not included in my plans for a rise to power."[14]

It is clear that this is Kissinger's preferred self-image. Was he unconsciously aware of another part of himself when, talking about the reasons why anyone in Russia would be willing to enter the atmosphere of suspicion surrounding the Communist leadership groups, he said, "Only an enormous desire for power can impel a man to enter such a career. Anyone succeeding in Communist leadership struggles must be single-minded, unemotional, unsentimental and dedicated."[15] While, obviously, the penalties for failure in Communist leadership struggles are greater than in equivalent contests in the U.S., the adjectives Kissinger uses would apply equally to himself. For example, as Kissinger had told Fallaci, "I'm not one of those people that allow themselves to be swayed by their emotions."[16] So, too, as we have seen, he was certainly single-minded and dedicated. Equipped by character for the struggle, did Kissinger also realize at some level that he had an "enormous desire for power"?

It would be naive for us to think that Kissinger did not have such a drive—or that most people who enter the political field are not equally driven. What is interesting about politics *is* power, and power-interested individuals. One of Kissinger's remarks is apropos here: "You know," he said during one of his shuttle flights, "most of these world leaders, you wouldn't want to know socially. Mostly they are intellectual mediocrities. The thing that is interesting about them is . . . *their power*" [my italics].

Kissinger, of course, is an intellectual who has also sought power. Part of his fascination lies exactly in his posing for us the intellectual-activist dilemma. How to participate in power without giving up one's intellectual convictions? How to accept the necessity to compromise and make hard choices in the real world without becoming a mere opportunist or losing one's soul?

From a fairly early age, Kissinger had had power of sorts thrust upon him. In the military, at age 22, he had administrative power over a district in Germany; at Harvard, age 28, he was in charge of the International Seminar. Such power may have been largely unsought, at least consciously. Kissinger's later career, however, suggests an unerring and tenacious "desire for power," manifested strongly from the time of his connection with the Council on Foreign Relations.

But not all power seeking is the same. Purposes may differ; as Kissinger said, it is a question of "what one can achieve with power." So, too, may motives, the personal reason so closely aligned with seemingly impersonal purpose. In my view, Kissinger's primary motive for seeking power was less to dominate others than to seek to prevent them from dominating him. It was a defensive "drive" (if one can so put it). Such an explanation dovetails with Kissinger's characteristic habit of identifying with his opponent. As we noted earlier, Kissinger was already aware in his B.A. thesis that such identification increases the individual's "power over himself . . . and over the environment."[17] In identifying with one's enemy, one also identifies with his power and thereby prevents its misapplication to oneself.

In part, this is the same mechanism we all experience in identifying with an entity more powerful than ourselves. Thus, if America is powerful, her individual citizens feel powerful, and if America is humiliated, that is, made to lose face as a power (for example, in Vietnam), then individual Americans feel impotent. Kissinger, as we know, also identified with a powerful America, as well as with erstwhile enemies. It is only in the latter respect that he differs from most of his fellow Americans.

Kissinger's desired purpose for the power he secured, partly by grasping it directly and partly by the identification mechanism we have just described, was to help establish or secure a world of stability and order. One can see immediately the difference from, say, a Stalin or a Hitler and their uses of power. Thus, Kissinger is not only intellectually but also psychologically a conservative, who wants power not to *do* something so much as to prevent *others* from doing something unstabilizing to him.

Aggressive and Libidinal Drives

In analyzing the personal power drive, political scientists have tended to follow the pioneering work of Harold Lasswell as he sought to explore the uses of psychoanalysis. Lasswell took as his inspiration the compensatory theories of Alfred Adler, rather than the theories of Freud per se. Adler had written about an inferiority complex and how an individual overcompensates for it. Lasswell worked this theory into one which asserted that political man displaced private motives onto a public object. The prime motive was that of low self-esteem, and political man compensated by seeking and exercising political power.[18] It was more or less this theory that the Georges employed in their fine study of Woodrow Wilson and Colonel House.[19]

If we were to look at Kissinger in these terms, we could make a case for his low self-esteem and his compensation in the exercise of power. The insecure, shy young German-Jewish refugee has obviously taken on the confidence of his rise to power. His policies, according to this theory, can be viewed as mere rationalizations of his personal needs.

As can readily be seen, any such interpretation relies on an analysis of aggressive impulses, which fit readily with an almost compulsive drive to power. Nowhere is there a mention of the libidinal impulses, which sit at the heart of Freud's work. In the entire course of the Georges' work there is no mention of sex. Aside from being prudential, the political scientist's use of Adler, who questioned the whole emphasis on sex in Freudian theory, clearly is functional, focusing as it does on the central concept of politics: power.

Kissinger has indirectly supported this procedure in his oft-repeated aphorism that "power is the ultimate aphrodisiac." It suggests, correctly, I believe, that power is of more concern to Kissinger than sex. Or, rather, that sexual relations are seen more in terms of conquest and domination than of pure libidinal desire. Here, Kissinger could appeal to a long tradition, embodied in the heroes of Laclos and Stendhal, which sees aggression at the heart of sex as much as of battle; indeed, we have the battle of the sexes. Kissinger, as a male chauvinist for whom women are a mere "hobby" or "pastime," as he confessed, would readily fit into this tradition.

For whom, however, is power the aphrodisiac? Obviously, Kissinger meant that because of his power women were sexually attracted to him. But one may also suggest that the aphrodisiacal aspect of power operates not only upon the opposite sex but upon one's self, in the form of self-love, or narcissism. Such self-love, often approaching megalomania, allows the political leader to exist without the immediate love or approbation of individual others (he still needs the love and esteem of the many, or of history, or posterity).[20]

Applying this theory to Kissinger, we can now see one of the sources of his unsentimentality. He could make his decisions without worrying about whether he would lose the love or even the services of his aides. Instead, he accepted the resignation of his closest assistants without sentiment. Such an analysis also fits with the notion that Kissinger was more comfortable in dealing with enemies than friends. With enemies he was dealing with power, and defending against its misuse. With friends, neither love nor power figured prominently.

Some combination of aggressive and libidinal drive analyses seems called for in the effort to understand political power. To speak merely of a "drive to dominate," as most political scientists do in talking of power, is to leave the matter asserted but unanalyzed. In the case of Kissinger, for example, his fascination with and drive to power is actually compounded of many motives: fear, need for defense, compensation, repressed and displaced sexuality, intellectual conviction, and other desires. Among these last is his own claim that, with power, he can do "splendid things."

The Moral Uses of Power

What are Kissinger's public purposes, as separate from his private desires, in his use of political power? To what public ends does he wish to use his position? One single and overwhelming answer emerges: to preserve a stable international order. For Kissinger, this preservation is also identified with America's national interest, which happily coincides with the good of mankind, now threatened with extinction. Thus, for Kissinger the highest public moral end is to serve this purpose, as he construes it (and we have already studied some of his particular policies).

Kissinger, however, has often been accused of having no higher goal than the achievement and preservation of power—especially his own—and of being either amoral or immoral. In short, it is said that he has no moral purposes, or, put another way, that his purposes are not moral, but purely pragmatic and power oriented.

Kissinger himself is very sensitive on this issue. During the pre-Christmas 1972 negotiations on Vietnam, Kissinger complained that his critics acted as if they had a "monopoly of anguish and a monopoly of moral sensibility. I don't say that somebody who disagrees with us is immoral, wrong, a traitor, or any of the things they tend to call their opponents. . . . No matter how unhappy we were with Dulles, for example, we didn't really think he was out of our moral framework."[21] Speaking to students during the events of 1970, Kissinger is reported to have said, "I think I know what concerns you all, it was not that long ago that I was a professor. I know that it is the morality that bothers you. I think I am sensitive to that."

One of Kissinger's critics, who knew him well, preferred to put it another way. What Kissinger is basically concerned with is not morality but honor. In this interpretation, Kissinger is concerned only with what other people think of him, which determines his own view of himself, i.e., in the terms of this book, self-esteem. He wishes to be seen as honorable and, in fact, does not like using the term "morality" at all. Honor, of course, is an aristocratic notion, and would fit with Kissinger's admiration for "seigneurial" men. Morality, we can suspect, is too close to mere goodwill, as we shall see.

In any case, Kissinger did threaten to resign at Salzburg unless his "public honor" was vindicated, thus giving support to the interpretation above. The word "honor," but not "morality," resounds through his news conference: "This is a question of my honor," he reiterated. The only indirect reference to moral purpose is when Kissinger rather passionately declared: "I have been generally identified, or it is alleged that I am supposed to be interested primarily in the balance of power. I would rather like to think that when the record is written, one may remember that perhaps some lives were saved and that perhaps some mothers can rest more at ease, but I leave that to history."[22]

If more concerned with his immediate personal honor, Kissinger did exhibit an awareness that a deep moral sense existed in America. In fact, he insisted on American moral superiority, say, to the Russians. But such morality was to be kept within bounds, and not allowed to eventuate in the moral idealism that had so blighted American foreign policy. In his speech to *Pacem In Terris III* in October 1973, Kissinger said,

"America cannot be true to itself without moral purpose. This country has always had a sense of mission." But then he hastened to add, "But when policy becomes excessively moralistic it may turn quixotic or dangerous. A presumed monopoly on truth obstructs negotiation and accommodation. Good results may be given up in the quest for ever elusive ideal solutions."[23] In shorter terms, Kissinger could have said, "The road to hell is paved with good intentions."

Kissinger was aware that, as a practical matter, the United States had to believe in itself and its moral goodness. Indeed, as we noted earlier in Chapter 5, George Cabot Lodge reported him as preoccupied with the need to revitalize America morally. America, Kissinger insisted, must act out of firm conviction in its own purposes, and not suffer loss of faith which leads to "a policy of the guilty conscience."[24] This was one reason why Kissinger was so disturbed by the student demonstrators, who seemed to believe that power, *any* power, was inherently immoral. Such a view left one with only goodwill, and Kissinger knew the dangers of that position from personal experience as well as intellectual conviction. As he told the French reporter, Danielle Hunebelle, "When you know history, how many tragedies have been touched off by men of goodwill, you have to admit the tragic elements of existence. And that's hard for an American. . . ."[25]

Kissinger, as more than an American, could accept the tragic necessity of having to *act*, and to act in a seeming amoral or immoral way in order to achieve a higher historical morality: the preservation of stability and order through the use of power. Intellectually, he defended his policy on many grounds, but the major form it took in foreign policy debates was the realism versus idealism argument. Thus, he linked his personal views directly with the mainstream of American foreign policy speculations.

In practice, did Kissinger's distrust of goodwill, which he seems to identify as the primary constituent of morality, actually lead him to immoral actions? To an identification with his enemies' definitions of morality, i.e., to immorality? These are exceptionally difficult questions with which to grapple, for if the concept of power is amorphous, that of morality is even more so.

A glance at another realist may help us pursue the question. George F. Kennan is a brilliant philosophical student of foreign policy, as well as a seasoned practitioner of diplomacy. Long before Kissinger, he, too, attacked moral idealism, and called for a more realistic American foreign policy. Yet Kennan could still quiver in moral indignation when he contemplated the American military occupation of Germany after World War II:

I had been twice in Germany since the termination of hostilities. Each time I had come away with a sense of sheer horror at the spectacle of this horde of my compatriots and their dependents camping in luxury amid the ruins of a shattered national community, ignorant of the past, oblivious to the abundant evidences of present tragedy all around them, inhabiting the very same sequestered villas that the Gestapo and SS had just abandoned, and enjoying the same privileges, flaunting their silly supermarket luxuries in the face of a veritable ocean of deprivation, hunger, and wretchedness, setting an example of empty materialism and cultural poverty before a people desperately in need of intellectual and spiritual guidance, taking for granted— as though it were their natural due—a disparity in privilege and comfort between themselves and their German neighbors no smaller than those that had once divided lord and peasant in that feudal Germany which it had been our declared purpose in two world wars to destroy.[26]

Ought one to compare this reaction with Kissinger's behavior in Germany in 1945? Having forgiven the "bad" Germans, had he taken on in part their mentality? Should one compare it with Kissinger's disregard of the similar American presence in South Vietnam?

So, too, ought one to compare the hardheaded Kennan's horror at the spectacle of bombed-out Hamburg and his question as to the rightness of the bombing, with Kissinger's attitude to, say, the Christmas bombing of Hanoi?[27] Such questions seem to point to a certain moral insensitivity in Kissinger, as if somehow he had overcompensated for his feelings of defenselessness when protected only by goodwill and not power.

Lord Acton had said, "Power tends to corrupt; absolute power corrupts absolutely." Kissinger, of course, never had absolute power. But what limits were there on the power he did have? Was he corrupted by it, in the sense of becoming absorbed only in its uses, and not its moral purposes? What are the limits, if any, to power? Kissinger's response has been a stress on the personal sense of limits, the conservative's necessity of self-restraint. Kissinger has expressed little sympathy for the democratic emphasis on accountability and the checks and balances written into the Constitution, which only hamper foreign policy formation and action. Thus, he has behaved in a fashion that allows a critic, such as Anthony Lewis, to say, "More than any past Secretary of State, he has maneuvered and tricked and distorted the law to get around what he knew was the will of Congress and the nation. He sent most of our food aid to Saigon; he juggled funds; he even asked his lawyers to see whether the War Powers Act, restricting Presidential war-making, might allow him to bomb Vietnam despite a flat legislative ban on bombing."[28]

If one follows this line of interpretation, Kissinger seems, in fact, to have been corrupted to a certain extent by his fascination with power. It is a paradoxical outcome to his desire to make goodwill effective. We appear to be in the presence of the old means-end dilemma, of another variation on the intellectual-activist dilemma. Kissinger's defense would be to claim that his seemingly amoral or immoral actions are simply means in the service of a higher morality; that the necessity of present power is juxtaposed with faith in future goodness. He would appeal to the judgment of history. His critics answer that morality is a matter independent of ends, to be judged here and now, in its own right. For such critics, power is power and morality is morality; but, ideally, the twain should meet. Unfortunately, in the judgment of many observers, they have not done so in the person and policies of Henry Kissinger.

Position or Person

Still, the question remains: Is it mainly the position that compels its occupant to what, in an individual, appear to be amoral or immoral stances? After the Nazis and Nuremberg, we are less sympathetic than we might have been to the sloughing off of personal responsibility by an appeal to the necessities of bureaucratic function. Yet, even if this be granted, the role clearly affects the way an individual behaves, at least in part.

Some critics believe that only if structure is changed will policy become more moral. Others place their faith in a change of values, or restoration of the right ones. Richard Falk, for example, has offered a mix of these two approaches in his thoughtful consideration of historical and futuristic perspectives on international law and drastic global reform.[29] Obviously, structural and value changes are interrelated, playing a leap-frogging game of cause and effect.

The same is true of personality and policies. There is a correspondence between them. Different personalities generally mean different policies, and vice versa. Morality and moral actions are not something "out there." They are an inward movement, culminating in specific actions and policies. In this sense, the fact that it is *Kissinger* who is Secretary of State, and not someone else, does matter. Given his own view of history as the revelation of personality, Kissinger would be the first to agree with this statement, and all that follows from it.

Chapter 13

A "HERO'S" TRAGEDY

A Life and Work: Overview

HENRY KISSINGER is not only a two-sided but a multisided, complexly motivated individual. It is extremely difficult, therefore, to come to balanced conclusions about him. He himself would appeal to the judgment of history for a fair assessment. But the judgment of history, while clearly of longer range than the immediate view of contemporaries, is itself not a fixed decision. Rather it is an accumulation of changing views, starting from the contemporary, and necessarily having to take the contemporary into account; indeed, as soon as events are past, "contemporary" judgment is itself "historical." Thus, even though our perspective is relatively limited, we may not be excused from the particular historical judgment that is available to us, and to us alone.

Nevertheless, though acting initially as historians, we have also a special psychological interest in our subject. And from this perspective, judging, especially in the sense of condemning, is less important than understanding. Hence, our "judgments" and "conclusions" are intended primarily as heuristic ones, put forth in the service of further insight into the personality, views, and policies of this intriguing man and important statesman.

We have tried first to sketch the main features of his life and his rise to political power. Treating Kissinger as an unusual kind of Eriksonian hero, we have looked at his early years in Fürth, Germany, at the Kissinger family, the Orthodox Jewish community, and the gathering Nazi storm, and asked what effect they had on young Henry. Following the Kissinger family to America, we studied his efforts to assimilate to his new country, involving especially his experiences in World War II and the army, and then at Harvard. Marriage, graduate school, the Council on Foreign Relations: these, too, played their shaping roles. Kissinger's work for the Council and the publication of *Nuclear Weapons and Foreign Policy* made him a figure of some importance on the foreign policy scene and also established his lasting connection with Nelson Rockefeller.

All of these developments, especially the last, gave Kissinger not only power but a whole new life style as well. The new life style did not include his wife, and separation and divorce followed in the early 1960s. Freer than ever to devote himself to his career, Kissinger, after service to Presidents Kennedy and Johnson, became by an ironic turn of events Nixon's special assistant for foreign affairs and head of the National Security Council. Now he had become part of history, not merely a student of it. In his new roles Kissinger also became the superman and culture hero of America and the world.

Watergate pulled Nixon down, but left Kissinger still standing in the debris. Appointed Secretary of State in the waning days of the Nixon administration, Kissinger became involved in the Middle East negotiations. Again he demonstrated his seemingly magical abilities. With the actual fall of Nixon, Kissinger became the strong man, gratefully retained by Gerald Ford.

Now, however, began a falling-out in Henry Kissinger's romance with the media. As evidence of Kissinger's personal endorsement of Nixon's policy of secrecy and force—the Cambodian invasion, the bombing of Hanoi, the wiretapping, the intervention in Chile—began to emerge, Kissinger lost much of his support in the press, if not in the country. At this time of renewed testing and criticism, he sought to defend his honor and to shift some of his priorities away from the personalism of his negotiations to the institutional problems of an emerging interdependent, economically based world, thus cutting the ground from under his attackers. It is a process that is still going on.

America and Europe

That, in summary form, is a bare-bones account of Kissinger's life and work. I have tried to suggest that the basic process is best seen as the Americanization of Henry Kissinger and, as one result, the Europeanization of American foreign policy. Kissinger, with his sense of tragedy, his feeling for history, and his notions of destiny, felt he had something special to offer his adopted country. When, after World War II, the dilemma of nuclear war confronted the United States, his character and views seemed to coincide with the needs of his adopted country. In a peculiar alchemy, Kissinger appeared to give to America skills and concepts which fulfilled American aims, but with a European accent.

Whatever the ultimate success of Kissinger's Europeanization of American foreign policy, his own Americanization is an extraordinary story of personal achievement. Though it lies within the general pattern of such achievements, we should note that Kissinger's story is also partly the story of one particular American ethnic group, the Jews, and their climb to assimilation and power. Only after World War II, did American Jews establish themselves in significant numbers in universities, such as Harvard, in governmental scientific advisory circles, and even in the State Department. This last institution, bastion of the WASP establishment, has had its first Jewish Secretary of State in the person of Henry Kissinger, who audaciously criticized the established Anglo-Saxon policy makers in terms of their own established values, yet another paradox of our story. For the unusual thing about Kissinger is not only that he is a refugee Jew who became Secretary of State, but that he is a conservative one.

Obviously, it is only a stereotype that Jews are radicals; many are conservative. Orthodox Jews are especially predisposed in this direction. What is unusual is that Kissinger became an intellectual and an academic, but unlike most of his fellow Jews in this category, he did not become a liberal. Instead, Kissinger became a conservative intellectual, and because of this unusual quality, he was acceptable to the Republican establishment and the military hawks. Thus, Kissinger's Americanization has had some very special features.

Personal Themes

A number of themes emerge from a consideration of Henry Kissinger's life and career. He believes, almost compulsively, that goodwill is not enough. For a person, or a nation, the only defense is power. Power is to be used to insure the preservation of order and international stability, and definitely not to achieve novel, revolutionary aims.

Pervasive throughout Kissinger's life is what I have variously called his identification with the opponent, the enemy, or the aggressor. This has been a key mechanism by which Kissinger has both acquired power and defended himself against the threat implicit in its possession by others. It lies, too, at the core of Kissinger's belief in accommodation and of his extraordinary negotiating abilities. Another means of achieving power for Kissinger has been the cultivation of patrons. Patronage means dependency, and Kissinger has been able to manage the unusual feat of maintaining his inward independence while moving upward by means of a dependency that he outwardly scorns. Kissinger is an activist, though an intellectual one. He believes in heroes who pursue their lonely course independent of the approval of the masses. Such heroes find their satisfaction in a future judgment by history; in the meantime, history is itself viewed as the unfolding and fulfillment of a personality, and hence its own reward. Kissinger sees himself as such a hero, necessarily manly, strong, and confident. He is also much concerned with his honor, and morality is often submerged in this more heroic, aristocratic quality.

Kissinger is notably arrogant, the other side of his noticeable shyness and insecurity. (The equation here has been changing, with success pulling both traits toward a more moderate expression.) The arrogance, at its full height, sometimes seems to approach megalomania, or what Kissinger calls his "Napoleon complex." On the other side, as a check, is Kissinger's constant preoccupation with limits, with the requirement of self-restraint.

"Paranoid" and "overly suspicious" are terms frequently used about Kissinger. There is no question that our lonely, independent hero is often unduly sensitive to criticism and deeply distrustful of those around him. Suspicious of others, he is himself sometimes duplicitous, or at least he skirts the edge of untruth. Yet he insists on the necessity of sincerity, of true conviction, if one is to persuade others. In the eyes of some of his critics, Kissinger goes so far as to persuade himself sincerely that someone else's work is his, Kissinger's own; in short, he is a plagiarist without knowing it.

Kissinger's strengths are those of a synthesizer, not an original thinker. He has the ability to marshal a great array of facts, order them logically, and then draw options from them. His memory is one of his strong points. He is a terribly hard worker, with great energy and stamina, thus laying a physical basis for his psychological domination. The latter takes the form of what we have called "presence" or "weightiness," wherein Kissinger convinces us of his brilliance and general abilities.

An intellectual, Kissinger is generally scornful of academics and "mere" intellectuals who do not have power. Kissinger is an active and conservative intellectual who has used the intellect as a way of coping with the threat of hostile power in the service of revolutionary and destructive aims. He has identified the enemy as communism and displaced onto it his feelings about Nazism, though he is able to accommodate himself to both evil forces and, indeed, often identifies himself with their behavior in strange ways. He is preoccupied with the possibility of holocaust, now made real as a result of the nuclear weapons threat. Aware that nuclear power, paradoxically, has made military power powerless, Kissinger is obsessed with the need for "credibility," i.e., the substitution of psychological power for the lack of truly effective military power.

Kissinger's approach to the analysis of power and international politics is not behavioral but historical and psychological. We will not repeat here the details of his view of history and its meaning, or of his own work, such as *A World Restored*. Nor will we reiterate the specific elements of his concern with psychology. Suffice it to say that the historical and psychological approaches, fused, lie at the core of Kissinger's entire world view.

Last, we must stress as a constant theme in Kissinger's life and career his ability to change and to develop. He is an assimilationist par excellence. His identification with his opponent also serves him in this matter. So do his intellectual abilities, his impressive capacity for synthesizing. As one informant remarked, Kissinger is "an extraordinary example of self-invention"; we would add that the invention seems continuous. His change and development, of course, take place within set, stable limits, as befits a conservative. It is this combination of change and constancy, of opposite and conflicting traits, that makes Kissinger so subject to differing evaluations— and so intriguing a historical figure.

The Mediating Force

Kissinger's personal traits are obviously fascinating. How much do they enter into his policy attitudes, and in what ways? My view is that they are extremely important, but must be seen as subordinate to his intellectualization, though, of course, they underlie it. Kissinger's personal needs for stability, identification, limitation, and so on, have been transformed into a coherent world view and style of acting. As such, the personal needs are now "distanced" from the policies, and if one wants best to understand the policies it must be in terms of Kissinger's ratiocinations, which have taken on a life of their own.

In many ways, this conclusion is a surprising one to me. In the case of Richard Nixon there was no intellectualization, no conceptual system worthy of the name, that mediated between him and his psychological impulses. He acted directly on the political process, uninspired by almost anything other than opportunism and his inner needs. There was no real Nixon policy; only a personality. And when events conspired to give a President of the United States extraordinary and often almost unlimited power (except for the self-restraint he might impose on himself), Nixon showed that he had few limits, of conviction or intellectualization, to serve as a check on his policy. As I remarked even before the Watergate revelations, in *In Search of Nixon*, "Nixon's 'philosophy' . . . is really his 'psychology.' . . . it does seem clear that, for example, welfare and unemployment for Nixon are not so much social problems as they are moral problems; and moral problems are largely the externalized form of his internal dynamic problems."[1] His internal dynamic problems were serious and ultimately unmanageable.

Kissinger is quite different. It is not that, like all of us, he does not externalize his internal dynamics and, therefore, the deepest understanding of his life and work is not given by a close study of his personality formation and expression, one of the major subjects of this book. It is simply that the form Kissinger's externalization has taken has assumed a consistency of its own and must be reckoned with in these terms. Kissinger's is a position strongly oriented to certain pressing realities of international relations and should be taken seriously in this regard. Whether or not one agrees with his policies, they exist in their own terms.

As a person, Kissinger may be duplicitous, in love with power, and so forth, and one may admire or dislike him for these and other qualities. But, as with an artist or a scientist, disagreeable personal qualities should not affect our evaluation of the work produced. Kissinger, in this sense, is an artist (and perhaps a "political" scientist) on the international stage. His personality has certainly shaped his world view, as we have tried to show, and his personal traits still permeate his work and policy. We cannot understand the latter fully without comprehending the former. One part of that comprehension, however, is the realization that Kissinger is a conservative intellectual and that his policies are animated by deep-seated convictions and beliefs. Between his personality and his policy stands his world view, his historical and psychological approaches, and it is this mediating aspect of Kissinger we must remember and take most seriously as we seek to evaluate his "life work."

Achievements: Specific and General

What are Kissinger's achievements or, at least, his claims to fame? Kissinger himself has made certain statements that can serve as grounds on which to judge his successes. As he remarked back in 1972,

Basically, thought Kissinger, the postwar foreign policy of the United States had once had a coherence—back in 1945 when it was first shaped. "It had a 'theory of power,' a 'theory of economics,' " said Kissinger, "and we saw the world as ours to defend against a monolithic Communism. Acheson and Dulles and Kennan all saw us as bringing our strength to a point where we could negotiate with the Communists. . . ." But what we needed now was another, different *concept* [my italics]. "How do you withdraw?" "How do you lessen the burdens and exposure and yet be the great international power? . . . How do you limit this exposure and yet keep America a force for peace?" [2]

What "different concept" has Kissinger put forth? He would respond that it is the idea that, in a world threatened by revolutionary communist power, where American nuclear power is made powerless by fear of retaliation, some combination of limited war and the psychological will to use it, and even go beyond if necessary—i.e., credibility—must be put before the enemy. Coupled with this assertion of our military and psychological power must be the offer to negotiate, whenever possible. Thus, a stable international order may possibly be reconstructed, based on a realistic assessment of forces and not a mere idealistic aspiration toward goodwill.

Yet Kissinger's "different concept" is hard to evaluate or to study in concrete application. There is no question that he has a coherent, consistent concept behind his various policies; the difficulty is in locating it in summarized form. Thus what is most important in Kissinger, I believe, is less a sloganized "different concept" than his systematized world view, such as we have sought to study it. One of his achievements, in short, an intellectual one, is the working out of a subtle, highly sensitized conservative world view in its application to international affairs.

As a full-time professional student of his subject (the first Secretary of State to be so), Kissinger, for better or worse, has brought Old World views to his work. He has added a special kind of Machiavellian and Bismarckian realism to American idealism (some would speak of complete substitution). He has injected a strong note of Kantian and Hegelian epistemology and philosophy of history into American foreign policy speculation, though largely undetected as such. Especially, he has followed Clausewitz, and placed military policy emphatically at the service of foreign policy.

As a European, Kissinger has been less impressed than most of his fellow citizens with the uniqueness of American experience. He believes that the general lessons of history can be applied to the United States, though he is aware that this cannot be done mechanically. Believing that there are some eternal verities in history, he knows that they can only be understood in relation to particular circumstances. On the basis of these historical convictions, Kissinger has then tried, conceptually, to bring the United States fully and centrally into the existing international system.

Critics differ as to the importance and originality of Kissinger's conceptual approach to American foreign policy. There is widespread agreement, however, that he has had great impact on the style of diplomacy. His "personalism" has come to dominate the international scene. His shuttle flights have captured the public imagination. More significantly, Kissinger's willingness to negotiate with anyone, and the content of his negotiating style, have left their impression on America's external relations.

What about his specific negotiations, the actual implementation of his concept? Kissinger adroitly managed the opening to China and has been the leading figure in pursuing détente with the Russians. These moves have been seen as a "revolution" in American foreign policy. Kissinger also received the Nobel Peace Prize for his efforts at ending the Vietnam War. For this, and for his Middle East negotiations, he has been acclaimed by the public as a magician.

Kissinger's critics do not accept these moves as true achievements. China, they say, was a door waiting to be pushed open;

besides, it was Nixon's idea. Détente was already a policy under Lyndon B. Johnson, though events were not propitious for pursuing it. As for Vietnam, it remained an American involvement four years longer than it should have. In 1973–1974, these critics would have seen the Middle East as Kissinger's only real success; today, they doubt even that. As for the rest of his specific diplomatic moves, they view them as botched, citing such instances as Chile and Cyprus.

One observer a while ago mimicked Kissinger, who likes to rate someone or something as having given a "B—" performance, and assigned grades to Kissinger's own performance. On that scorecard, Kissinger did not do brilliantly.[3] However, given the intractability of most diplomatic issues, it is difficult to know how well anyone would do, and critics may be holding Kissinger to an unrealistically high standard. China was apparently Nixon's idea, but Kissinger carried it off in high style (though paying the price of a tilt versus India). Détente, surely, is the only policy a sensible Secretary of State can seek to pursue vis-à-vis Russia; whether Kissinger is pursuing it foolishly—that is, adopting the wrong stance on Jewish emigration, the wheat sale, and so on—is another matter. On the Middle East, passions run high, in the face of no obvious solutions. While Kissinger's accommodation policy at the terrible expense of Israel may not succeed, there is no reason to believe that a policy of intransigence on Israel would better preserve that state in the long, if not the short, term. (Besides, Kissinger is Secretary of State of the United States of America, not Israel.)

One can, and should, debate endlessly the specifics of Kissinger's foreign policy and its implementations. Opinions will vary greatly, depending on the particular observer. Such debate, however, is not our object here. Rather, our aim is to set such debate in the framework of the largest possible understanding of Kissinger's personality, world view, and policies. In this context, a paradox emerges: Kissinger's greatest public triumphs—in Vietnam, in China, and in the Middle East—have either been failures *on his own terms,* and/or have occurred in those areas of the world where he was least prepared, intellectually, to deal with the problems.

Vietnam was a failure because time and again Kissinger's psychological understanding of his opponent turned out to be wrong. It is a failure because, after four years of additional expenditure of Vietnamese and American lives and fortune, and the near collapse of the American domestic fabric, South Vietnam was lost to the North, as Kissinger's critics said it would be. It is a failure because none of the dire consequences Kissinger kept predicting—the blood bath, the disaster supposed to emanate from the falling dominoes, and so on—has come into being. Kissinger's only excuse for this extraordinary failure of judgment and foresight could be that it was Nixon's policy, which Kissinger merely carried out. Unfortunately, the record is clear that it also was or became Kissinger's policy.

China was a triumph of Kissinger's negotiating style, but the substance of Chinese history and politics was not at his command when he began. The same must be said of the Middle East. In part, then, Kissinger's real triumph in these areas was due not so much to the special expertise he brought to them, but to his ability to learn, and to deal with these countries in terms of his peculiar negotiating skills and his larger views on the whole of American foreign policy.

Kissinger's real achievement, once one moves beyond particular negotiations, is that he has justified his own claim to have given to American foreign policy a consistent, coherent, "conceptual" basis. He has imposed on America his world view in the international arena. It is a world view different from that of Presidents Nixon and Ford and their homegrown American domestic and foreign perceptions, but highly compatible with them. Insofar as Nixon and Ford represent American public opinion—and Nixon did get 60 percent of the vote in 1972—

Kissinger may be said to be the Secretary of State America has wanted. Given the structure of American political and military life, Kissinger is a most successful exponent and implementer of its values. Depressing as this conclusion may be to Kissinger's critics, one may have to join one of them when he confesses, "I believe that Kissinger is about the best that the American political system can produce under present circumstances, given prevailing beliefs and consciousness."[4]

An Intellectual Judgment

It is ultimately on the intellectual level, the level of Kissinger's conceptualization, that one must seek to evaluate him most comprehensively. Here, on his own favored terrain, there are serious charges to be leveled against Kissinger. His entire concept of foreign policy is immersed in history and psychology, and if these are deeply flawed, the long-range outcomes are also likely to be flawed. Kissinger's policies are presumably based on understanding the "Meaning of History," on comprehending what Kraemer called the currents of history overwhelming his people and, by extension, all of us. The device by which Kissinger has sought to understand and extract lessons from history has been analogy, and, cautious as he is about using the technique, his analogies seem wrong.

Commenting on Kissinger's choice of the nineteenth century, Richard Falk declares that "Kissinger, along with many others of his generation, has chosen the wrong historical analogy."[5] The correct one, according to Falk, is the seventeenth-century transition to the modern state system. At that time, there occurred a shift from the earlier concept of a world order based on central moral guidance by the Christian Church to one based on territorial states guided by a natural law version of the balance of power. In Falk's view, the twentieth century is necessarily swinging back to a world order based on some new form of central guidance and nonterritoriality. Kissinger, however, remains wedded to the traditional balance of power concept, in its nineteenth-century rather than seventeenth-century dress.

Falk's criticism is a thoughtful, high-level version of what others have criticized as Kissinger's mere personalization of foreign affairs and his neglect of larger economic and social forces inundating our world. I would make a different, or at least additional, criticism of Kissinger's choice of analogy. In my view, Kissinger's reading of twentieth-century history, specifically the Nazi period and World War II (about which he writes so little, but which acutely shaped his life), is what forms the basis of his historical understanding, such as it is. The nineteenth century is merely the displacement, the distancing, of his absorption in his own time, as he himself admits in *World Restored*.

Kissinger's error in reading his own experiences, I believe, stems from his projection of a personal experience of the failure of goodwill—his father's and his people's—onto history at large. It is an error embraced by many of his generation, and the one just before it. It assumes that the existence and expansion of Hitler's power was abetted by foolish men of goodwill, the appeasers, whose lack of power and of forceful action allowed Hitler to rise and flourish. Munich is its symbolic expression. This interpretation of history focuses on short-range factors and neglects the deeper causes going back to the Treaty of Versailles. Here, however, at the negotiations ending World War I, hard, vindictive men, void of goodwill, established a settlement which brought about the eventual desire by Germany for revenge, an economic depression, and ultimately the rise of the Nazis. One has only to read Keynes' *Economic Consequences of the Peace*[6] for the details.

Kissinger, to his credit, learned the lesson in part. He realized that settlements must be reached by accommodation, not imposition. But he shared the view that "aggression" must be stopped by force. (Incidentally, a view with which, *in principle*, I concur.) In Vietnam, like so many others, he thought he saw communist aggression at work. Not really understanding the revolutionary forces surging through the non-European parts of the world, Kissinger mistook a Vietnamese civil war for a communist conspiracy. The result of Kissinger's hardnosed but misguided Vietnamese policy (the equivalent of the hard, vindictive policy of the Versailles Treaty) was, initially, death and destruction in Vietnam, and broadening of the war to Cambodia; then, at home, came domestic disturbances; at a further remove, the American involvement in Vietnam was reflected as a weakness in the Middle East, leading to an Arab oil embargo, which contributed to a critical inflation in the West, the end results of which are incalculable. These are the true domino effects. Can one really believe that a settlement in Vietnam, even a withdrawal, in 1968, as promised by the Nixon administration and constantly prophesied by Kissinger, would have weakened America more than the policy pursued?

In my view, then, Kissinger's long-range historical and strategic understanding has been faulty. It has been flawed by his conservative world view. His mind is simply not attuned to the new world of revolutionary political, social, and economic developments and aspirations. Nor does he fully understand the new world of science and technology. His desire for stability has led him to make a false analogy of our problems with those of the early nineteenth century and of the 1930s and 1940s. On the short-range, tactical level, his skills are excellent. Alas, because of his frozen historical vision, his identifications and empathy—good and useful in themselves—have been employed in short-sighted fashion.

We touch on another limitation (and here we are using the term in a pejorative sense, different from Kissinger's use of the notion) to Kissinger's historical vision if we consider his treatment of Napoleon. In *A World Restored* Kissinger sees only Napoleon's foreign policy, his limitless ambitions, and not the carrying forward of the freedoms of the French Revolution, for example, to the Rhineland, and the consequent freedom and civil liberties for the Jews, Kissinger's own people. Kissinger makes not the slightest effort to see what Hegel saw: that Napoleon was not only a despotic adventurer but an embodiment of revolutionary ideals in spite of his betrayal of them. Kissinger is right in his judgment on Napoleon as a tyrant, but it is not the only judgment a historian should be making. It demonstrates a narrow conception of history.

Such a narrow conception points to another limitation in Kissinger. One of his achievements was to remind Americans of Clausewitz's formulation that war is policy pursued by other means. But this formulation points directly to the question of what "policy" is being pursued. Any such policy must be rooted in the domestic aims and values of a people. Kissinger's disregard for or ignorance of American domestic policy and values points to a vacuum or worse in his international policy, since the consequence of his position is that America's purposes are only those of Kissinger's desire for stability and order. In the case of Vietnam, it is clear that Kissinger neither foresaw, nor understood, nor cared an iota about the domestic implications of his policy, other than as an impediment to its being carried out. The fact that he was not alone in this lack of concern does not mitigate the fact that this very intelligent man lacked a broader vision and understanding.

We can see Kissinger's blindness in this area exhibited blatantly in the Solzhenitsyn affair. Kissinger advised President Ford not to receive Solzhenitsyn at the White House because it might be interpreted by the Russians as a repudiation of the policy of détente. Kissinger's only worry was that it would be a wrong "signal" to the Russians. (A similar instance was the reception of an Italian neo-Fascist at the same time as the rejection of an Italian communist's visa application to the United States.) It simply never occurred to him that the matter would also be a "signal" to the American people, repudiating our entire domestic value system of open and free exchange and display of divergent beliefs.[7] Kissinger's world is a world of signals in an international order hermetically sealed from American liberal, domestic values.

His failure here also touches on the limitations of his psychological approach. He not only misunderstood Vietnamese psychology, as he eventually admitted; he also misunderstands the American people. His eye is always on right-wing reactions, which he fears, again in a misapplied analogy to Germany of the 1920s and 1930s. He has absolutely no sympathy for liberal or radical Americans, who at their best are rooted in the traditions and aspirations of the founders of the Republic. In tones suspiciously like those of the Nazis, he has complained about Americans' lack of discipline, of immediate acceptance of order and authority. He distrusts any signs of the idealism and morality so characteristic of Americans, though paying them lip service. His understanding of America, in short, is not so much wrong as it is one-sided. Here, at home, his capacity for empathy and accommodation is conspicuously lacking.

It is, therefore, in the realm of historical and psychological insight, on which Kissinger prides himself, that his deficiencies loom largest. The failure of his declared aims, for example, to institutionalize his policies in the State Department, or even to foresee certain problems and handle them effectively, are minor flaws in an otherwise rather spectacular performance. In the end, however, harsh as the evaluation may be, one must conclude that Kissinger's present successes are vitiated by his failure to view the past and the future with sufficient insight.

Kissinger's Future

What of Kissinger's personal future? At some point, presumably, he will no longer be Secretary of State. Kissinger himself has declared that after eight years, anyone in his position needs to recharge his batteries. His friends speculate as to what he will do. Some see him as a roving ambassador, a sort of Harriman, but Kissinger's difficulties in sharing power with others casts this role in doubt. Others see him as a grey eminence of American foreign policy and any future President, but his enjoyment of the limelight and the trappings of power speak against this. Obviously, too, this possibility depends on the circumstances under which he leaves and the new people who come into power.

Kissinger has been inundated with offers from the outside. He has been, and will be again, asked to serve as president of universities and foundations, and even to be the head of the Motion Picture Association of America. Most observers agree that if Kissinger so desires, the Rockefellers would probably set up a whole new foreign policy organization for him to direct.

There is another possibility. Though he likes the good life, Kissinger could, under certain circumstances, see his destiny as one of withdrawing from public life, like de Gaulle, and waiting to be called back. His wife, Nancy, with her leanings to a private life, might push him in this direction, and he is young enough to think of returning to a position of power. But all this, too, seems fanciful.

The most likely future is that Kissinger will retire for a time to write his memoirs. In the past he has spoken, with a kind of ambivalence, of his desire to write a great book on the history and evolution of the international system. Such a volume would serve as his life work as a scholar, standing in place of the books he has already written, which, in this mood, he has described as journalistic and ephemeral. This magnum opus, "The Theory and Practice of International Affairs," was most in Kissinger's mind after his disheartening experience as an adviser to John F. Kennedy and in the bitter aftermath of Rockefeller's failure to defeat Goldwater in 1964. If another such mood should come over Kissinger, he might rejuvenate his scholarly ambitions.

Most probable is that he will subsume his ambition to write a great theoretical work in the writing of his memoirs. Here person and policy, life and reflections, would come together. Kissinger has thought of going to Oxford to write his book, and at one time even entered into negotiations to buy a house in London. One friend thinks he will retire to Switzerland, where John Kenneth Galbraith and the jet set go. By now, his geographical horizons are much enlarged and location an open matter.

Beyond the memoirs, it is difficult to guess at Kissinger's future life. One can be confident that he will not fade from the public scene. His abilities and ambitions are too great for that to happen. Moreover, we know that one of Kissinger's major demonstrated traits has been his ability to grow and develop. It would be an injudicious biographer, then, who would guess at Kissinger's probable future after the writing of his memoirs. That is a matter best left to his destiny.

The Future of America

And what of America's destiny? The problems of being a major power in a world of nuclear weapons, revolutionary movements, increasing interdependency, and have and have not confrontations are here to stay for the foreseeable future. To cope with these problems and their like, what is needed is an end to the false dichotomy between idealism and realism in American foreign policy and inauguration of a new policy of idealistic goals, realistically pursued. Such a policy, in turn, requires a healing of the split in the American psyche. Our professed values must be clearly reexamined and enunciated, and honestly and effectively pursued in action. The word and the deed must be brought into reasonable correspondence.

Kissinger has repeatedly emphasized the union of thought

and action so badly needed in foreign, not to mention domestic, policy. On many occasions he has brilliantly exemplified this credible belief. In a revealing, though slightly cryptic statement, he has declared that he entered the Nixon administration because "I felt that with my particular background I had a special obligation to understand the dangers of national division and to do my best to overcome them."[8] There is no reason to doubt the sincerity of this statement or to question the fact that by his lights he sought to overcome not only national but international division. The question is whether he understood realistically either the divisions in his own life or the domestic divisions of idealism and realism in American life.

Kissinger tried, in the journal *Confluence*, to join two currents of thought symbolizing his own divided life experiences, the European and the American. It is our thesis that, intellectually, he never succeeded in fusing the two traditions. Kissinger has not been a de Tocqueville. On the personal level, he has tried desperately, but again unsuccessfully, to heal the divisions in his own soul, and to amalgamate the impulses of goodwill and power. The lack of success is why he leaves us with the impression of a "Dr. Kissinger and a Mr. Henry" personality. His effort to overcome the divisions in himself has been dramatic and impressive, and in this sense he has been a true historical hero, wrestling with his own tragic destiny. In the end, however, unless he can once again exhibit his great power of change and self-invention in unsuspected ways, reintegrating a latent commitment to goodwill, we must conclude that Kissinger is a hero too deeply flawed to serve as inspiration for America in its grappling with the awesome problems that face it. Because he is so remarkable a man, this is not only Kissinger's tragedy, but America's as well.

Notes

Introduction

1. Yet we must concur with Sigmund Freud, describing one of his cases, that "it still strikes me myself as strange that the case histories I write should read like short stories and that, as one might say, they lack the serious stamp of science. I must console myself with the reflection that the nature of the subject is evidently responsible for this, rather than any preference of my own"; "Studies on Hysteria," in *The Standard Edition of the Complete Psychological Works of Sigmund Freud*, ed. James Strachey, 24 vols. (London: Hogarth, 1953–1974), vol. 2, p. 160.

2. Edwin Diamond, "Would you Welcome, Please, Henry and Liv and Jackie and Erica!", *Columbia Journalism Review* (September–October 1975): 46. This is an interesting and lively article on how the media have turned events and issues into "stars" whose most trivial actions are presumably of breathtaking interest. Thus, one reporter has scavenged in Kissinger's garbage for newsworthy events.

3. Thomas L. Hughes, "Foreign Policy: Men or Measure?" *Atlantic Monthly* 234 (October 1974): 53.

4. Quoted in the *New York Times*, March 25, 1974.

5. The translation used is given in the *New York Times*, July 13, 1975.

6. *Time*, April 1, 1974.

7. *New York Times*, June 3, 1974.

8. *Rolling Stone*, November 8, 1973, p. 35.

9. *Boston Globe*, May 3, 1974.

10. Marvin Kalb and Bernard Kalb, *Kissinger* (Boston: Little, Brown, 1974), p. 97.

11. Edward Bok, *The Americanization of Edward Bok* (New York: Scribner's, 1920).

12. In addition to the Kalb book, there are such other serious works as Stephen R. Graubard, *Kissinger; Portrait of a Mind* (New York: Norton, 1973), and David Landau, *Kissinger; The Uses of Power* (Boston: Houghton Mifflin, 1972). Ralph Blumenfeld, staff and eds. of the *New York Post*, *Henry Kissinger, The Private and Public Story* (New York: New American Library, 1974), is a useful source of raw data. Dana Ward, "Kissinger: A Psychohistory," *History of Childhood Quarterly* 2 (Winter 1975): 287–348, is an unsympathetic effort at psychologizing Kissinger, as is Garry Wills' rather more perceptive "Kissinger, Personality," *Playboy* (December 1974): 122ff. The magazine in which Wills' article is published seems suitable for Kissinger as sex symbol! Neither Ward's nor Wills' article undertakes to study Kissinger in the sense or in the ways I am employing here.

13. Bruce Mazlish, *The Riddle of History* (New York: Harper & Row, 1966).

14. As the reader will see, there are one or two exceptions, such as the identification of Kissinger's college roommate by name. The reason for this last exception is obvious; there is no way of keeping his identity confidential (I might add that he has consented to the use of his name).

15. George F. Kennan, *Memoirs: 1925–1950* (Boston: Little, Brown, 1967), p. 278.

Chapter 1

1. Erik H. Erikson, *Young Man Luther* (New York: Norton, 1958); idem, *Gandhi's Truth* (New York: Norton, 1969).

2. *New York Times*, November 14, 1971.

3. "Kissinger: Action Biography," ABC Television Network, June 14, 1974, produced by Ted Koppel and Stan Opotowsky, p. I–2.

4. Ibid., p. I–3.

5. The *New York Post* article on Kissinger tells a different story. It claims that Zionism "had a strong foothold in Fürth ever since the first Zionist Congress was held in the Bavarian capital, Munich, in 1897" (June 4, 1974, p. 37). I can only state that *all* my interviewees from Fürth emphasized the prevalent anti-Zionism of the Jewish community. Faith in the *Post* allegation is also shaken by the fact that the first Zionist Congress was held in 1897 in Basle, Switzerland (cf. Peter Loewenberg's fascinating piece on "Theodor Herzl: A Psychoanalytic Study," in *The Psychoanalytic Interpretation of History*, ed. Benjamin B. Wolman [New York: Basic Books, 1971], pp. 150–191). (My criticism is only partially mitigated by the later correction of the *Post*'s "fact" in the book version of the series; Ralph Blumenfeld, staff and eds. of the *New York Post*, *Henry Kissinger, The Private and Public Story* [New York: New American Library, 1974].) For a full treatment of the assimilationist, and therefore anti-Zionist, position of the German Jews under the Weimar Republic, see Sidney M. Bolkosky, *The Distorted Image: German-Jewish Perceptions of Germans and Germany, 1918–1935* (New York: Elsevier, 1975).

6. "The Israel Press Highlights," *Hadassah Magazine* 55 (March 1974): 33–35.

7. *New York Post*, June 4, 1974, p. 37.

8. For similar cases in which the son repressed all conscious criticism of an authoritarian father see Alexander L. George and Juliette George, *Woodrow Wilson and Colonel House: A Personality Study* (1956; reprint ed., New York: Dover, 1964); idem, *The Autobiography of Charles Darwin* (New York: Dover, 1958). On the latter, compare my article, "Darwin and the Benchuca," *Horizon* 17 (Summer 1975): 102–105.

9. Oriana Fallaci, "Kissinger: An Interview," *The New Republic* 167 (December 16, 1972): 22.

10. Paula apparently had no siblings, but a number of aunts and cousins;

the genealogy is hard to establish precisely. Apparently, two aunts initially worked in the butcher shop, then both went to England. They are now dead. One cousin, one gathers, went to Uruguay, and yet another is in New York, living in the same building as Louis and Paula Kissinger. Fortunately, exact establishment of the family tree is not crucial, as there is no hint, for example, that the aunts played a significant role in young Henry's life. He did visit his mother's cousin, a successful periodontist in London, during the war, and has kept up relations with that family to this day.

11. *New York Post*, June 4, 1974, p. 4.

12. "The Israel Press Highlights."

13. Ibid.

14. Ibid.

15. Accounts differ here. Some of Henry's childhood friends claim he always played the wings, and rather awkwardly. Cf. *New York Post*, June 4, 1974, p. 37. In such matters childhood memories often err, either enlarging or playing down reality.

16. According to one childhood friend, John Sachs, Kissinger "was very knowledgeable about religion but he did not have the same conviction as others. He was observant more for his parent's sake than his own" (*New York Post*, June 4, 1974, p. 37).

17. Ernest Jones, *The Life and Work of Sigmund Freud* (Garden City, N.Y.: Doubleday-Anchor, 1963), p. 8.

18. Fritz Kraemer caught part of what was involved when he remarked, "Imagine what it means when your father, who was your authority, the father you admire . . . is suddenly transformed into a frightened little mouse" (*New York Post*, June 3, 1974, p. 4). Of course, Louis Kissinger was always shy and gentle, but Henry would have perceived as a child only the strict, authoritarian side of his father; thus, Kraemer's analysis stands.

19. Kissinger was not alone in his reaction. Raymond Aron, in many ways his teacher, when face-to-face with Hitler's evil in Germany between 1931 and 1933, concluded that the policy of "goodwill" pursued by Leon Blum was of no use.

Chapter 2

1. "Kissinger: Action Biography," ABC Television Network, June 14, 1974, produced by Ted Koppel and Stan Opotowsky, p. I–3.

2. Stephen R. Graubard, *Kissinger: Portrait of a Mind* (New York: Norton, 1973), p. 2.

3. Marvin Kalb and Bernard Kalb, *Kissinger* (Boston: Little, Brown, 1974), p. 387.

4. *New York Post*, June 6, 1974. Cf. Kissinger's own account in "Kissinger: Action Biography," p. I–4. Cf. Kalb and Kalb, *Kissinger*, p. 41, for yet a different account.

5. But compare Kissinger's account in "Kissinger: Action Biography," p. I–5.

6. Back in America, Kissinger, Rosovsky, and Springer all joined the reserves, as officers. When the Korean War broke out, the last two were called back to service, with Rosovsky actually sent to Korea. Kissinger seems to have escaped being called up again.

7. *New York Post*, June 6, 1974.

8. Henry Kissinger, "The Meaning of History; Reflections on Spengler, Toynbee and Kant" (B.A. Thesis, Harvard University, 1951), p. 343.

9. Identification, defined as a complex unconscious process whereby real or imagined characteristics of another person, e.g., parents, become permanent components of the personality, or, more simply, as "the psychological assimilation by one individual of some emotional attitude or trait or idea of another personality," is a standard, normal aspect of development; see Ives Hendrick, *Facts and Theories of Psychoanalysis* (New York: Delta, 1958), pp. 374, 160. Identification with the aggressor is a defense mechanism whereby the person masters anxiety and fear by taking on the attributes of the threatening source—e.g., a small child afraid of ghosts or lions pretends to be one, and flits about or roars in imitation; see Anna Freud, *The Ego and the Mechanisms of Defense* (New York: International Universities Press, 1946), pp. 118 ff.

10. Bruno Bettelheim, "Individual and Mass Behavior in Extreme Situations," *Journal of Abnormal Social Psychology* 38 (1943): 417–452.

11. Joseph Kraft, "In Search of Kissinger," *Harper's*, January 1971, p. 57.

12. More recently, Kraemer has predicted the failure of Kissinger's Middle East policy—but without giving a date.

13. Quoted in Bernard Law Collier, "The Road to Peking, or How Does This Kissinger Do It?" *New York Times Magazine*, November 14, 1971, p. 107.

14. Ibid., p. 106.

15. Kraemer is strongly opposed to "analysis," the critical approach (meaning, literally, to "distinguish" or "take apart"), and skepticism. In this, of course, he is at one with most conservative thought (cf. Burke or de Maistre). Since academics are given to analysis, criticism, and skepticism, often to the detriment of espousing vigorous action, it is easy to see why Kraemer, and eventually Kissinger might scorn them.

16. Quoted in Kraft, "In Search of Kissinger," p. 58.

Chapter 3

1. *The Harvard Yearbook* (Cambridge, Mass., 1950).

2. Ibid.

3. Ibid.

4. Ibid.

5. Ann Fleischer's name is spelled on occasions with an "e," but more usually, and lately, without it.

6. Joseph Kraft, "In Search of Kissinger," *Harper's*, January 1971, p. 57.

7. See, for example, Stephen R. Graubard, *Kissinger: Portrait of a Mind* (New York: Norton, 1973), for a convenient paraphrasing of Kissinger's writings.

8. Report of the 1965 Harvard International Seminar, p. 1.

9. I am grateful to my colleague, Lucien Pye, for the reference to Sadat.

10. Henry Kissinger, *Nuclear Weapons and Foreign Policy* (New York: Harper & Row, 1957).

11. Graubard, *Kissinger*, p. 115.

12. Townsend Hoopes' description of Bowie is worth contemplating: "Robert Bowie, whom Dulles recruited from the Harvard law faculty to be director of policy planning, played the role of chief devil's advocate (one aide called him 'the paid hair shirt'). He served up a variety of 'think pieces' to challenge the conventional wisdom and debated issues face to face with Dulles, displaying a sinewy mind that showed no particular deference to the position of Secretary of State. As Dulles relished a real argument when he respected his opponent, Bowie became an important catalyst on a range of major issues. The Dulles-Bowie arguments tended always to move around a central point: whether or not to be a little more forthcoming, a little more magnanimous, a little more accommo- dating—with Moscow, Peking, Cairo, London or Paris—than the im- mediate power realities required. By his own account, Dulles always took the hardest line. Bowie's imagination and relative liberality, which he did not disguise, made him an increasing target for dark innuendo from absolutist cold warriors in the Pentagon (later, he and Admiral Radford each referred to the other as a 'devilishly clever' man)"; *The Devil and John Foster Dulles* (Boston: Little, Brown, 1973), p. 147.

13. Graubard, *Kissinger*, p. 114.

14. Henry Kissinger, *A World Restored* (Boston: Houghton Mifflin, 1973).

15. Kissinger, *Nuclear Weapons and Foreign Policy*.

16. Guido Goldman, quoted in Ralph Blumenfeld, staff and eds. of the *New York Post*, *Henry Kissinger, The Private and Public Story* (New York: New American Library, 1974), p. 122.

17. Graubard, *Kissinger*, p. 115.

Chapter 4

1. Klaus Werner Epstein, *The Genesis of German Conservatism* (Princeton, N.J.: Princeton University Press, 1966).

2. "Henry" lends itself to a "swinger" image; "Dr. Kissinger" makes for heavy going. As my work progressed, I also found myself thinking of my subject as "Henry," whereas Richard Nixon had never been anything for me but Mr. Nixon.

3. Cf. Chapter 8, p. 180.

4. Dana Ward, "Kissinger: A Psychohistory," *History of Childhood Quarterly* 2 (Winter 1975): 287–348. Interestingly, Daniel Ellsberg, in his *Rolling Stone* interview, pt. 2, no. 149 (December 6, 1973), says "I recently read an article in *Psychology Today* on depressed behavior and was interested to see an interpretation of classic personal depression as a state of mind in which the person feels helpless, feels that he has no impact on the world outside, that he can't affect anything or change

anything" (p. 43). Ellsberg is referring to the state of many Americans faced with American involvement in Vietnam during the Nixon administration; the description hardly applies to Kissinger personally, one of the participants in that policy.

5. Henry Kissinger, "The Meaning of History; Reflections on Spengler, Toynbee and Kant" (B.A. Thesis, Harvard University, 1951).

6. Kissinger, of course, is hardly unique, even as a Secretary of State, in some of his traits. Compare, for example, Dean Acheson's description of Cordell Hull: "Suspicious by nature, he brooded over what he thought were slights and grievances. . . . His brooding led . . . to feuds. His hatreds were implacable" (p. 9), and, on Hull's exacting work schedule, "For many years he would summon his principal assistants to a Sunday-morning conference in his office, a practice which should have been forbidden by the constitutional prohibition against 'cruel and unusual punishment' "; *Present at the Creation* (New York: Norton, 1969), p. 742.

7. Henry A. Kissinger, "The White Revolutionary: Reflections on Bismarck," *Daedalus* 97 (Summer 1968): 898, and Oriana Fallaci, "Kissinger: An Interview," *The New Republic* 167 (December 16, 1972): 21. In his *The Necessity for Choice* (New York: Harper, 1961), Kissinger makes a comment on revolutionary leaders that is also very self-revealing: "But empirical reality is much less significant for individuals whose *raison d'être* is the desire to *change* reality. For them 'true' reality consists not of what empirical study reveals but rather of the world they wish to bring about. To them, the vision of the changed world for which they are striving is much more 'real' than the circumstances against which they are rebelling. It is much too easy to say that a Castro—or Nasser or Lumumba —is lying. It would be more nearly true to say that they have different standards of truth and reality than we (p. 327)."

8. For the extreme complexity of this whole moral problem see my article, "History and Morality," *Journal of Philosophy* 55 (March 13, 1958): 230–240.

9. Cf. Chapter 10, p. 221, of this present book, and see Bruce Mazlish, *In Search of Nixon* (New York: Basic Books, 1972).

10. This incident seems to echo the end of *Confluence*, when contributors to the suspended last volume were also, so to speak, left hanging.

11. Another, slightly more flattering, way of looking at this trait is to compare Kissinger to the character, Jacobovsky, in Franz Werfel's play, *Jacobovsky and the Colonel*. Jacobovsky is the prototypic Central European Jew, who lives by his wits. In contrast with the Colonel, who, along with his rigid character, has a "14th-century mind in a 20th-century body," Jacobovsky always sees "two possibilities" in every situation. Courtly and contriving, Jacobovsky also seems duplicitous because of his clever willingness to exploit different possibilities, to entertain both sides of an argument, and to live in a world of "two possibilities." The analogy—it can be no more than that—with Kissinger is obvious. Cf. Franz Werfel, *Jacobovsky and the Colonel*, tr. Gustave O. Arlt (New York: Viking, 1944).

12. Fallaci, "Kissinger," p. 21.

13. To another person Kissinger remarked, "I don't let too many people get close to me."

NOTES

Chapter 5

1. Cf. Marvin Kalb and Bernard Kalb, *Kissinger* (Boston: Little, Brown, 1974), p. 49.
2. Henry Kissinger, *The Necessity for Choice* (New York: Harper & Row, 1961), p. xi.
3. Cf. Stephen R. Graubard, *Kissinger: Portrait of a Mind* (New York: Norton, 1973), pp. 60–64, for a detailed description of the membership.
4. Council on Foreign Relations, *Annual Report of the Council on Foreign Relations, 1954–1955* (New York: Harold Pratt House, 1955), p. 19.
5. Ibid, p. 21.
6. Ibid., p. 20.
7. Ibid., p. 21.
8. Kalb and Kalb, *Kissinger*, p. 51.
9. Council on Foreign Relations, *Annual Report of the Council on Foreign Relations, 1955–1956*, p. 9.
10. Henry A. Kissinger, *Nuclear Weapons and Foreign Policy* (New York: Norton, 1969), chap. 2.
11. See Chapter 4, p. 95.
12. Henry Kissinger, "The Policy-Maker and the Intellectual," *The Reporter*, March 5, 1959, pp. 30–35, the substance of which can be found in Kissinger, *Necessity for Choice*, pp. 340–358.
13. Kissinger, *Necessity for Choice*, p. ix; Cf. Graubard, *Kissinger*, p. 111, for the "connections" resulting from Kissinger's own connection with the Rockefeller Brothers Fund reports.
14. Dean Acheson, *Present at the Creation* (New York: Norton, 1969), p. 112.
15. David Halberstam, *The Best and the Brightest* (Greenwich, Conn.: Fawcett Crest Book, 1972), p. 419.
16. Cf. account in Ralph Blumenfeld, staff, and eds of the *New York Post*, *Henry Kissinger: The Private and Public Story* (New York: New American Library, 1974), pp. 108–110.
17. Blumenfeld et al., *Henry Kissinger*, p. 108.
18. David Landau, *Kissinger: The Uses of Power* (Boston: Houghton Mifflin, 1972), p. 44.
19. Kalb and Kalb, *Kissinger*, p. 53.
20. Ibid., p. 55.
21. Blumenfeld et al., *Henry Kissinger*, p. 116.
22. *Prospect for America: The Rockefeller Panel Reports* (Garden City, N.Y.: Doubleday, 1961).
23. See Blumenfeld et al., *Henry Kissinger*, p. 120.
24. Kalb and Kalb, *Kissinger*, p. 56.
25. Blumenfeld et al., *Henry Kissinger*, p. 120.
26. Kissinger, *Necessity for Choice*.
27. Kalb and Kalb, *Kissinger*, p. 64.
28. Henry A. Kissinger, *The Troubled Partnership* (New York: McGraw-Hill, 1965).

29. Kalb and Kalb, *Kissinger*, p. 67.
30. Ibid.
31. Henry Kissinger, "What Should We Do Now?" *Look*, August 9, 1966, pp. 27–28.
32. Kalb and Kalb, *Kissinger*, p. 69.
33. Blumenfeld et al., *Henry Kissinger*, p. 167.
34. Ibid., p. 109.
35. *New York Times*, September 24, 1974, p. 34.
36. *New York Times*, October 6, 1974, p. 58.

Chapter 6

1. Ralph Blumenfeld, staff, and eds. of the *New York Post*, *Henry Kissinger: The Private and Public Story* (New York: New American Library, 1974), pp. 108–110.
2. Marvin Kalb and Bernard Kalb, *Kissinger* (Boston: Little, Brown, 1974).
3. Stephen R. Graubard, *Kissinger: Portrait of a Mind* (New York: Norton, 1973).
4. See, for example, Charles R. Ashman, *Kissinger: The Adventures of Super-Kraut* (New York: Dell, 1972); and Monroe Rosenthal and Donald Munson, *President Kissinger* (New York: Freeway Press, 1974).
5. Interestingly, the Kissingers had a real maidservant of sorts, that is, an *au pair* girl for the children; and, most interesting, this live-in girl was from Germany, and not Jewish.
6. See Chap. 9, p. 196, for some suggestive evidence that Kissinger had sought, even if briefly, professional psychotherapeutic advice for himself as well.
7. Kalb and Kalb, *Kissinger*, p. 9. According to Kissinger, "When I get nervous, I eat." Loss of weight, then, would indicate a general lowering of tension.
8. Oriana Fallaci, "Kissinger: An Interview," *The New Republic* 167, (December 16, 1972): 22.
9. After her remarriage to a more traditionally Jewish professor, Ann apparently has returned to her original faith and stopped going to the Ethical Culture meetings. Curiously, in 1967, before her remarriage, Ann had arranged for Henry Kissinger to address the Ethical Culture group to which she belonged. In his address he attacked L.B.J.'s bombing of North Vietnam!
10. See Kalk and Kalb, *Kissinger*, p. 146, for details about Kissinger's emergence as a swinger.
11. Danielle Hunebelle, *Dear Henry* (New York: Berkeley, 1972).
12. Fallaci, "Kissinger," p. 22.
13. Ibid., p. 22.
14. See Henry A. Kissinger, *A World Restored* (Boston: Houghton Mifflin, 1973), pp. 41 and 273, for Kissinger's view of politics as a form of theater.

Chapter 7

1. Henry Kissinger, "The Policy-Maker and the Intellectual," in *The Necessity for Choice* (New York: Harper & Row, 1961), pp. 340–358.
2. Cf. Stephen Graubard, *Kissinger: Portrait of a Mind* (New York: Norton, 1973).
3. A "world view" is basically what it says: a general view of the world which colors the whole approach to external reality. The German word, *Weltanschauung*, is more impressive, of course. "Ideology" relates to the consciousness of an individual, class, or group by which it structures its activity in the world. It generally has the connotation of a set of dogmas which allows its holder to defend his power position. (For a history of the emergence of the term, and thus its meaning, see George Lichtheim, "The Concept of Ideology," *History and Theory* 4 (1965) no. 2: 164–195.) "Operational code" suggests a formal code, consulted like a cook book by the political actor, but as Alexander L. George argues, "the term 'operational code' is a misnomer. It really refers to a general belief system about the nature of history and politics; it is *not* a set of recipes or repertoires for political action that an elite applies mechanically in its decision-making. The beliefs and premises that comprise what [Nathan] Leites called 'operational code' have a more subtle and looser relationship to decision-making. These general beliefs serve, as it were, as a prism that influences the actor's perception of the flow of political events and his definition or estimate of particular situations. The beliefs also provide norms and standards that influence the actor's choice of strategy and tactics, and his structuring and weighing of alternative courses of action." ("The 'Operational Code': A Neglected Approach to the Study of Political Leaders and Decision-Making," Rand Corporation, 1967, p. 1.) As can readily be seen, however, though "world view" is the most comprehensive and "operational code" the most limited term, all three phrases—world view, ideology, and operational code—share a more or less common meaning.
4. For one recent effort, however, see Richard A. Falk, "The Sherrill Hypothesis," unpublished manuscript, Princeton University, June 1974.
5. Henry A. Kissinger, *American Foreign Policy* (New York: Norton, 1969), p. 79. Cf. Henry A. Kissinger, *The Necessity for Choice* (New York: Harper & Row, 1961), p. 279.
6. Henry A. Kissinger, *Nuclear Weapons and Foreign Policy* (New York: Norton, 1969), pp. 28, 4.
7. Hans J. Morgenthau, *Politics Among Nations* (New York: Knopf, 1948), p. 22.
8. Ibid.
9. For the relation of one great conservative thinker to change and even revolution, and his willingness on occasion to be allied with these movements, see Bruce Mazlish, "The Conservative Revolution of Edmund Burke," *Review of Politics*, 20 (January 1958): 21–33.
10. Cf. Kissinger's division of politics solely into conservatives and revolutionaries—liberals don't exist—in *A World Restored* (Boston: Houghton Mifflin, 1973), p. 329.

11. Ibid., pp. 338, 339.
12. Kissinger, *Necessity for Choice*, p. 357.
13. Ibid., p. 327.
14. Henry A. Kissinger, "The Meaning of History; Reflections on Spengler, Toynbee, and Kant," B.A. thesis, Harvard University, 1951).
15. Henry A. Kissinger, *The Troubled Partnership* (New York: McGraw-Hill, 1965), p. 251. As an example of how Kissinger created reality, we are told that during the Middle East crisis of October 1973, when the Russians seemed to be trying to take advantage of the Israeli weakness owing to losses of equipment, Kissinger explained: "We tried to talk in the first week. When that didn't work, we said, fine, we'll start pouring in equipment until we create a new reality." (Quoted in Marvin and Bernard Kalb, "Twenty Days in October," *New York Times Magazine*, June 23, 1974, p. 50).
16. Karl Mannheim, "Conservative Thought," in *Essays on Sociology and Social Psychology*, ed. P. Kecskemeti (New York: Oxford University Press, 1953).
17. Kissinger, *World Restored*, p. 191.
18. Ibid., p. 193.
19. Ibid.
20. Ibid., p. 194.
21. Kissinger, *Necessity for Choice*, p. 349.
22. Ibid., p. 353.
23. Kissinger, "Meaning of History," p. 1. The citations in the text that follow, unless otherwise stated, are from this work.
24. Kissinger, *Necessity for Choice*, p. 2. The citations in the text that follow, unless otherwise stated, are from this work.
25. On another level, however, Kissinger's dismissal of attitude, i.e., of good or bad will, implicitly undercuts his own stress, elsewhere, on psychological disposition and intention.
26. George F. Kennan, *Memoirs: 1925–1950* (Boston, Little, Brown, 1967), p. 322.
27. Ibid., p. 54.
28. Kissinger, *Nuclear Weapons*, pp. 4, 42. The citations in the text that follow, unless otherwise stated, are from this work.
29. Kissinger, *Necessity for Choice*, p. 2.
30. Ibid., p. 5.
31. Ibid., p. 198.
32. Ibid., p. 287.
33. Oriana Fallaci, "Kissinger: An Interview," *The New Republic* 167 (December 16, 1972): 19.
34. Ibid., p. 21. In fact, Machiavelli does not talk specifically of the Prince's will—it is impossible even to guess what passages Kissinger might have had in mind—and it appears that Kissinger is relying on various German interpretations of Machiavelli, itself a revealing fact.
35. Niccolo Machiavelli, *The Prince and the Discourses*, intro. by Max Lerner (New York: Modern Library, 1950), chap. 15 of *The Prince*, p. 56.
36. Kissinger, *Troubled Partnership*, p. 63.
37. Kissinger, *Necessity for Choice*, pp. 7, 3. The citations in the text that follow, unless otherwise stated, are from this work.

38. Fallaci, "Kissinger," p. 21.
39. Ibid., p. 210.
40. Henry A. Kissinger, "Peace, Legitimacy, and the Equilibrium: A Study of the Statesmanship of Castlereagh and Metternich" (Ph.D. diss., Harvard University, 1954), p. 6. World Restored, the published version of the dissertation, differs from the original in terms of both omissions and additional material.
41. Kissinger, World Restored, p. 28.
42. Kissinger, Troubled Partnership, p. 63.
43. See Kissinger, "Peace, Legitimacy, and the Equilibrium," p. 1.
44. Kissinger, World Restored, p. 326.
45. Ibid., p. 328.
46. Cf. Kissinger, Necessity for Choice, p. 9.

Chapter 8

1. Henry A. Kissinger, "The Meaning of History; Reflections on Spengler, Toynbee, and Kant" (B.A. thesis, Harvard University, 1951), p. 348.
2. See the New York Times, July 3, 1975, for a Chinese view on the similarities between the Soviet system and Hitler's.
3. Henry A. Kissinger, Necessity for Choice (New York: Norton, 1969), p. 31.
4. For further speculations along these lines on the psychological effect of the nuclear threat, see Bruce Mazlish, "What is Psychohistory?" (Paper delivered to the Royal Historical Society, September 22, 1970), and published in the Transactions of the Royal Historical Society, 5th ser., vol. 21 (1971), pp. 79–99.
5. Henry A. Kissinger, American Foreign Policy (New York: Norton, 1969), p. 57.
6. Henry A. Kissinger, A World Restored (Boston: Houghton Mifflin, 1973), p. 1.
7. Henry A. Kissinger, "Peace, Legitimacy, and the Equilibrium," (Ph.D. diss., Harvard University, 1954, pp. i–ii). Note that the construction of the new international order in 1815 was the result of Napoleon's "revolutionary" ambitions; in 1945 it was a result of Hitler's, with the threatened resurrection of the revolution—the equivalent of the return of Napoleon—this time in the form of communist nuclear war.
8. Henry A. Kissinger, Nuclear Weapons and Foreign Policy (New York: Norton, 1969), pp. 3, 15.
9. John Newhouse, Cold Dawn. The Story of SALT (New York: Holt, Rinehart, 1973), pp. 1–2.
10. Ibid., pp. 2–3.
11. Ibid., p. 18.
12. Kissinger, Necessity for Choice, p. 312.
13. Kissinger, World Restored, p. 63.
14. Kissinger, "Peace, Legitimacy and the Equilibrium," p. 128.
15. Kissinger, "Meaning of History," p. 382.
16. Ibid., p. 1. It is interesting to compare Kissinger's statement with

Karl Marx's youthful essay, "Reflections of a Young Man on the Choice of a Profession," in *Marx and Engels. Collected Works*, (New York: International Publishers, 1975), vol. 1, pp. 3–9, where Marx wrestles with a similar problem.

17. Kissinger, "Meaning of History," p. 1.

18. Ibid., p. 26.

19. Ibid., p. 27.

20. Kissinger, "Peace, Legitimacy, and the Equilibrium," p. ii.

21. Ibid., p. 6.

22. Kissinger, *World Restored*, p. 322.

23. Ibid., p. 213.

24. *New York Times*, October 13, 1974, p. 35. Of course, once aware of the statements made in this book, a self-conscious Kissinger may not say anything further about "limits," thus falsifying any future validation of my assertions.

25. Henry A. Kissinger, "Reflections on Cuba," *The Reporter* 27 (November 22, 1962): 21.

26. Kissinger, *Necessity for Choice*, p. 40.

27. Ibid., pp. 45, 46.

28. Marvin Kalb and Bernard Kalb, *Kissinger* (Boston: Little, Brown, 1974), p. 205.

29. Daniel Ellsberg interview in *Rolling Stone*, November 8, 1973, pp. 37–38.

Chapter 9

1. Alfred North Whitehead, *Adventures of Ideas* (New York: Macmillan, 1933), p. 369, quoted in Henry A. Kissinger, "The Meaning of History; Reflections on Spengler, Toynbee, and Kant" (B.A. thesis, Harvard University, 1951), p. 349.

2. Henry A. Kissinger, *A World Restored* (Boston: Houghton Mifflin, 1973), p. 186.

3. Ibid., p. 174. Elsewhere Kissinger offers a third definition: "The tragic aspect of policymaking . . . lies precisely in its unavoidable component of conjecture"; Henry A. Kissinger, *The Necessity for Choice* (New York: Harper & Row, 1961), p. 355.

4. Henry A. Kissinger, *The Troubled Partnership* (New York: McGraw-Hill, 1965), p. 249.

5. Kissinger, *World Restored*, p. 82.

6. Kissinger, *Necessity for Choice*, p. 356.

7. Ibid., p. 1.

8. See ibid., p. 175.

9. Kissinger, *Troubled Partnership*, p. 250.

10. Ibid., p. 251.

11. Kissinger, *World Restored*, p. 74.

12. Kissinger, *Troubled Partnership*, p. 24.

13. Ibid., p. 25. In "Domestic Structure and Foreign Policy" (1966),

Kissinger makes the same point, criticizing American decision makers for placing "a relatively low valuation [on] historical factors. Nations are treated as similar phenomena, and those states presenting similar immediate problems are treated similarly" (*American Foreign Policy* [New York: Norton, 1969], p. 33).

14. Ibid., pp. 48, 251.
15. Ibid., p. 47.
16. Kissinger, *World Restored*, p. 331.
17. Ibid.
18. Henry A. Kissinger, *Nuclear Weapons and Foreign Policy* (New York: Norton, 1969), p. 16.
19. Ibid., p. 121. In the preface to the original, full text of *Nuclear Weapons and Foreign Policy* (New York: Harper & Brothers, 1957), p. xi, Kissinger puts the point more negatively: "We can draw only limited guidance from previous experience because much of it has been made irrelevant by the very enormity of modern means of mass destruction. (Reference to this edition will be in the form of *Nuclear Weapons*, Harper ed.)
20. Kissinger, *Necessity for Choice*, p. 65. In *Nuclear Weapons*, Harper ed., Kissinger declares that "Contemporaries are in a peculiarly difficult position to assess the nature of revolutions through which they are living. All previous experience will tempt them to integrate the new into what has come to seem familiar. They will have difficulty understanding that what is most taken for granted may be most misleading because a new order of experience requires new ways of thinking about it" (p. xi).
21. Kissinger, *Troubled Partnership*, p. 5.
22. Kissinger, *Necessity for Choice*, p. 300.
23. Kissinger, *World Restored*, p. 329.
24. Ibid., p. 332.
25. Ibid., p. 30.
26. Ibid., pp. 41, 51.
27. Ibid., p. 76. In *Troubled Partnership*, Kissinger says of the United States and France that they acted "as if each had a psychological need to use the other as a foil" (p. 21), and, at another place, that Adenauer's German policy gave France "the psychological support it needed for excluding Britain from the Common Market" (p. 72). These are random examples of Kissinger's constant interest in the psychological.
28. A comparable example is John Maynard Keynes' masterly handling of the leading personalities, Clemenceau, Lloyd George, and Woodrow Wilson, involved in the Versailles Treaty negotiations. See *The Economic Consequences of the Peace* (New York: Harper & Row, 1971), chap. 3. In general, there is something about peace settlements that allows for this enormous weight of personalism.
29. *New York Times*, November 14, 1971.
30. Kissinger, "Meaning of History," p. 26.
31. Kissinger, *Troubled Partnership*, pp. 197, 96, 141.
32. In "Central Issues of American Foreign Policy" (1968), included in Kissinger, *American Foreign Policy*, Kissinger does use the term "psychotherapy" once more.

33. Nevertheless, CIA Director Richard Helms testified that it was at Kissinger's request that a psychiatric profile was done on Daniel Ellsberg (eventually executed by Bernard Melloy). Kissinger, however, has flatly denied any role. See *Rolling Stone*, November 8, 1973, p. 40.

34. Oriana Fallaci, "Kissinger: An Interview," *The New Republic* 167 (December 16, 1972): 22. As Agatha Christie has the wise Poirot point out, talk reveals the person, even if unintended: "And then, . . . we will talk! *Je vous assure, Hastings*—there is nothing so dangerous for any one who has something to hide as conversation! Speech, so a wise old Frenchman said to me once, is an invention of man's to prevent him from thinking. It is also an infallible means of discovering that which he wishes to hide. A human being, Hastings, cannot resist the opportunity to reveal himself and express his personality which conversation gives him. Every time he will give himself away"; *The ABC Murders* (New York: Pocket Books, 1974), p. 152.

35. Kissinger, *World Restored*, p. 129.

36. Kissinger, *Necessity for Choice*, p. 12.

37. Kissinger, *Nuclear Weapons*, p. 93.

38. Ibid., p. 79.

39. Ibid., p. 42.

40. Erik H. Erikson, *Insight and Responsibility* (New York: Norton, 1964), p. 57. Erikson repeats the story, in a slightly different version, in *Identity: Youth and Crisis* (New York: Norton, 1968), p. 29.

41. Kissinger, *Necessity for Choice*, p. 60.

42. Kissinger, *Troubled Partnership*, p. 25.

43. Kissinger, *Necessity for Choice*, p. 139.

44. Ibid., p. 209.

45. Kissinger, *Troubled Partnership*, p. 204.

46. Ibid., pp. 67–68.

47. Kissinger, *World Restored*, p. 42.

48. Kissinger, *Necessity for Choice*, p. 48.

49. Ibid., p. 50.

50. Cf. Marvin Kalb and Bernard Kalb, *Kissinger* (Boston: Little, Brown, 1974), p. 102, for linkage as a new form of balance of power.

51. Kissinger, *Necessity for Choice*, p. 139.

52. Kissinger, *World Restored*, p. 319.

53. As various people have observed, there is generally a pecking order among the personalities involved in negotiations. Thus, though Adenauer behaved as a superior to American and British negotiators, he felt junior to de Gaulle. Whereas Kissinger behaves as junior to Brezhnev, he is senior to Sadat; and so forth. Although it came to my attention only while this book was in press, for a specific analysis of Kissinger's style of negotiating in the Middle East, see Amos Perlmutter, "Crisis Management: Kissinger's Middle East Negotiations (October 1973–June 1974)," *International Studies Quarterly* 19 (September 1975): 316–343.

54. Cf. Richard Holbrooke, "Kissinger: A Hero, Perhaps, But Not a Model," *Boston Globe*, September 15, 1974, p. 32, for comment on Kissinger's sense of timing in negotiations.

55. Kissinger, *Nuclear Weapons*, p. 29.

56. Ibid., p. 36.

57. See Kissinger, *Necessity for Choice*, p. 135, for a definition and discussion of persuasion.

58. Cf. David Landau, *Kissinger: The Uses of Power* (Boston: Houghton Mifflin, 1972), p. 5, for the way in which talking and arguing figure as part of Kissinger's persuasive powers.

59. Cf. Richard A. Falk, "What's Wrong with Henry Kissinger's Foreign Policy?" Policy Memorandum no. 39 (Princeton, N.J.: Center of International Studies, Princeton University, July 1974), p. 29, for the way in which Kissinger's style also operates so as not to make his opposite numbers in a negotiation feel guilty over what is, possibly, their indecent behavior.

60. Fallaci, "Kissinger," p. 21.

61. Max Lerner has made the observation that "the result is a kind of transference that takes place in Kissinger and each of the leaders, helped by the hours after hours of close intensive discussion in which inhibitions are worn down. It is a kind of therapy—through diplomacy" (*New York Post*, June 3, 1974).

62. Kissinger, *Necessity for Choice*, p. 207.

63. Ibid., p. 183.

64. See Erik H. Erikson, *Gandhi's Truth* (New York: Norton, 1969).

Chapter 10

1. Oriana Fallaci, "Kissinger: An Interview," *The New Republic* 167 (December 16, 1972): 20. In the famous accidental airing of his remarks during a Canadian state dinner, a year or so after Nixon's resignation, Kissinger was overheard to comment that Nixon was "an odd man but he was very decisive in his own way . . . not a bad President—quite a good President" (*Boston Globe*, October 17, 1975, p. 11). As for Ford, Kissinger has remarked, "Humanly, I feel closer to Ford than I did to Nixon," Joseph Kraft, "The Rising of Lowered Expectations," *New York Times Magazine*, August 3, 1975, p. 38. See this article generally for the view that Ford has almost no foreign policy independent of Kissinger's advice.

2. Fallaci, "Kissinger," pp. 20–21.

3. Marvin Kalb and Bernard Kalb, *Kissinger* (Boston: Little, Brown, 1974), p. 14.

4. Ibid., p. 15, for a full account.

5. Ibid., pp. 15–16.

6. Fallaci, "Kissinger," p. 20. Cf. the full account of Kissinger's remarks at the Canadian state dinner, *Boston Globe*, October 17, 1975, p. 11.

7. Kalb and Kalb, *Kissinger*, p. 83.

8. Cf. the case of William Saxbe, who also made devastating remarks about President Nixon's competence and yet received an appointment in the administration.

9. Kalb and Kalb, *Kissinger*, p. 91.

NOTES

10. "60 Minutes," 3, no. 3 with Harry Reasoner and Mike Wallace, as broadcast over the CBS Television Network, October 13, 1970, p. 7.

11. "Kissinger: Action Biography," ABC Television Network, June 14, 1974, produced by Ted Koppel and Stan Opotowsky, p. III–1.

12. William Safire, "Puppet as Prince," *Harper's*, 250 (March 1975): 16.

13. Kalb and Kalb, *Kissinger*, p. 95.

14. Ibid., pp. 108, 375.

15. Ibid., p. 221.

16. Ibid., p. 344.

17. In the remark at the Canadian state dinner, Kissinger also referred to President Nixon as "an unpleasant man . . . nervous . . . He made people uneasy" (*Boston Globe*, p. 11).

18. Henry A. Kissinger, *A World Restored* (Boston: Houghton Mifflin, 1973), p. 19.

19. According to Danielle Hunebelle, Kissinger claimed it was "too dangerous" to keep a personal diary: "Suppose I died or got robbed. . . . Even so, when you're permanently under pressure and in control of yourself, you really feel like opening up sometimes. So, at night, I often go up and chat with the President." *Dear Henry* (New York: Berkeley, 1972), p. 43. As Richard A. Falk, who alerted me to this passage, comments, "Little did Kissinger realize that while he was 'opening up' Nixon was evidently taping their conversations!" "What's Wrong with Henry Kissinger's Foreign Policy?" Policy Memorandum no. 39 (Princeton, N.J.: Center of International Studies, Princeton University, July 1974), p. 25. If these tapes ever become available to scholars, we shall know more about the true nature of the Kissinger-Nixon relations. As for his potential memoirs, Kissinger responded with his usual wit to the observation that he could earn a great deal of money with them by saying: "I don't know whether I can make more money not writing them, or writing them. There may be some people who will pay me for not writing them . . .";
Boston Globe, p. 11.

20. See, for example, James David Barber, *The Presidential Character* (Englewood Cliffs, N.J.: Prentice-Hall, 1972), chaps. 11 and 12, and Bruce Mazlish, *In Search of Nixon* (New York: Basic Books, 1972).

21. Lyndon B. Johnson, of course, with his appointment of Walt Rostow anticipated Nixon. But the general point still stands.

22. Fallaci, "Kissinger," pp. 18, 20.

23. *New York Times*, March 27, 1975.

24. For Nixon's depressive moods and especially his unconscious reaction to success see Bruce Mazlish, *In Search of Nixon* (New York: Basic Books, 1972), passim.

25. For a revealing comparison of Kissinger, rather than Nixon, with the British Prime Minister, see Garry Wills, "Kissinger as Disraeli?" *Moment* 1, no. 2 (July–August 1975): 14–20. The stress in this article, however, is on the way Disraeli and Kissinger dealt with the fact of their being of Jewish background.

26. For a description of the NSC under the Nixon administration, see I. M. Destler, *Presidents, Bureaucrats, and Foreign Policy* (Princeton, N.J.: Princeton University Press, 1974), pp. 118–132.

27. Kalb and Kalb, *Kissinger*, p. 78.

28. Cf. Destler, *Presidents*, pp. 95–118.

29. For details, see, for example, the *New York Times*, July 13, 1975.

30. *New York Times*, June 12, 1974.

31. Safire, "Puppet as Prince," p. 17.

32. Bernard Law Collier, "The Road to Peking, or How Does This Kissinger Do It?" *New York Times Magazine*, November 14, 1971, p. 110.

33. Fallaci, "Kissinger," p. 22.

34. Jack Anderson comments that "he [Kissinger] is convinced that Egypt's President Anwar Sadat and Saudi Arabia's King Faisal are *sincere* [my italics] in their offer to accept the pre-1967 Israel"; *Washington Post*, December 16, 1973, Section B, p. 7, quoted in Gil Carl Alroy, *The Kissinger Experience. American Policy in the Middle East* (New York: Horizon, 1975), p. 151. Is Kissinger being shrewd or overtrusting? Alroy, whose book is hostile to Kissinger, believes the latter.

35. In his remarks at the Canadian state dinner, Kissinger said, "In the last nine months he [Nixon] barely governed"; *Boston Globe*, p. 11.

36. Destler, *Presidents*, p. 64. Cf. Graham T. Allison, "Conceptual Models and the Cuban Missile Crisis," *American Political Science Review* 63 (September 1969): 689–718; and Morton H. Halperin, *Bureaucratic Politics and Foreign Policy* (Washington, D.C.: Brookings Institute, 1974).

37. Destler, *Presidents*, p. 75.

38. Quoted in Halperin, *Bureaucratic Politics*, p. 232.

39. *New York Times*, April 26, 1974.

Chapter 11

1. Theodore Draper, "Détente," *Commentary* 57 (June 1974): 25, 27.

2. Martin Kalb and Bernard Kalb, *Kissinger* (Boston: Little, Brown, 1974), p. 22.

3. Ibid., p. 549.

4. Ibid., p. 116.

5. Ibid., p. 124.

6. Henry A. Kissinger, "The Viet Nam Negotiations," *American Foreign Policy* (New York: Norton, 1969), p. 100. The article in question originally appeared in *Foreign Affairs* 47 (January 1969): 211–234.

7. Kissinger, *American Foreign Policy*, p. 112.

8. Ibid, p. 123.

9. Ibid., p. 134.

10. Oriana Fallaci, "Kissinger: An Interview," *The New Republic* 167 (December 16, 1972): 17.

11. Kalb and Kalb, *Kissinger*, pp. 136, 285, 299, 183.

12. Ibid., pp. 162, 288.

13. Ibid., p. 168.

14. Ibid., p. 169.

15. *New York Times*, May 4, 1975.

16. Cf. Tad Szulc, "Behind the Vietnam Cease-Fire Agreement," *Foreign Policy*, no. 15 (Summer 1974): 21–69.

17. Henry A. Kissinger, *The Troubled Partnership* (New York: McGraw-Hill, 1965), p. 60.
18. Henry A. Kissinger, *The Necessity for Choice* (New York: Harper & Row, 1961), p. 253.
19. Henry A. Kissinger, *Nuclear Weapons and Foreign Policy* (New York: Norton, 1969).
20. Kalb and Kalb, *Kissinger*, p. 241.
21. Fallaci, "Kissinger," pp. 19–20, 18.
22. Kalb and Kalb, *Kissinger*, p. 255.
23. Kissinger's respect for Indira Gandhi may have increased as a result of her assertion of more authoritarian power in mid-1975. In any event, to the distress of his critics, he refused to criticize her recent policies, on the grounds of noninterference in Indian domestic affairs (though, as his critics point out, he was willing publicly to criticize the Allende government in Chile). Cf. Bernard Gwertzman "U.S. Silence on India: Nonintereference or Immorality," *New York Times*, August 13, 1975, p. 2.
24. *New York Times*, March 27, 1975.
25. An additional explanation for Kissinger's position may be found in the view he confided to a selected audience to the effect that his optimal goal was to preserve the peace in the Middle East for another ten years. By then many factors would have changed, such as oil, the position of Europe, and the relations of America and the Soviet Union.
26. "Kissinger: Action Biography," ABC Television Network, June 14, 1974, produced by Ted Koppel and Stan Opotowsky, p. III–12.
27. Though the CIA, according to highly reliable information, spends millions of dollars, employs numerous agents in gathering materials, and has an excellent cadre of psychiatrists preparing psychiatric profiles on the leaders of every conceivable country (and even of the second and third level of leadership), the use of these expensive "tools" by our own foreign policy leaders seems highly erratic. As one highly placed State Department official replied, "Now that you mention it, I suppose I should have consulted the profile before the negotiations; I'm sure the Secretary [Kissinger] did." Unlike psychohistorical studies, however, the psychiatric profiles (good in themselves, from what I can judge) are cut off from policy studies; thus, the gap between psychology and policy must be filled in, intuitively, by the policy maker, if he bothers.
28. "Kissinger: Action Biography," p. III–13.
29. Cf. Kalb and Kalb, *Kissinger*, p. 515.
30. "Kissinger: Action Biography," p. III–13.
31. Kalb and Kalb, *Kissinger*, p. 525.
32. Cf. Garry Wills, "Kissinger as Disraeli?" *Moment* 1 (July–August 1975): 14–20, for the attraction of Christianity for Kissinger. As Wills points out, however, "There is no evidence that Kissinger ever considered baptism" (Disraeli had been baptized), p. 18.
33. Cf. the account in Ralph Blumenfield, staff and eds. of the *New York Post*, *Henry Kissinger, the Private and Public Story* (New York: New American Library, 1974), p. 62.
34. Kalb and Kalb, *Kissinger*, p. 529.
35. Henry A. Kissinger, *A World Restored* (Boston: Houghton Mifflin, 1973), p. 153.

36. See Henry R. Nau, "Interpreting U.S. Foreign Policy on Food and Energy" (Paper presented at AAAS Annual Meeting, 26–31 January 1975, New York City), p. 6.

37. For a cogent statement of these objections, see, for example, *Trialogue* 7 (Summer 1975): 13.

38. In addition to the Kalbs' account, see Edward N. Luttwak and Walter Laqueur, "Kissinger and the Yom Kippur War," *Commentary* 58 (September 1974): 33–40. William B. Quandt, "Kissinger and the Arab-Israeli Disengagement Negotiations," *Journal of International Affairs* 29, (Spring 1975): 33–48, considers the accounts of both the Kalbs and Luttwak and Laqueur as contributing to erroneous myths; the real reason for the delay was a function of diplomatic and bureaucratic moves that had nothing to do with *either* Schlesinger or Kissinger trying to delay the arms resupply. Whatever the true story, it is clear that Kissinger was pleased with the situation that opened up to him as a result of the war.

39. *New York Times*, December 9, 1974.

40. John Hersey, *The President* (New York: Knopf, 1975).

41. Henry A. Kissinger, "The Meaning of History; Reflections on Spengler, Toynbee, and Kant" (B.A. thesis, Harvard University, 1951), p. 333.

42. Dean Acheson, *Present At The Creation* (New York: Norton, 1969), p. 7.

43. *New York Times*, December 7, 1974.

44. Kalb and Kalb, *Kissinger*, p. 347.

45. *Boston Globe*, February 6, 1975.

46. *New York Times*, May 29, 1975.

47. Ibid., p. 1.

48. Nau, "Interpreting U.S. Foreign Policy," pp. 1–2.

49. Kalb and Kalb, *Kissinger*, pp. 428–429.

Chapter 12

1. Hans J. Morgenthau, *Politics Among Nations* (New York: Knopf, 1948), pp. 13, 15, 17.

2. Ibid., pp. 13, 14.

3. Bertrand de Jouvenal, *On Power*, trans. J. F. Huntington (New York: Viking, 1949), p. xvi.

4. Ibid., p. 18.

5. See J. Bronowski and Bruce Mazlish, *The Western Intellectual Tradition* (New York: Harper, 1960), chap. 3.

6. Quoted in Richard A. Falk, "The Sherrill Hypothesis," June 1974, unpublished ms., Princeton University, pp. 31–32.

7. Henry A. Kissinger, *The Troubled Partnership* (New York: McGraw-Hill, 1965), p. 18.

8. Henry A. Kissinger, *The Necessity for Choice* (New York: Harper, 1961), p. 32.

9. Ibid., p. 41.

10. Ibid., p. 46.

11. Needless to say, the idea of continuing growth is more complicated than as stated—one thinks of the arguments about limited growth, no growth, and so on—but the general point still stands.

12. Jeffrey Race, "Toward an Exchange Theory of Revolution," in *Peasant Rebellion and Communist Revolution in Asia*, ed. John Wilson Lewis (Stanford, Calif.: Stanford University Press, 1974), pp. 169–204, contains an interesting and novel effort to view power as an expanding entity, tied to emergent structures, rather than as a given, static matter. Thus, Race views power as something that can be created, in an expansive way. Its aim, however, is still domination over others. Race's ideas, nevertheless, seem worth pursuing.

13. Marvin Kalb and Bernard Kalb, *Kissinger* (Boston: Little, Brown, 1974), p. 201.

14. Oriana Fallaci, "Kissinger: An Interview," *The New Republic* 167, no. 23 (December 16, 1972): 20.

15. Kissinger, *Troubled Partnership*, p. 195.

16. Fallaci, "Kissinger," p. 18.

17. Henry A. Kissinger, "The Meaning of History; Reflections on Spengler, Toynbee, and Kant" (B.A. thesis, Harvard University, 1951), p. 343.

18. Harold D. Lasswell, *Psychopathology and Politics* (1930; reprint ed., New York: Viking, 1960); idem, *Power and Personality* (1948; reprint ed., New York: Viking, 1962).

19. Alexander L. George and Juliette George, *Woodrow Wilson and Colonel House: A Personality Study* (1956; reprint ed., New York: Dover, 1964).

20. For a fuller treatment of this notion as one aspect of a larger concept, see Bruce Mazlish, *The Revolutionary Ascetic* (New York: Basic Books, 1976).

21. Kalb and Kalb, *Kissinger*, pp. 352–353.

22. *New York Times*, June 12, 1974.

23. Quoted in Richard Holbrooke, "Kissinger: A Hero, Perhaps, But Not a Model," *Boston Globe*, September 15, 1974, p. 34.

24. Kissinger, *Necessity for Choice*, p. 208.

25. Danielle Hunebelle, *Dear Henry* (New York: Berkeley, 1972), p. 24. Although unreliable and suspect in many ways, this book, according to most of Kissinger's close acquaintances, is unusually revealing of a Kissinger not normally seen by the public.

26. George F. Kennan, *Memoirs: 1925–1950*, (Boston: Little, Brown, 1967), pp. 428–429.

27. Cf. ibid., pp. 436–437.

28. *New York Times*, January 16, 1975.

29. Falk, "Sherrill Hypothesis"; idem, "What's Wrong with Henry Kissinger's Foreign Policy?" Policy Memorandum no. 39 (Princeton, N.J.: Center of International Studies, Princeton University, July 1974).

Chapter 13

1. Bruce Mazlish, *In Search of Nixon* (New York: Penguin Books, 1973), p. xxviii.
2. Theodore White, *The Making of the President 1972* (New York: Atheneum, 1973), p. xii.
3. See Zbigniew Brzezinski's "Report Card," as of February 1974, in the *New York Times*, March 14, 1974. For a more favorable evaluation, cf. John D. Montgomery, "The Education of Henry Kissinger," *Journal of International Affairs* 29 (Spring 1975): 49–62.
4. Richard A. Falk, "What's Wrong with Henry Kissinger's Foreign Policy?" Policy Memorandum no. 39 (Princeton, N.J.: Center of International Studies, Princeton University, July 1974), p. 3.
5. Richard A. Falk, "The Sherrill Hypothesis," unpublished manuscript, Princeton University, June 1974, p. 2.
6. John Maynard Keynes, *The Economic Consequences of the Peace* (New York: Harper & Row, 1971).
7. I might add that, personally, I happen to disagree with Solzhenitsyn's views, insofar as I am acquainted with them. For the embarrassment stirred up by the Italian neo-Fascist's meeting with members of the National Security Council, which could only have occurred with Kissinger's approval, tacit or otherwise, see the *New York Times*, October 5, 1975.
8. *New York Times*, June 12, 1975.

Index